The Big Healing

Praise for *The Big Healing*

"McKeon is a master of new-age teachings . . . offer[ing] a refreshing and enlightening perspective on personal growth and transformation . . . *The Big Healing* is not just a book, it's a powerful tool for transformation . . . a beacon of hope for anyone seeking personal growth and healing . . . With McKeon's guidance, you'll learn to tap into your inner wisdom and intuition to create a life that aligns with your true purpose . . . Embark on a transformative journey with Chris, Ayako, and El, renowned spirit mediums who offer a unique and intriguing approach to guide you on a path of healing and self-discovery." —*Midwest Book Review*

"At the work's core, there is an emphasis on why it is necessary to question and not simply take what is presented to you as the ultimate truth . . . the genuine belief the author and his children possess is sincere and may possibly prompt readers to take a leap of faith to experience the same feeling of awe and release, resulting in a thoroughly cathartic experience." —*US Review of Books*

Other Books by Christopher McKeon

The Story of Life
Victim to Victor

The Big Healing

*A Fantastical True Story of Liberation, Hope,
and Healing to Empower Your Life*

Christopher McKeon, M.Dıv.

Tőteppit Press

Tőteppit Press
Rico, Colorado USA

thebighealing.storyoflifebook.com
www.toteppitpress.com

Publisher's Cataloging-in-Publication Data
McKeon, Christopher D. A. author.
The big event : a fantastical true story / Christopher McKeon.
First edition. | Rico, CO : Tőteppit Press, 2024. | Includes bibliographical references
    and index. | Also available in ebook and audiobook format.
LCCN 2024905097 (print) | ISBN 979-8-9864707-7-1 (hardcover) | ISBN
    979-8-9864707-3-3 (paperback) | ISBN 979-8-9864707-8-8 (EBOOK)
LCSH: Spirituality. | Spiritual life. | Healing. | Inspiration. | Channeling (Spiritualism)
    | BISAC: RELIGION / Spirituality. | BODY, MIND & SPIRIT / Channeling &
    Mediumship. | BODY, MIND & SPIRIT / Healing / Prayer & Spiritual | BODY,
    MIND & SPIRIT / Inspiration & Personal Growth.
LCC BL73.A73 .M35 2024 (print) | LCC BL73.A73 (ebook) | DDC 299/.9–dc23.

Unless otherwise indicated, scriptural quotations are from the Holy Bible, New
International Version (NIV), various publishers and dates. Those labeled KJV are from
the King James Version, various publishers and dates. Quotations used per applicable
copyright law.

Cover design by rebeccacovers
Text set in EBGaramond, Latin Modern Roman Dunhill

Net sale proceeds from this book support the *Story of Life* free paperback program
(PDF ebook is free online and at toteppitpress.com).

As of 13 October 2017, each emergently birthed person's mindset addiction and the Negative Collective Consciousness animating it are no more; you are free to heal and at liberty to experience Life in absolute autonomy.

There is no purpose to this life,
You make your own purpose;
That's what makes life beautiful.
— El

For my beloved daughters who elevated this experience for me from weird to real.

And in memory of every manjack who e'er sought reality o'er the veil of belief.

Contents

12 ET as a Mode of Inquiry

Preface

THIS BOOK COMPRISES chapters 1–12 of the *The Story of Life*'s forty-two (*SOL*; McKeon 2022). We abridged the preface, introduction, and chapters 11–12; other edits are typographical. The idea is to present my two middle daughters' and my testimony in a shorter, more accessible and readable book. It's a revelatory tale, not reasoned, researched, or imagined. A result of real-time conversations with God (henceforth, *Mina*);[1] the so-called angels Gabriel, Lucifer, Michael, and others;[2] Jesus; Sun-myung Moon;[3] Buddha; Muhammad; Abraham; Zoroaster, and many more; plus family, friends, and others living in spirit world,[4] the real and surprisingly simple nature of which you'll read here (and in detail in *SOL*).

---

1. Creator, Father, Lord, Master, Allah, Jehovah, YHWH, Brahman, Ahura Mazda, First Cause, Source, Universal Force, or whatever and in whichever faith language you use. He asked us to knock off calling him God and all the rest because they reference painful behaviors that distort what he is. We generally address him by his preferred name on Earth, Mina (see his full name in *SOL* § 1.1:336).

2. These aren't their birth names but bestowed by humans (*SOL* Table 17:523).

3. Korean evangelist (d. 2012) and founder of the Holy Spirit Association for the Unification of World Christianity (HSA–UWC, or Unification Church). Turns out, he played an important part in this story while alive and then afterward, too.

4. We use pseudonyms except where individuals, as noted, permitted our use of their real name.

What you'll read is revelation in that spirit persons conveyed it but, using a modality we call *energy testing* (§ 1.2.1.3:172), we still had to get out of our own heads just to range through the possibilities and then *ask*. So, this book is also *learned* knowledge. PART I, *The Big Event*, narrates our extraordinary first two days and the week-long circumstances leading up to it, the universal transformation it sparked, some of what we learned, and its effect on us. We found out the hard way that an extrapolation may logically and consistently follow a revelation with eminent sense, but isn't necessarily true at all. Therefore, what you will *not* read in this book are our own inferences, opinions, and beliefs masquerading as revelation. Rather, we analyze and interpret in concert with Mina and other relevant spirit persons.

The genesis of this book was our, perhaps naïve, desire to know The Truth. We couldn't foresee that things we thought firmly rooted and plainly sensible were not true while others we never even imagined were. I joke about my jaw-hitting-the-floor comedy routine, but our schooling was anything but a barrel of laughs. The answers profoundly shocked us. My daughters took it mostly in stride with the aplomb, I suppose, that befits their jaded millennial youth. I felt the ground quake beneath my Judeo-Christian feet. Questions—*disbelief!*—poured out of me, occasionally accompanied by my children's exaggerated eyes to the heavens.

"You have to think like Captain Jack Sparrow, Dad," my girls, in all gravity, urged in mopier moments.

I wasn't even sure what that meant. "Isn't he a drunkard?"

Eye rolls.

Having less baggage to jettison, they thought I should more easily flush away decades of faith, learning, and enculturation instead of hammering the same questions from every angle to assure belief we were talking with *the* Creator, not to mention everyone else, and to reconcile what they were saying with what we thought we knew. Well . . . we had a lot of fun, too. Mina, the 'angels,' and family and friends in spirit world are for the most part wonderful, kind, considerate, happy, and caring people. But what they had to say was ofttimes dry gravel down our gullet. We couldn't just ignore their testimony, though—weren't *we* interrogating *them*?—especially when we'd reason it through and find no substantive chinks.

Our revelation-and-response comes on the heels of my sixty-year trek through Christianity (my daughters, since birth), forty some years of it caught up in varying degrees with Rev. Sun-myung Moon's deep spirituality and his vapidly chaotic Unification Church.[5] But right from this story's October 2017 beginning we found only loving, embracing energy, logical consistency, common sense, simplicity, hope, and above all, *liberation*. Our feelings upon release from millennia of human delusion and fatuous complexity felt like draining a dirty bathtub.

You'll see how this amazing opportunity appeared not through grace, benevolence, providential timing, holier than thou-ness, the Call, or some mystical lottery but simply from our curious, out-of-the-box thinking unbounded by religion and philosophy's blinders. We rang and Mina answered. So, too, with you if you learn energy testing, which introduction you'll find in PART II. Then, you can verify our story for yourself.

The *The Story of Life* is an axial moment challenging socioculture's norms. *We* aren't that axial moment, it's God—well, Mina. We are, let's say, his cogitative messengers. In addition to money-making and volunteer professions, I've been a missionary, minister, pastor, and military/law enforcement chaplain all my adult life. Yet, here I am having found religion, faith, philosophy (except its critical reasoning toolset) and its subset theology[6] all largely albeit not entirely, as you'll see, faulty; illusion if not delusion.

We encountered our revelations a typical, oft fractious American family only to find ourselves a more healed team. I penned this book, but couldn't have done it without my two middle daughters. Their ability to intuit, sense energies, feel spirit persons' emotions like body language, utilize clair senses, grasp concepts I stumbled over, figure out better questions when I'd driven myself into a ditch, be a compass when I'd get lost, and validate what, on my own, I certainly

---

5. Read *Victim to Victor* (McKeon 2024) for the first 21 years of this wildin' tale.

6. Religion (theology) relies on revelation and philosophy (reason) to frame it; philosophy (not its pure reason toolset) relies on reason and theology (revelation) to frame it.

could have only doubted, was invaluable. Thank you, girls, for your help as I wrote *The Story of Life*, especially our wonderful experiences at Wild Flower Lane discovering its beginnings. It immensely challenged us. We got on each other's nerves. Dug up the rawest emotions. Flayed our hearts. At times, put us to tears. We shared the foxhole. I'm proud of you both.

Subscripted endnotes (example$_{52}$) and superscripted footnotes (example[78]) are citations and discussion containing clarifications and pertinent information. Cross-references to footnotes [endnotes] use the format *FN[EN]:note#:page#*. References directing you to another [chapter]section use the format *[CH.#]§#:page#*, sometimes prepended by *CHAPTER-NAME* for clarity. *Important note*: where this book cross-references a passage from *The Story of Life* (which seems better left in than out of this book), the reference is prefixed by *SOL* so you're pointed to the correct book.

Dialogue is verbatim when it really stuck in our minds or we wrote it down, otherwise it's the speaker's approved paraphrasing. "Double quotes" indicate spirit person dialogue, or as noted. 'Single quotes' and *italics* indicate phrasing and emphasis. Italics also indicate energy-test responses like *yes*, *no*, *maybe*, and other words or phrases (*SOL* CH. 41:623). In a citation, *io* and *ia* means italics original or added, respectively.

Regarding ebooks, Mina's caveat is that electronics (electricity, generally) disrupt spiritual 'energy' such as chakras, reducing spiritual awareness, intuition, and ability to cognize this content.

Thank you for acting on your curiosity, interest, or intuition to consider this material. Just reading it broadens humanity's awareness of the universe in which we live and, in so doing, promotes healing. In your own way you're contributing to reducing pain and suffering, which seeds a better future.

Christopher McKeon
Southwest Colorado, USA
July 2024

Introduction

OUR STORY IS the tale of how the walking disaster that's life—which we're all just trying to grin and bear our way through to its Wagnerian finale—did a one-eighty October 13, 2017; what changed that day and how, some of why life sucks, how it actually is, and how it all affects *you*. Details in *The Story of Life* (SOL).

"Dad," my daughter El said in deadly earnest on the heels of my *yes* to writing Mina's book, "make absolutely sure you tell them this is totally *not* a new religion or any kind of dumb philosophy."

Palms out, I said, "Okay, I promise."

"That they don't have to listen to it, or worship anything, or—"

"Yes, of course I will, sweetie."

"Because people are totally, absolutely *free*."

"El, I got you."

"I'm just saying, Dad." Her eyes toyed with a roll. "Cuz that's the *last* thing we need!" A strong *Yes!* from Mina (God).[7]

Our tale is simply the story of life. Not how we'd like it to be in our happiest fantasies or self-loathing expiatory flagellations, but how it really is. You might feel a profound feeling of *free*. Liberated.

---

7. See how he's communicating with us in THE BIG EVENT (for his name: FN 1:*i*; SOL § 1.1:336).

Released. Empowered. *Relieved.* You might surprise yourself to encounter a natural capacity for love and acceptance you never seriously imagined in actuality existed.

That's what's in it for you. And you needn't do a single just-change-yourself-this-or-that-way thing to experience it. Relax and consider fairly this story of life. It will happen naturally. That's how it went for us, anyhow; at least even odds for you, too.

Taking on existential reality is like growing up where we need come to grips not only with the world as it is instead of how we thought it should be till it punched us in the mouth, but with our parents too as they really are and the world they constructed for us throughout our childhood as it really is. The six stages of grief—denial, anger, bargaining, depression, acceptance, wring-and-repeat—are how we traverse this inescapable demand of life; it keeps psychiatrists in business anyway. We all follow this trajectory. Some wallow or restart if-then-else loops or lurch through to the promised land only to bang into the ongoing confusion, faith, hope, belief, or delusion of an uncertain world while hoping, praying, and striving to make it through to death with some semblance of happiness toward a brighter deceased tomorrow. Like all merry-go-rounds, it can dizzily spin one into puking or entirely off into the weeds.

Wouldn't it be convenient just to get off? You do that by understanding what's really going on to gain a clear awareness of where you stand as a physically alive person in the larger universe. We've never reliably been able to do that, hence all our competing revelations, theologies, and philosophies. Now we can. For that, we introduce *energy testing* (ET; § 1.2.1.3:172), a reproducible physiological method for getting the real skinny from the horse's mouth. You can do exactly what we did: discover energy testing; then through your own visceral, physiological experience decide if you're actually feeling the spiritual energy of Mina, 'angels' (spirit-born humans), family, friends, or others in spirit world answering your questions; and finally, follow up the answers your queries deliver.

All this may quite naturally concern the religious or philosophical. If it makes you feel any better, it challenged us on all counts, too. The reaction is natural though not inevitable, and is certainly amenable. Before judging, consider: fallacious, religion and philosophy certainly are; but rubbish, 'God' and rationality absolutely are not. 'God' is real. Not deitic or divine nor magical but a human person; it's how *we* come to *be* human. Via principles of reality that sol describes, he created this universe for us to live in absolutely, unconditionally, and unequivocally *free*. Not free within reason, or as a duty, under law, responsibly, morally bounded, or so long as we keep it on the straight and narrow thus on the road to judgment and punishment if we don't, but utterly, perfectly, *a*judgmentally free. This book is just an introduction. *The Story of Life* provokes you to wrap your head seriously around the concept of *free*. You might find it less easy than maybe it ought to be.

So, turn the page to THE BIG EVENT and discover our October surprise. Then in PART II a bit about what came afterward and energy testing as a means to interact with spirit persons. If our story grabs you, check out *The Story of Life* for the whole enchilada. Discover how you can spin this wheel yourself so that instead of having only faith or hope this book isn't pulling your leg, you come away with knowledge and liberation that, indeed, it's not.

Part I

The Big Event

All Shook Up

Thursday October 12, 2017 ca. 5 pm

O f all the days in all the months in all the year, Friday the 13th just had to be the day the world as it was all sort of just blew up in our face. My two daughters and I. . . well, we quite lit the fuse when, about sixteen hours before that cool October morning, we'd tramped through the garage door of our woodsy rural log cabin home following an afternoon of errands and posed a simple question. Atop a wild, spiritually hectic week culminating in our long afternoon in the car talking over God, ancestry, life, and surprises from dear dead friends, my two-days-eighteen daughter El froze mid-step in our living room and blurted, "Creator,[8] do you have a family?"

And he answered.

We all three traded surprised eyes at the *yes* response.

She was on a roll. "Do you have a wife?"

---

8. How we addressed him before he said he prefers Mina (for his real name: *sol* § 1.1:336).

Yes.

"Do you have children, not just us?"

Yes.

She paused a few seconds, thinking through the logic. "Do you have a *mother?*"

Yes!

While I jacked my jaw up off the floor, she looked at me. "Dad, I can literally *feel* his joy that we've just discovered this! He's really happy! Can we meet her?" she added, not to me. "Can we talk to her?"

At which point El swiveled to her right, face and eyes cranking upward as though at a much taller person. Her expression transformed, aglow with delight and excitement. A smile burst across her cheeks as her hands flew to her heart. She sucked her breath.

"*Hi*, Mother!"

Yeah. I gawped, too.

Even a wizened skeptic like me could tell my younger daughter was having a moment, an experience, a—well, a revelation. Chills, tingles, and heat shivered me timbers stem to stern. Energy and pleasure radiated from El. I could see her gleam. There was no mistaking her profound joy and rapture. We, too, felt the presence of 'Mother' fiercely blazing with happy excitement. Communicating. In our *home*. To *us*. Who were *aware* of her. My older daughter and resident spiritualist Ayako, now two days from her twenty-first year, twisted round a blue-upholstered, high-backed dining chair and plopped into it facing El with a knowing curiosity, feeling all the energy we were experiencing and more. We incessantly questioned Mother and Mina—'God' (FN 1:*i*)—into the night; you'll encounter it all here and in *The Story of Life* (SOL; McKeon 2022).

That wasn't even the really exciting part. But before we got to that, our curiosity slanted us through some scary hours later in the night that left my exuberant daughters tearful and terrified, and me wondering just what can of worms we'd pulled the pop-top on. For now, though, we enthusiastically pushed our envelope of reality and the eye-popping responses snowballed. A lifelong

Irish Roman Catholic, Protestant Christian, Unificationist,[9] and now post-Unificationist, it soon registered that my worldview, my *lifeview*, was in some real distress here. Stuff needed clarifying if not a little unmitigated arguing. Yet, for all that, Mina's answers were coherent, consistent, and sensible. Only good, loving, calm but excited energy bathed the room. With that, it seemed as wise a time as any to get down to the suddenly apropos nitty-gritty.

I said, "Creator, is the Bible true?"

No.

---

9. A follower of Sun-myung Moon's Divine Principle, the core of his Unification Church.

I pulled a hard breath, astonished, though as a graduate of divinity school maybe not all that surprised. Even so, a linchpin of my lifeview clattered to the wide-planked floor.

"What about the New Testament? Is Jesus' teaching in that true?"

"Dad, he said—"

No.

"*All* of it?" I gave my girls each a once over, but if you could wear a body shrug like a pantsuit, they were. *Kids*, I thought. Always jaunty at the start of a march across somebody else's Bataan.

No.

"So, some of it, then, is true."

Yes.

"How 'bout Jesus," El said, "is he a real person?"

Yes.

Well, that was a relief. I think. Anyhow, the girls looked copacetic. We quizzed Mina on this topic awhile until, inevitably, it led to the issue most pressing me.

"Is Rev. Moon's teaching in *Divine Principle* true?"[10] I mean, I'd largely bet the farm on it in 1981.

No.

My ribs fell in. There went another linchpin. I let out a wheeze like I'd just downed a shot of two-hundred proof. Bleary eyes landed on each daughter, but saw in them none of my own jolt.

"Jeez, girls," I yawped, "that's my lifeview purt' near forty years!"

Ever sassy, Ayako said, "Welcome to the next wave, Dad."

Unlike Jesus, I *knew* Sun-myung (he eschews titles, now). His theologically ultra-modern Divine Principle was more real to me than worn out, foggy old Christianity, its grand morsels of wisdom and Jesus notwithstanding. Sure, Divine Principle reposed upon the biblical witness, but to me it more sensibly elucidated its core truths. It underwrote the full scale of my adult life. I might be perennially at war with Sun-myung's pigheaded church institution but not his Divine Principle, not by any stretch.

I said, "*All* of it?"

---

10. His codified theology published in Korean (1954, 1966) and English (1973, retranslated 1996).

I had to ask because, like everyone in spirit world communicating with a non-conversational medium[11] in the physical world, Mina must needs be literal in our mode of communication. Absent face-to-face or even voice-to-voice, it's nigh impossible to gauge what a person means by words alone. Consider how the misunderstanding curve rises proportionally to one's metaphorical distance from the speaker. Words (rooting in shared definitions) need convey precisely what's meant. It's a tough row to hoe for humans, wedded as we are to contextual word play. You might think Mina could simply know our thoughts, but that creates complications of its own that *sol* tackles. What it boils down to, Ayako pointed out, is that we had to formulate our questions thoughtfully into unambiguous inquiries and confirmations that backed up our responses.

No, Mina answered me through El.

Huh. Once again, only some of my lifeview was true. Was that good? Who could know. As with the Bible, I could only wonder, *which freaking part?* The *Divine Principle* is a weighty *vade mecum* in its own right. Being young, unformed, and like many in their generation rejecting religion generally though not God specifically, my daughters *looked* okay—my eldest like an old soul hearing something she'd long suspected and her kid sister charmed in high cotton—but *my* cosmology was melting apart like Icarus' wishful wax job. This conversation was sweeping away a lifetime of hard-won truths, from the nature of the universe and God to Jesus and Sun-myung's messianism and the spiritual verity and providential histories that went with them (likewise with all religions), not to mention what I'd sacrificed—wasted?—for it all. My head was spinning. I was anything *but* okay. But dammitall if that would throttle my interest; perish the thought. Come hell or high water, I'm nothing if not the cat tempting curiosity.

By and by, we worked our way to the crux of the Abrahamic religions: the Fall of Man. Original sin territory and their *raison d'être*. After some unexpected and perplexing responses from Mina, we needed to get a few things straight.

---

11. One not able to converse voice-to-voice with spirit persons as in spoken conversation.

I said, "Are you saying the Fall never happened?"

Yes.

"So..." dittoed El, finally sounding a tad betrayed, "there *was* no Fall of Man?"

No.

"Satan never persuaded Eve to eat the 'fruit'?" she continued. "Lucifer never fell—never had a wrong sexual relationship with Eve like Rev. Moon said? People never tried to be God and 'fell' from grace or perfection, or whatever?",

No, no, no.

"Well," said I, "fuuu—!"

No.

Ayako shifted round to me with disapprobation. "That 'no' means negative energy resonates, Dad."

Great.

After more give-and-take—during which Mina recast 'the Fall' as *The Corruption* in which humans self-manifested our selfish, harmful world and self-alienated ourselves from God (I mean, Mina) without any help from anybody, including our evolutionarily left-over, full-blown-batty reptile brain—El perceptively said, "Wait. Are Adam and Eve even real people who actually lived?"

No.

Ayako and El traded stares. It seemed their own lifeviews were at last meeting some unexpected renovation. About time.

I choked. "Um, they don't exist?"

No. They don't exist.

"Then, is Satan a real being, a fallen angel, or . . . whatever?"

No. No . . . no.

"Wait, wait." Just. *Wait.* I needed a minute to *think.*

El didn't. "You mean Satan doesn't even *exist*? There's no devil, no evil force or being that—"

No, no.

"So, no war in heaven," she went on in obvious offense, practically ticking through Revelations (12:7–9) on her fingers and giving me, her ministerial, semi-Bible-thumping father a flinty eye, "no angel

rebellion, no beings cast down to earth, no ancient good vers—
none of these stories religion taught us are true?"

No. Sorry.

El blew off a heavy breath, threw up her hands, and tromped
in a circle. Oaths welled up in my brain so fast they had to take a
number.

A little hostile, I said, "What about Darwin, then?"

"Not Darwin, Dad," said Ayako, ever the schoolteacher, "Darwin-
ism. Unless you mean the guy, you're talking natural selection."

"Uh, sure... but is he—it—true?"

No.

"What? But then—?"

"So, evolution is *wrong*?" said El.

Yes.

"All of it?" I added, pretty much expecting the obvious.

No.

Yep. Here we go again. "So, basically, *everybody's* explanation for
humanity's existence and miserable condition is total bullshit?"

"Dad..."

"False?"

Maybe...yes.

Ayako said, "Remember, Dad, he said not *every* single thing."

"Yeah, but everybody's?"

"Like, all religions and philosophies?" El said plainly.

Yes.

She let out a low, gruff whistle. "*Waaah*—when your whole
existence is just a fat lie."

"So, Islam, too?" I said. "And Buddhism, Confucianism, Hindu-
ism, Animism—"

Yes, yes, ye—

Ayako gave me an eye. "He said all religions, Dad. Come on."

Yes.

"I'm just being thorough." And not taking sides, I didn't say.

No.

El barked a laugh and rolled a few eyes.

"I'm not? But I . . . wait," I said toward El, who was doing our energy testing, "are you pulling my leg?"

Yes.

"Well. Isn't he just a barrel of monkeys. Never took God for a joker," I said to Ayako, though a medium once claimed it to me.

"Lots of things you never thought of, Dad," she chirped, queen of the snappy comeback and earning my tight-lipped stare-down. My mood was a little nettled, frankly.

A flurry of questions and statements followed as we plunged ever deeper down our rabbit hole. I put evolution aside for now. It only dealt with our bodies anyhow. We had *cosmic* issues on the table. But now, a few other things in my head about the human 'fall from grace' were rising to the fore and clashing with Mina's assertions. It occurred to me we'd need to pull in somebody else, the very somebody who off and on since late summer had purveyed through a local medium a seemingly clear, unambiguous spiritual reality that included a very real Adam and Eve: Archangel Michael.[12]

1.1 SEVEN WEEKS EARLIER . . .

See, back on August 27, 2017 my 'woo-woo' spiritualist church friend, Moth Man[13]—always going on about spirit world, Mother God, the Divine Feminine, angels, spirit animals, and the like— sauntered up to me after church in Bowie, Maryland with a friend of his whom I didn't know particularly well. He said, "Hey, we have this thing going on in a few minutes where we're going to use Emotion Code [an alternative healing modality$_2$] to heal Archangel Gabriel and Michael. You like angels, right?" All I had for that was a body shrug. "Why don't you join us?"

I blinked, nonplussed. "Uh . . . what's wrong with them?"

"They have trapped emotions." Moth Man's eyes flitted to his nodding companion. "Gabriel came to my buddy here in a dream last night, asking him to do an Emotion Code healing."

---

12. No such thing as *arch*angels. We use it for clarity and convenience (see *SOL* § 1:520).

13. My Moonie best friend and 'spirit animal' expert, his own being the moth.

Ohhh-kay, then. I didn't really hang around the goofy new-agey types but, as we'd been acquainted since 1982, I'd made him the exception. I've always been a somewhat cutting-edge theologian though apparently a little conventional in my angelology. If you wonder why angels would even need healing much less humans to do it for them, well, I did, too.

I said, "What's 'emotion code' and why do they need us?"

Moth Man launched into a quick overview, noting they'd lined up a local Unificationist 'mental medium'[14] in a breathless 2 AM phone call who also happened to be a certified Emotion Code practitioner. The stars were aligned. He wore an expectation I'd say yes the way a dog starts chewing while chow's still airborne twixt the bag and bowl. I'm really *not* the new-agey type, did I mention that? On the other hand, I'm always game for something interesting and unusual and this scored about a hundred-forty on that scale. The four of us sat down at a faux wood-top table in a quiet, closed room in the church. Our local *Ms. Medium* (whom I'd only just met scant weeks earlier) laid out her Emotion Code three-ring handbook, composed herself as we all sat on tenterhooks, and then gently asked the room if Gabriel was present.

Well, of course he was.

Our 'Angel Code' meetings that followed this initial gathering (during which Ms. Medium averred Michael "pushed Gabriel aside" to grab the healing benefit "all for himself"[15]) was shaping up to be a deuce of a book in its own right until Mina and these self-same angels later cratered the whole episode's veracity, but more on that later. The gist of this backstory is that it's here the dichotomy arose between Michael and Mina's revelations that began tickling my mind at the news there'd been no human Fall. It began during our third Angel Code meeting at Moth Man's house when Michael was lamenting, through Ms. Medium's anguished tears, how Lucifer provoked the Fall of Adam and Eve and that he loathed himself

---

14. One who experiences spirit world mainly via the clair senses such as hearing, seeing, feeling, or a combination.

15. And here's where Mina says all the trouble started with these Angel Code meetings.

for not doing more to stop it. How paralysis had gripped him till he'd ultimately done nothing. How, afterward, Lucifer arrogantly strutted through spirit world striking fear into the hearts of the stoutest angels (Michael, anyway) with his intimidating bluster and caused a rift, or 'war,' between the many soon-to-be-fallen angels flocking to his new-way standard and those clinging steadfast to God. How *our* fault lay in giving Lucifer all his venal power by adopting his self-centered philosophy. And so on. Michael had plainly painted Adam and Eve, the Fall, and Lucifer-*cum*-Satan as thoroughly real.

This had been some heady stuff for me, practically an elixir. It sure triggered my Moonie humans-ruined-the-universe-and-stabbed-God-in-the-heart guilt reflex that makes stereotyped Catholics to say nothing of Jews look like dabblers in the stigmatic arts. As Ms. Medium narrated Michael's torpedoed feelings during this third meeting, my heart clutched at my ribs, squeezed in viselike empathy as I contemplated this forlorn angel's suffering. My own traitorous chest crushingly proclaimed my own *personal* responsibility for it. This direct physical experience with such a powerful energy left me feeling profoundly *woke*. I went from skeptic to believer in two seconds flat for three reasons. First, I implicitly trusted Ms. Medium's integrity that imparted the certainty she was indeed speaking with *the* Archangel Michael. Second, I felt my body and the atmosphere ever so energetically and emotionally charged. And third, his story was logically consistent with Divine Principle (my spiritual lifeview, which had emitted a too-good-to-be-true flicker of caution I'd rather too casually tamped down). Unhappily, Michael's thrilling drama seven weeks ago was now colliding head-on with Mina's cold, hard layout of reality.

1.2 THURSDAY, OCTOBER 12, 2017 CA. 11 PM

Having skipped dinner, we'd been in spiritual conversation with Mina and Mother for about six hours by now. Except for Ayako sometimes hand testing[16] from her dining chair, El and I had been swaying on our feet the entire time. My stiff lower back burned in knotty resentment. Trembling legs tottered from the fatigue of Mina's energetic answers. Here in my house this crazy evening with him thrashing so many cornerstone beliefs, the contradiction with Michael's pious professions through Ms. Medium resolved into focus. It opened a new line of inquiry I couldn't resist and demanded explanation in any case.

There was little doubt in my mind we were receiving outside-of-self answers to our questions. Besides astounded to my core by this wholly unexpected turn of events, the spiritual energy in the house and coursing through our bodies was electric even for a two-dimensional guy like me who saw himself amongst the more spiritually dense of the species. It was all too strong, too real, certainly nothing my body had ever experienced. And this wasn't merely me observing Ms. Medium's clairvoyance, but my daughters' and my own. The three of us double-checked, validated, and corrected each other. Ayako was a regular genius sorting out the confusion of my oft-vague query formulations. As a historian, pastor, chaplain, theologian, research writer, software engineer, deputy sheriff, and all-around seeker of truth, the one thing I can't abide is illogic, irrationality, inconsistency, and complexification. They point only to confusion and untruth. Contradiction's a fair beast to slay or one can't claim to *know* anything. Aside from simply defaulting to 'divine' authority, how was I to resolve the apparent contradiction

---

16. Using the subtle energy in the hands to replicate sway, or push, test results (*SOL* § 2.2.1.1:626).

between this evening's new information and Michael's from our Angel Code meetings seven weeks ago?

I thought the solution was obvious. "Creator, would you ask Archangel Michael if he'd come so we could ask him a few things?"

Yes. You bet.

We expected a friendly Q&A. We got something else entirely.

The Fracas

2

Thursday October 12, 2017 ca. 11 pm

Both girls felt Michael's energy enter the room. El described it as calm, quiet and unassuming. I thanked him for coming. Ayako still lounged in the open dining area facing El, standing in the open living room. She was leaning on the opposite side of the peninsular kitchen counter from me rocking on my feet in the open kitchen in front of our double-door fridge. I sensed, or rather felt, Michael alternately rooted stock-still then pacing from one side of El to the other. Ayako considered herself already plenty experienced interacting with spirit world since childhood—as, too, did El since the previous weekend (§ 1.2:59)—and felt his presence was the real deal.

For starters, we put Mina's new information about the no-Fall and Adam and Eve, Cain and Abel, and Satan's non-existence along with Lucifer's amazing innocence to Michael. Enthused over the evening's events and our minds expanding beyond albeit still boxed into many preconceived notions, none of us imagined what we were about to unleash.

"Did you know about any of this before now?" El straight up said, some cross-examination in her voice.

No, Michael said. *I'm only learning about it this very moment.* His response felt less energetic—less confident, maybe?—than Mina's and slower besides, as if hesitant, perhaps temporizing.

"What about the stuff you told us in the Angel Code meetings?" I said, and not just a little skeptically, either. "How you saw the Fall happen, about Lucifer's violence and arrogance . . ."

No.

"No? You didn't tell us those things?"

Yes.

"What?" I scowled across the counter at El, looking a tad quizzical herself. "I don't—"

"Come on, Dad," Ayako said, "you have to remember he's being literal. He means yes, he *didn't* tell you those things."

Ah, jeez. I'd stumbled again over my own poorly phrased question—"vague," Mina later called my grammatical convolutions. "Well, if you didn't tell us those things . . ."

"Michael, are you saying Ms. Medium lied?" said El.

"Whoa," I said. "How'd you get to *that*?"

If eyeballs could shrug. Two-for-two cutting straight to the point, though.

She pressed on: "So, did she, Michael?"

Yes.

I felt a sucker punch to the chin. "Creator, is that true? She *lied*?"

Yes.

My lungs vacuumed the room through my slack-jawed mouth. That was such a hard pill to swallow I could only set it aside for the moment. Instead, I said, "But, Michael, you just told us you *didn't* know the Fall never happened or that Lucifer was *never* guilty of wrecking the universe. That's exactly what Ms. Medium said."

"You have to ask a yes or no, Dad."

Bah. The whole discussion was already feeling queer.

El said, "Did you know the Fall never happened, Michael?"

No.

"Or that Lucifer never 'tempted' or 'fell' with anybody, especially not with Eve who never even existed?" El was giving me that epic-pastor-fail look again.

No. I didn't know a thing about it. I'm totally surprised!

I said, "You told us you watched it happen!"

Yes. His answer was consistent but felt more like a shrug, to be honest. And after all it was Ms. Medium who'd actually said it.

El's eyes were on me, a little viper behind her lashes. "Dad thinks you're lying, Michael."

"What? No! I wasn't saying—I mean, that's not..."

"*Are* you lying, Michael?"

"For God's sake, El! I'm trying to find out—"

No.

"Somebody's lying,"—Lordy, but I'd raised a snappy little trial lawyer—"either Michael or Creator. The Fall happened, or it didn't. Adam and Eve exist, or they don't. Michael saw it go down, or he didn't. Lucifer—"

"Yeah, yeah, I got it." I contemplated things a tick or two. "There's something we're not understanding."

"Well, there's only one way to—"

I palmed a hand at her. "Just gimme a minute, will you?"

"So, Michael," she declared, ignoring the parental hand, "for sure you did *not* know Lucifer's innocent. Is that correct?"

Yes. I didn't know.

But, really, how? It's preposterous that falsehoods like the Fall or Adam and Eve's existence or Lucifer's rebellion could endure from the beginning of time, hidden from Mina's own archangels, from their very eyeballs as they traversed the cosmos in service to humanity. Was there something Michael *wasn't* saying? *Was* he lying? Did angels even lie? And right in front of God? If *God* was lying...well, what for? Why would anybody—well, except Adam, Eve, or Lucifer—lie about any of this? *Cui bono?*[17]

---

17. *To whom is it a benefit?* From Cicero, " 'cui bono' fuisset" in *Pro Roscio Amerino* (80 BC), § 84.

I felt entirely perplexed. Perspicacious El seemed flummoxed, too. Ayako just looked content to referee. As I mulled it over, arms folded and head absently bowed to my inner investigator, I tried to formulate some rational follow-on query. Movement caught my eye.

1.1   Lucifer Arrives in a Fury ...

El stiffened. Fear flashed across her face. Facing me, she twisted her torso round and jerked her eyes toward the front wall of the house. My own eyes followed but met only our two cavernous living room windows, inky black portals to the utterly Stygian forested Virginia night that had so terrified the girls when we'd first moved in from the luminous suburbs four years earlier. We could've been floating inside a black hole. She flinched, cried, and faltered backward, colliding with a counter stool.

"It's Lucifer!" she hissed. In that instant, her spiritual senses had opened wide. She perceived Lucifer huge and swelling and in a fury blasting into our house through the exterior living room wall. She felt his seething energy. Saw "his eyes raging with murder and squarely fixed on *me*!"

Ayako shrank transfixed into her chair, eyes locked on her sister and Michael beside her. I sensed his nebulous shape or lambent presence standing to El's left but moving fast to her right. My own feet felt magically stapled to the pine floorboards. I didn't understand my daughters' reactions because I neither spiritually saw nor intuitively perceived their experience. All the same, icy fingers fluttered over my skin as a ball of lead sank in my gut. El burst out crying as she described a spiritual blowout.

"Dad! Lucifer and Michael are fighting!" Her eyes tracked them struggling down along the length of the peninsular countertop. "They're right in front of your bedroom door now!"

"I don't see anything," I said.

"You can't feel the heat?" said Ayako with accusation, eyes fixated on the vestibule where my bedroom entry cornered off the basement stairs.

"They're really fighting, Dad!" Panic and tears lit El's voice. "I mean, *ohmigod*, it's a full-on battle!"

She scooted round the kitchen counter's end and latched hard onto me. Her eyes refused to relax their grip on the unseen tableaux at my bedroom door. I felt her quaking and hugged her close with my left arm, wondering just what I should do. What I *could* do. Not in the parenting manual, this. Ayako was mute, rigid against her chairback, knees locked, legs straight out in the air, hands white-knuckled on the seat's edge. Her eyes bored a beeline over her toes to the angelic battleground at my bedroom door. Though we didn't know it then, spirit persons Taiji, Hideto, *Obāsan*,[18] and Ayako's own two guardian angels protectively surrounded her. Then seventeen *other* angels 'jumped into' Ayako to shield her from the fierce energies spiritually scorching the room. Taiji screamed. Hideto froze in fear. El's and my guardian angels, along with my dad (d. 2012) and his mother (d. 1992), shielded the two of us., El's countenance was darkly furious.

She clamorously *commanded*, "Mina, get them out! Right now! Take your fight out of here, Michael! Go on! Get out! Get out!" She angled iron, mutinous expectations up at Captain Dad.

"Creator!" I bellowed, my voice hard yet feeling stupid all the same because, to me—except for their terror and my persistent icy, bony fingers, leaden feet, and some vague Spidey sense—the house was calm as ever. "Please, get them out of the house right away. *Now.* They're scaring everybody!"

In moments, my children relaxed. El reported the archangels gone and Ayako that their blistering heat had waned. She slowly unwound, legs deflating feet to floor and color returning to her hands. Her welling eyes shifted to me. I sharply felt my dimwitted helplessness.

With a strident tone El said, "Will you keep Lucifer out of our house, Creator?"

Yes.

"You promise he can't come back inside?"

Yes.

"You'll keep him out if he means *any* harm to me or wants to fight?"

Yes.

She looked none too placated to me. But how militant does one really get with the world's creator? Well, maybe plenty, judging by El's clamant attitude.

---

18. Japanese (お祖母さん): *grandmother.* Taiji Sawada and Hideto (Hidé; *hee-deh*) Matsumoto are dead Japanese rock stars. *Obāsan* is my children's great-great grandmother. More on them later and in the endnotes (EN 54:184; EN 56:185; EN 59:185; see also page 64).

"I feel burned up, Dad," Ayako said, verging on tears. "It was like a blowtorch shooting over from your bedroom. I thought I was gonna catch fire!"

El echoed her big sister's perception.

I said, "Why didn't you move, or just come over here with me?" I was already feeling heelish not yanking her out of the line of fire myself. Even if I couldn't see it or feel it, she could and it showed. That should've moved me to snatch her from her chair, dammit.

She blinked, flipping her palms up in her lap. "I couldn't move. It was too terrifying. You can't imagine. I felt, you know . . . I don't know, locked in place."

"Jeez."

Then El squealed in full panic. "*Ohmigod*, they're fighting in the spirit world! They're scaring *everybody*! Dad! Spirit world's emptying out . . . the angels are taking sides! People are running away to Earth to escape the war!"

"Wha—?"

With a guilt-ridden expression, wet eyes beseeching my soul, El breathed, "You don't think we broke the world, do you, Dad?"

I mean, seriously? The world's been here a long time and people have done a lot dumber stuff than this. I paced, massaged my neck. All I could finally muster was, "I don't know, honey. I'm sure it'll be okay."

What El was actually sensing, we learned, were hundreds of *quadrillions* of what we then thought of as angels flocking from across the universe to the epicenter of Michael and Lucifer's unprecedented, ferocious pulse of raw, supercharged mind 'energy' (we later termed it *L*ife force; *SOL* § 6.11.4:198; *SOL* § 2.3.2.1:241), a colossal macroburst that clobbered our universe. Arriving in various states of concern, curiosity, and uproar, they literally packed the planet and solar system's 'spiritual plane' to capacity. This titanic energetic disruption pushed the, on average, ten-plus billion potently weaker spirit people here minding their own (or maybe your) business right off the Earth the way a light bulb scatters roaches. At that moment, however, this was all beyond our ability even to imagine.[4]

Agog with worry, we peppered Mina for insight. El found Mother and him in seemingly grave spirits over the fallout from the chaos in spirit world (not exactly; not in the way we construed things, but we thought so, then). That revelation only cranked El's fears higher. Her blood ran cold in dread of billions on gazillions of fear-crazed or outright 'evil' spirits fleeing angelic bedlam wreaking havoc on Earth's innocent like wandering barbarian hordes. She nagged Mina for our house to be the safest refuge in the world—he promised it now was—because, by this time of the night, she was examining her unfortunate need to sleep, unconscious and vulnerable, and not liking her prospects.

Not gazillions, but quadrillions of guardian angels garboiling all round the planet now left their physical human charges on the back burner to pile into this crowd—El's and mine chose later that night to leave us because of how we'd interrogated Michael—to directly witness and focus their collective attention on this situation. Ayako's were older and more sober. They'd interposed before her like angelic Marines.[5] Although the guardian angel coterie left many people across our world and the universe in the lurch that night, Lucifer mobilized temporary replacements within 36–48 hours and permanent replacements in a week.[6]

When Mina revealed all this to us—we were surprised, to be sure, though instinctively felt *au courant* to know Lucifer oversaw guardian angels—and how dire he and Mother had viewed a celestial 'war' cooking off in spirit world . . . well, we might've had *Ghostbusters* (1984) on the brain. While the overall situation seemed an epic crisis for the angels and scattering humans, Mina didn't take the angelic uproar or the human spirit world's manic panic as a crisis the way we did at all. He understood the emotional outburst as normal if not orderly or productive. Of course, the questions we'd posed, especially framing them in terms of 'war,' and how we'd interpreted the answers, had a lot to do with our mindset at the time.[7] When it occurred to us to ask, we learned war can't achieve anything in spirit world. Celestial war and angelic rebellions are the personification of physical world concepts. Violent struggle isn't an angelic proclivity anyway, even though angels do emote and fight and spirit humans do play war.[8]

A plot twist blew out this 'heavenly storm' the next morning. But the mood in our home this night was grim. We—particularly El—felt responsible for blowing up spirit world to rival (in our minds) anything vedic or biblical, all because of our cat-killing curiosity.[9] Yet, for all that, my children were adamant that Mother and Mina hadn't lost their immense joy and excitement that we'd productively uncovered these realities for the first time, even if the initial outcome seemed to us wholly counterproductive. Master compartmentalizers those two are, we reckoned.

On the other hand, my daughters' joyous feelings and (probably cavalier) excitement had evaporated. Ayako, for all her airy *sangfroid* throughout the evening, was feeling the shock of her life as Mother mused over a 'providential' response that might've asked her—to paraphrase Lucy Baldwin's sharp 1940s wit—to "just close your eyes and think of England."[10] El's earlier exuberance and steely prosecutorial persona shattered. She was frantic spirit world would descend any moment on our gloomy forest home thrusting torches and pitchforks high, convulsing with fury to 'get' the instigator of their travails.

Our energy now about as insolvent as the Weimar treasury, we finally called our talkathon a night near on one o'clock in the morning. Ayako quietly cried herself into a fitful sleep somewhere near dawn. Her sister bolted her basement door with a chair under the knob and trembled 'neath her sheets. Me, I instantly passed out, obtuse head to pillow.

Michael's Reveal

3

Friday October 13, 2017 ca. 6 am

I **awoke Friday the** 13th to a whispery house a little wrung out a few ticks past six, the sky just lightening into sunrise still an hour away. I lay awhile sprawled under warm, embracing blankets pondering our big event now dawning into an unheralded PART DEUX. Eventually, I found myself in my just-bought plush and comfy swivel desk chair with a steaming homemade Indian *masala* tea lubricating the brain wheels and studying last night's shocking events, especially Michael's odd-sock behavior that seemed to be what set off the fracas. If I was to bet money, something there was going unspoken—were I to take it all at face value, that is. What were my options, realistically? Flush it out the back of my head or drop another nickel in the slot, is what I figured.

I climbed to my feet and free-ranged questions with Mina—still there, so I wasn't hallucinating—trying to grasp the Fall of Man biblically and in Sun-myung's Divine Principle interpretation in light of what we'd learned the previous evening. It was a slow and laborious process for me. I wasn't near as adept at this conversational method as my daughters had tirelessly made themselves in the single short week just passed. However, I could literally feel Mina's energy pulsate through my body, so I had that going for my credulity. His answers were plain but came torturously slow, sometimes so languid I wasn't sure I'd even got one. I asked and re-asked questions and statements just to satisfy myself I'd received what I thought I'd received. More than once I apologized for being tedious. More than once he pushed back, *no problem*.

1.1   El Rises to the Occasion . . .

Despite his ungrudging answers, I couldn't yet see any bigger picture. Whatever train of thought I needed to follow eluded me. I felt stuck. Exasperated. I dropped into my chair and nursed the remains of my tea. Not much later, I heard a peeved clomping on the stairs—El rising uncharacteristically early from her basement dwelling as her older sister still lay dead to the world.

"What are you doing, Dad?" she grumped as she staggered in barefoot. "Archangel Gabriel just *literally* pulled me bodily out of my warm, toasty, loving bed and told me I was needed upstairs."

I'm sure I sort of gaped at her. "Really? He *pulled* you out of bed? Like, physically?"

"Yes! I could feel him tugging on my ankle, like I had no choice. So . . ." She crossed her arms and cocked a hip not unlike some pointy-head schoolmarm, I thought. "What have you started?"

I snorted tea. Boy, children! Wait. I'd forgot: she was entering day three of her eighteenth year today . . . and artlessly trying out its pre-adult powers.

After explaining my investigative effort, she took over receiving answers while I sat back in my deluxe leather seat, eyes lidded like Roman Rudenko scaring up another prosecution for Stalin. With my daughter as Mina's stand-in, I threaded my way through humanity's supposed fall from grace as Divine Principle and Judeo-Christo-Islam (and humanity generally) typically understand it juxtaposed against the new data we'd encountered the night before. El emotes the spiritual energy and feelings that she intuits with an esprit as entertaining as informative. As she vocalized Mina's responses, she couldn't help aping his heart and personality the way she did Mother the previous evening. This natural ability of hers is what really elevated this experience for me from a pretty-hard-to-believe curiosity that might've simply fizzled to a serious revelatory experience meant to be seriously taken. As I watched her work, it seemed Mina himself was poised in her, well, bare feet.

I picked my way through the process and motivation of the Fall as Mina confirmed or rejected the various theological elements I raised. Each validation or repudiation then spawned entirely new directions to pursue. Hope I was actually getting somewhere started brewing, yet there was a lot of institutional confusion to work through. I caught myself wondering if my investigative effort was the sort of process by which Sunmyung, if not Jesus too, had come to understand the Fall as he did.[11]

It's worth saying that even in such a serious moment as this Mina was not above kidding around. He's simply not overwhelmed by life the way our spiritually immiserized existence creates the impression we're circling the drain. He has a long view that makes ours myopic. However momentous an event this was for us, it could've been just another day at the office for him. How often has he been disappointed? I had to wonder. Were we going to be just another flat tire? Well... he *was* excited, we could tell that. But worried? vexed? Not really, more like neutrally observing. El occasionally stopped herself with a, "was that a joke?" or, "are you laughing right now?" and we'd have a jocular sidebar until she'd soberly ask, "So, what's your serious answer to Dad's question, Creator?" Or I would. Patience isn't always my strong suit.

Then El set flat eyes on me. "Michael just arrived," she said.

1.2 Michael Arrives...

"He's here? Right now?" My own eyes quested through the room. I said, "Uh...hi, Michael," and to El, "Where's he standing...or whatever?" I mean, he could be floating in the lotus position, right?

"I think he's sitting on the bed."

"What, like, right in front of me?"

"That's my impression. I can kind of see him where he is, but not quite. You know what I mean?"

My shaking head said not even close. It later turned out her impression was not of Michael but Taiji, who'd slipped in to watch our efforts. I imagined his irreverent self bringing popcorn to make it a show. Michael, on the other hand, had only briefly stepped into my bedroom to trip El's antennae to his presence before closeting himself in Ayako's bedroom where he could feel out of prying eyes. She reminded him of someone he'd loved and trusted, which after all his volleying with Ms. Medium and Lucifer, as well as his own fears, gave him a sense of safety and comfort. Initially, Gabriel had attempted to rouse Ayako to help me talk with Mina, but Michael stayed his hand for reasons we detail farther on. He'd pulled El from her slumber, instead, and sent her upstairs to me.

I said, "Could I ask you some more questions, Michael?"

El swayed and nodded. As I queried him, I couldn't help but feel myself, maybe irreverently, looming over Boss Tweed's 1870s New York City Chambers Street witness rail in a sober, inquisitorial three-piece. Keeping my attitude friendly and respectful was job one, I reminded myself. Badgering angels wasn't on my bucket list. Neither was shooting down possibly my one opportunity to plough the world's oldest unbroken sod. Nevertheless, Ms. Medium's flagged narrative—especially last night's protestations of ignorance in spite of Michael faulting her misrepresentations (which I was far from ready to call lying)—had my mind on rails. I homed in on how he could possibly have not known there'd been no human Fall, let alone Adam and Eve's very central absence from the scene. There's a certain hierarchy of credibility here. Discrepancies between versions could realistically be resolved only one way. Absent better evidence, I defaulted to Mina's.[12]

The more I dug into the Fall and Michael's role, the more I sensed some level of evasion, or at least an ulterior theme. Not outright obfuscation, really—certainly not lying—but avoidance, I supposed, a preference to beat around the bush. In our experience, angels tell the truth when it's put right to them (and they're not winding you up with a grin). This morning I couldn't tell myself angels don't lie because Michael's discrepancies last night would've had me whitewashing a truth. So, it wouldn't be they can't or don't lie, just that (following Michael's Reveal) they haven't to *us* . . . that we could detect.

Increasingly, I was seeing Michael playing some untoward role in germinating the very concept of the Fall. Not to mention the ancient accusations that Lucifer deceived Man to become "God of this world" (2 Cor. 4:4 KJV), tore down the heavens in war and rebellion and, in Divine Principle's more recent indictment, that he'd statutorily raped (a now non-existent) Eve and utterly corrupted human nature till we hated our own selves worst of all. Goosebumps surged and prickled as I examined his answers through my unexpectedly sagacious daughter.

1.3 LUCIFER INTRUDES . . .

Startling me in my ruminations, El jumped and gulped a breath. She shrank into the wall. "Lucifer's here!" she yelped. "Creator! You *promised* Lucifer couldn't come back in our house!" Fear and accusation fairly roared from her tight throat.

"Hang on," I said, flying to my feet. "Creator, *is* Lucifer here?"
Yes.

In fact, he'd planted himself in Ayako's room and was eyeing Michael nose-to-nose. I fisted hands on hips. "Does he mean any harm? Is he going to fight with Michael?"

No.

"He's agreeing to be peaceful?"

Yes.

"So he's here with your permission, then?"

Yes. Of course. A little *duh* crept out of his response but that might've just been me.

Hunched flat against the wall, El's eyes circled the room like prey. "You'll kick him out if he makes any trouble?"

Yes.

"But not," I clarified, "if he's being peaceful."

Yes.

"Is that true, Lucifer?" I added for El's benefit. I wasn't feeling any threat myself. "You're going to behave yourself?"

Yes.

I know! It sounds ridiculous, considering who's in the house. But my daughter whom I *loved* now looked election-night panicked. Ayako's forsaken, imploring face from last night smoldered fresh in my mind. This was my house, so my rules. Just because I'm an earth-bound human doesn't mean I have no authority, even with an angel—though, since they're invisible beings, it's not like my authority goes far. Frankly, sometimes the authority you have is the authority you take. Nobody respects a weenie. Anyhow, Unificationism taught me that God created human beings higher than he did angels and I was still operating on that premise. We have since learned that human beings and angels are equal in all respects because both are human beings. There's no higher–lower, superior–inferior, or even authority amongst angels themselves or between angels, humans, and Mina. That's physical humanity's vogue. We're each of us, altogether, the human 'race,' a veritable family vast and universal (we use 'angel' here for clarity).

El still cringed all saucer-eyed. As I talked it through, she got a better feel for our home's energy and slowly uncoiled as she more clearly felt Lucifer's intentions. She plainly trusted Mina. And me. But if Lucifer chose to rampage, there wasn't anything I could practically do about it. I couldn't exactly go toe-to-toe like Jacob at the Ford of

Jabok$_{13}$ ... not without a Sam Colt in hand, and what good would that do? Her own fear and misgivings vying with trust in Mina, she accepted Lucifer's reassurances and pulled herself together to carry on. After all, she'd seen and felt his thunderous wrath seemingly bullseyed right on her just last night. Who wouldn't residually quail from that? Whether his real intent was accidental or indicated some hellish true nature was beside the point. Sure as eggs is eggs, it was real enough for her.

If indeed Lucifer was framed for the Fall, then bringing that lie to the surface should've been a welcome relief to him. In that light, his volatile behavior perplexed me as much as Michael's equivocation. But, at the end of the day, El was a just-eighteen young lady thoroughly awed by who he was and his imposing size and fury. Later that evening, and for several days thereafter, he would profusely apologize to us all for that wild night. He especially comforted El till her anguish melted in his arms. That story comes farther on.

At this point, Michael said he wanted to talk about the Fall and his role regarding it, but not with Lucifer in his face. What he wanted to get out he preferred said in private without Lucifer right there possibly reacting with anger.

Anger? I could almost hear Lucifer's echo.

A moment of unheard angel–God conversation later, Lucifer exited Ayako's room exuding much obvious misgiving, annoyance, and suspicion, and cooled his heels on a counter stool in the main room. Gabriel had been here awhile already, and together they waited on whatever it was to come off Michael's chest. I turned my attention back to Michael when I'd verified Lucifer's departure (to the degree possible). He answered a long series of questions which only bore witness to just how human angels are.

1.4 THE TALE MICHAEL TELLS ...

Here's Michael's tale as he now amended it, told on unsteady feet over Ayako's sleeping countenance, a seraphic image of comfort, trust, and non-judgment he could pretend was his only audience.

1.4.1 THE FALL OF MAN THAT WASN'T

There was indeed no original couple, he admitted, and he (along with Mina, Lucifer, and Jesus) fully well knew it. No Adam and Eve from which sprang the human race with some inherent duty to obey or worship God.[14] No providential responsibility to perfect themselves (Matt. 5:48; Moon 2006, 78) and bear perfected children (Moon, 34, 64). No disobedience or attempt to be "like God" (Gen. 3:5) or some other 'failure' that doomed as-yet-unborn humanity to physical death, eternal suffering, or some loathsome compromise with both without, as in many human traditions, some complex and ever-postponed salvific process. This goes for every human creation myth, not just the Abrahamic religions. Sure, Mina guided our physical bodies from microbe to swaggering biped but humans were and are naturally, *divinely*[19] human in accord with our intrinsic way of being. And then physical humanity's nineteenth generation[20] produced a woman—Mnèèptē (pronounced 'muuh-ne-ehp-tee'), in her language,[15]—whom Michael came to love.[16] As. Did. Lucifer. She chose Lucifer. Yeah, *boi*.

"Oh, my God," I mumbled, "are you kidding? It's a classic love triangle!" My angelology was no-joke getting a sobering upgrade. El's face was a panoply of expressions I had some trouble deciphering. Did she even know what a love triangle was? Maybe. Probably. Kids today are sadly more savvy than we parents might care to know and mine did plenty of reading. . . I elected to worry later.

Bereft, Michael had felt inferior, as anyone who's ever loved unrequitedly knows. Coincidentally, it was at just this point in human history that angels were increasingly noticing that, as a 'race,' they'd transformed from how they were at their inception to what today we call *fallen* or *Corrupt* but, for those back then, was yet unclear.

---

19. Not a turn of phrase Mina wholeheartedly approves owing to the implications in *divine*. We want to convey the intangible distinction between humanoid and human when, from the apparent fossil record, we can't perceive the difference.

20. Not on Earth, but at the time it was more or less the same generation everywhere because angels guided our coetaneous development across all human-inhabited worlds. Mina wanted none of his children to fall behind any others due to factors outside their control, although the human factor has since naturally thrown off that little dream.

This was a source of real concern and angst amongst the angels who after all had taken on the task to raise, educate, and protect humans in the physical world. Yet, humans and angels both only knew they were becoming...well, different, and not a good different. No one understood why what Mina calls The Corruption was happening because it was already confusing them. Humans and angels didn't perceive it for what it was or even act to nip it in the bud.

Mina laments that, although they could have, no one turned to him for guidance. They'd already forgot, or transposed, or got hazy on a lot of his story of life including him as an accessible parent, grandparent, and friend. Without their cooperation, Mina had no practical means to alter mindsets, though he was far from tightlipped. And even if he did, he'd never quash their freedom to be whatever they wanted to be. That's ultimately what it means to be free and loved. The Corruption's allure is strong, exquisitely gossamery, and comes across sensible and right. It has a short-term quality all its own but none of its presumed benefits—a cotton candy in the rain, one might say. The justifying delusions we create render it self-sustaining.

In this insidious milieu of *Accountability*[21]—its minions morality, justice, fairness, law, judgment, punishment—young Michael$_{17}$ for the first time encountered a self-negating inferiority in his beloved Mnèèptē choosing Lucifer (obviously, the better man in *her* eyes and something of an accusation in its own right) over him. Surely, her inexplicable choice meant Lucifer must have said or done something nefarious to harm her feelings for him. He lashed out in wounded 'justice,' as a wrongheaded youth might, to subtly discredit Lucifer as the better man not only in her eyes but in all. Like a cartoon anvil, Michael dropped the same heavy weight of hurt, loss, and accusation he was feeling times a million on Lucifer. Up to this point, there'd been no love relationships between physically alive humans and

---

21. Divine accountability; accountable to the universal moral standard—one's Divine Creator—for one's behavior in Thought and deed that causes harm in violation of our Creator's universal truth. Its nature necessarily requires blame and shared enforcement of the universal moral standard (divine Will) to compel living in accord with the Creator's divine (ultimate) altruism, i.e., harmlessness (SOL § 1.1:362; SOL § 4.1.2:378).

spirit world angels nor the dysfunctions we take as usual. This was unknown territory for both. Already alienated from Mina by The Corruption (the physically alive also estranged by a diminishing spiritual awareness), humanity lost touch with many core principles of life by which the universe, Mina, and humanity operate. In that vein, a human–angel relationship seemed unnatural to angels. It could be made to appear *morally* wrong. A penal offense, even.

Michael initiated a deception amongst the angels that it was Lucifer's relationship with Mnèèptē[18] that proximately caused what, in truth, was only the coincidental Corruption now twisting (especially a spiritually atrophying physical[19]) humanity into, Mina emphasized, "malevolence." It was not a rumor traceable to its source because Michael insinuated it as inexplicitly as The Corruption itself had. And really, like any good con amongst a willing or gullible audience, it needed only an impetus and the occasional reinforcement whilst it matured. As with The Corruption, Michael's deception self-reinforced. Angels naturally intensified and embellished it in the thinking and telling akin to the game *Chinese Whispers* or *Telephone* no different from humans. Some angels, of course, knew Lucifer well enough to scoff at the very notion. Yet his own childhood[22] was itself marred in a way that encouraged even their contemner.

Gradually, and without consulting Mina—indeed, as comprehension of Mina's nature metamorphosed from reality to delusion—many in the angelic world blamed Lucifer for The Corruption they were all feeling in themselves and seeing in physical humanity. They rejected him even as he lived amongst them and oversaw the work of guardian angels. Michael's fake news percolated into physical humanity's consciousness despite The Corruption degrading the connection between our spiritual mind and physical brain. The human belief that Satan–Devil–Lucifer rebelled against God, evilly deceived Eve, precipitated the human Fall thus corrupting our nature and creating death and all evil, seized our birthright, and rallied the troops to fight an actual war against courageous Michael and his own stalwarts until being "hurled down" (Rev. 12:9)[20] persists to

---

22. Angels are born babies and grow up in families, as they're human not a separate 'angelic race.'

this day, along with its countless derivations spread throughout humanity's creation myths. All of it spewed from the elements of Michael's Lie, itself rooted in The Corruption's very premise. Physical humanity saw in this two-pronged delusion, allied to our singular imaginations,[21] the reason for life's toil and trouble, death and distress, and our inability to live up to a preternatural 'divine' nature and its hippie-dippie perfection—the whole problem of evil in a nutshell, really. Out of this dirty bath trod Religion and Philosophy, all shiny and neat and wearing sensible shoes.

Educing Michael's story was truly labyrinthine. Its terribly divergent nature, our own mindset, and the tedious, literal means of our communication were so many traps and pitfalls.[22] In the course of nitpicking through the many questions, blind alleys, and apparent contradictions, Michael hesitated, prevaricated, and obfuscated, for sure. He never lied, though. We give him a pass on the former because his fear and shame was a tough nut with a preferably avoided Mina figuratively standing ('dialed in long distance') right there. Too, our communication constraints prevented him volunteering information except through our intuitive faculties—certainly less helpful then than now. Contradictions or illogic that might've indicated fraud he cleared up with sensible, logical consistency when we zeroed in on the right queries. He framed the preceding story and resolved its arcana. Mina, Gabriel, and Lucifer fleshed it out over time.

1.4.2 Why Michael Told His Tale

We're talking epochal time scales here. Why did Michael only now want to get this story out? Even as a far-out, wrong-way Moonie[23] you could've knocked me over with a feather when Michael allowed that part of the reason was that, as the great Ibn Sina might say, Sun-myung's *wājeb-al-wujud*[23] produced actual, tangible spirit-world

---

23. Arabic: *necessary being* (واجبالوجود; coined by Avicenna (d. 1037) to inject Persian ontology into ontologically bare Arabic); principally, Sun-myung's ontic 'is-ness' (Persian: *hasti*) of loving without condition what necessitates being unloved: Satan. His way wasn't wishful make-believe after all. Mina credits him the only human (spirit unaware; no direct access like Jesus (and another)) to arrive at this core apprehension of love despite Earth's never critically examined admonition to "love your enemies" (Mt. 5:44). A supremely torturous path to 'level up' this way.

effects. He literally altered universal reality. Staggeringly counter-intuitive considering how wrong he'd got God, Lucifer, most of his Divine Principle including the Fall of Man, his bombastic procla-mations, and (it goes without saying) a corrupt, abusive church institution he built from scratch and failed to curb. All the same (and it just goes to show), one of his effects was to rouse Lucifer in 1999[24] to let go his obdurate pain of condemnation "and just move on" by at last accepting Mnèèptē's hand, which he'd held at arms' length since the accusations sprang up so long ago, and to start a family.[25] The first substantive improvement in human reality since The Corruption—because it made what's coming next possible— and it was globally disparaged Sun-myung Moon who'd kicked it off with universally shunned Lucifer. Well, it stole my breath.

Lucifer's change of heart jolted Michael as if from a stupor. After all this time, he didn't love Mnèèptē the same way anymore, nor was she the reason he'd now decided to set things right and clear his heavy guilt. But like me feeling woke from Ms. Medium's storytime, Lucifer's new reality *woke* Michael. Then, like anyone dreading owning such an epic cock-up, he got cold feet—and here's why he stayed Gabriel's hand from waking up the far defter Ayako to help me energy test: El's unseasoned skill would delay the chopping block that much longer, and in any case Ayako, for reasons below, was now his indispensable muse. Accepting since 1999[26] how egregiously he'd acted and fearing everyone's reaction to the news, he couldn't bring himself to sidle on up to Lucifer and let it rip. That seemed like dumping water onto quiescently boiling oil. Lucifer only reinforced the image when, clueless, he'd overheard Michael's obvious lies the night before and apoplectically, if tentatively, tallied two and two.

1.5 Michael Reflects . . .

After their brawl and our retiring for the night, Lucifer had button-holed Michael to come clean even more doggedly than he'd done after Mina had 'broadcast' the truth throughout our 'quantumly entangled' universe[27] at the very start of this ancient drama, and Jesus himself had confronted the issue. Unfazed, yet paralyzed by indecision, Michael held fast his denials despite Lucifer hearing his inculpating palter *in flagrante delicto*. As evenings went, I thought his own sounded pretty bleak, tense, and scary, but he disagreed when we talked it over many months later.

I said, "So, Lucifer wasn't some raging bull like he was earlier but actually calm and reasonable?"

Yes. He was calm.

"He wasn't looming over you with his fists? Screaming in your ear? Pushing you around?"

Michael laughed. *No.*

"Kinda like two brothers talking, maybe."

Yes.

"Just a long, tedious harangue, then?"

Yes, pretty much.

"After I asked Creator to call you and asked my first question, did you know where it was going. . . like, the writing was on the wall?"

Yes.

"No backing out then. This was it."

Yes.

"On account of Creator being there?"

No.

"The Angel Code discrepancy, then?"

Yes.

I barked a laugh. "Just that?"

No.

Dang. These guessing games. Intuition took a minute. "Umm. . . well. . . there was no backing out because you'd irrevocably committed yourself to getting this out, coming clean?"

Yes.

"But, by now, I guess your plan for that was fairly shot to hell— um, so to speak, I mean."

Yes. Boy, yes!

"Uhh, sorry about that?" But was I? Probably not.

No. So, neither of us then.

It wasn't that Michael preferred humans to angels for his mea culpa. Just that physical humans were, by dint of ignorance, the only neutral ones in his view. He'd recognized that the Unificationism-derived (though faulty) belief the so-called Fall had traumatized the angels could meet his need. Moth Man's friend had embraced it, so he'd persuaded Gabriel to call him forth in a dream. It seemed a perfect venue. In the midst of expressing his pain, he could "just let slip" the sordid truth in a safer, therapeutic environment with Gabriel at his back that might mute the inevitable raving shitstorm. Instead, Ms. Medium hijacked his effort for her own wicked reasons and produced her dodgy divergence between Michael's alleged account and Mina's own—plus, scotched that marvelous Angel Code book I was dreaming up.[28] Worse still for Michael, the girls and I came away all boozed up on Ms. Medium's pious sham, but had now asked him to his face all the wrong questions in front of the decidedly wrong crowd like a disappointed tosspot bellowing right at the bar over cut whiskey.

Even though Ms. Medium put words in Michael's mouth, his denials to us last night were, on their own, a bundle of contradictions that, for me, cracked his credibility. Lucifer saw it, too, but in a land of unaccountability, what's a stonewalled angel to do? By October 2017, Michael's come-clean plan was in ruins. Ms. Medium had ice-picked him in the neck, the Angel Code folks had deviated into futility, and a spirit world TV exposé was a never-gonna-happen. Michael's easy options had narrowed to nil. Maybe he'd never get his penitence out and the universe would go on reeling immutably onward in its half-baked way. Then, yesterday, El went straight to the Source and we'd dragged him into it for the Sixty-four Dollar Question.

"But Creator said Jesus learned all about it and tried to help," I said, referring to Mina. "You didn't want him to mediate?"

No.

For crying out loud, why not? "Uh, let's see . . . well, you denied everything when Jesus confronted you during and after his lifetime, right?"

Yes.

"Did you see him as a neutral party at this point?"

No.

Never catching a break, that Jesus. "But you wanted the whole mess out and done with."

Yes.

"So . . . why'd you lie to *us*, then?" I wondered.

It was simple, really. Michael didn't like how we'd pulled him into this very public powwow with Mina. Even a half-wit could see it was an arrow straight between the eyes. He knew Lucifer's ear would catch it and, like snatching off a Band-Aid to 'soften' the pain, he just didn't want to go there, not like this, a raccoon trapped in a garbage can. He wanted to put us off track, gain himself some breathing space, control his situation. Bald-faced lying about Adam and Eve and Satan to our revealing queries would almost certainly provoke Lucifer into a fiery blow-up—who had his own reasons—and produce immense confusion. Maybe we'd get too scared and just let it go. If he was lucky, he might just deflect the whole thing until he could make more suitable arrangements that (perhaps foolishly setting aside his prior bad experience) involved a private confession through a mediator.

To that end, he'd wanted to go through Mnèèptē because of his sense of connection. Recently wed to Lucifer, she'd seemed the perfect go-between. Who better to tamp down ol' Lucifer's certain outrage? Then he imagined the inevitable horror and betrayal on her face for what he'd done and that plan seemed a whole lot less perfect. He felt just too ashamed to put it to her. That route was out. Sure, he wanted to scare off El and me like some *Scooby-Doo* scamp. On the plus side, he'd then intended to approach Ayako privately the way he had Ms. Medium in 2004. Mina said he'd often babysat Ayako and, minus his framing-Lucifer fiasco, she spiritually knew him pretty well (news to me). Michael calculated that her newfound energy testing—not as direct as Ms. Medium would've been, but sufficient for the task at hand—made her a suitable stand-in for his ideal intermediary.

She looks enough like Mnèèptē, affirmed Mina later, *the average person would think them sisters.*

Plus, Ayako snubbed her own judgmental tendencies where Ms. Medium gave them full rein. In Michael's mind, it added up to a win-win. Safe to approach and reminiscent of his former flame, Ayako was an ataractic for his much-daunted heart. Yes, the perfect muse, she was.

Well, we'd surprised Michael openly talking over the Fall with Mina. That hadn't happened since Jesus, and he'd done it privately, face-to-face, without serious controversy. Over time, The Corruption coupled to Michael's deceit converted Mina, in the minds of angels, into what we call an *Accountableist*[24] deity few found pleasant to contemplate. Michael hadn't even considered confessing to Mina in this sorry state of affairs. An eventual victim of his own deception, he'd come to fear a divine Accountability that never even existed.

"Hoist on your own petard," I said, clowning around.

Yes.

But he wasn't laughing. He hadn't welcomed our involving Mina until *after* the fat lady sang.

---

24. One concerned with accountability in all its forms. Basically, your typical god.

The Big Healing

4

Friday October 13, 2017 ca. 9 am

Is **that it**, Dad?" griped El, and stifled a (maybe fake) yawn. "You done? Can I go back to bed now?"

Wasn't she at least going to marvel a minute? "Hang on, sweetie. First, I'd like t—"

Her spine arched. "*Dad!*" she yowled in fear and anger. "Lucifer's back!"

With the bare bones of Michael's admission only barely out, and me off cogitating, Lucifer (low-key taking in Michael's stunner in the main room with Gabriel) bolted back into Ayako's room and startled Michael. El felt it, and could've jumped right out of her socks if she'd been wearing any. Suited up in a spirit world version of casual Friday that did sport socks, Michael practically did. He braced himself for Lucifer's long-dreaded, outraged, savage onslaught. He'd exactly predicted his clichéd reaction.

Hadn't he?

1.1 LUCIFER AND MICHAEL...

"Creator! You promised...!" But then El stopped. Listening via her intuition and *energism*[25] to take the measure of the room while quietly asking Mina questions, she instead said, "Wow, Dad! Lucifer's sitting on the bed with Michael... and—"

"He's on my bed now, too?"

Like me still learning the nuances of spiritually communicating, El assumed it was Lucifer she'd sensed on the bed from her intuition and scanty queries—until we got it sorted later—but it wasn't. Out in the main room, Hidé had been eyeballing Lucifer's darkening expression—surprise tangled up in hurt and betrayal—with a sinking soul at another fiery battle in the offing. He hadn't reacted too well the first time and wasn't hip to an encore. But he didn't want to desert us. Nestled in my bedroom with Taiji when (or *if*—nothing's sure till it's sure) a scrap kicked off had looked to Hidé a shrewd move, so in he'd fled. El sensed him enter and position himself on the bed alongside Taiji, facing me, about the same time she sensed Michael react to Lucifer barging in to brace him in Ayako's bedroom. Still presuming Taiji was Michael sitting on the bed, she figured the second person she'd sensed must be Lucifer. Instead, Lucifer and Michael were now shuddering cheek by jowl at Ayako's bedside. In these early days, El's sense experience sometimes intermingled with her energy test answers. If we weren't paying attention, we'd get confused until the inevitable contradictions pushed us to sort out corrections.

"—and... they're *embracing*! Michael's apologizing to Lucifer... he's in tears... and now so is Lucifer..." Her voice now quavered. "*Ohmigod*, Dad! They're just hugging and crying."

Lucifer had burst into Ayako's room with a tornado of emotion tearing through him. Yet, Michael's bared heart and the sheer intensity of his sorrow, regret, repentance, fear, self-contempt, grief, and despair carved across his countenance and buzzing through his

---

25. A term we redefine here to reflect the combination of skill, talent, experience, and receptiveness to encounter spiritual energy, in this case translating it to cognizable communication analogous to vibes and body language.

energy, all lumped into something that amounted to an unadulter-ated "I deserve it: taze me, bro," stopped Lucifer cold. He'd stormed into a choice—"When you come to a fork in the road, take it," Yogi Berra once quipped—with an instant to decide. Before he knew it, the past with all its hurt melted like hot beeswax out of each ferociously walled-up cell of the honeycomb bursting in his chest till all he knew and felt for Michael was *how Michael felt*. If he hadn't already reconciled his feelings for Mnèèptē and his overall situation back in 1999 (thanks to Sun-myung), then what was now happen-ing would've crashed and burned on the runway. It had altered Michael, made space for him to forgive himself and consequently accept Lucifer's forgiveness, which is what it takes for two people to reconcile (*SOL* § 4.2.1.3.3:381). Lucifer grabbed for Michael who dissolved into his unjudging, thoroughly *un*Accountableist embrace that lanced Michael's own pus-drowned *nous* like a boil.

Kicked back and possibly a little too relaxed in the saddle, I took in the empty, blank room—ignorant the real fireworks bloomed and thundered on the other side of the wall behind my chair and above Ayako's sleeping "shell," as she oft jested of her dormant body—and marveled at my younger daughter's sensitive perception. I'd long known Ayako was spiritually sensitive, but El's hit me from left field. A well of love and esteem gurgled up from the marrow at her unexpected empathy. I prized her in that instant like oxygen to the soul. We didn't know it yet, but even as Michael and Lucifer repented, forgave, and loved, and I perceived El in a new light, the universe began its own transformation as a great, stultifying 'mental layer' beguiling every thought and feeling since The Corruption—the very warp and weft of every person—spontaneously dissolved (*SOL* § 4.2.1.4:382).

El kept up her running commentary as Mina's answers swayed in. She sensed the bright, loving energy and intuited the appropriate queries. "Lucifer says Michael's apology is all he needs to hear," she said.[29] "He doesn't bear him any ill will at all. It's like the whole thing is just washed away."

Jeez, I thought, *just like that?* I said, "Just like that?"

She nodded, teeth broadly gleaming, eyes glued to my bed.

I'd belatedly activated the record function on my phone amidst Michael's interview, but later found it had failed to save. Our couple hours of conversation were lost. This technical failure would recur with a depressing persistence; a recording would fail to save, fail to activate, or simply get 'lost,' even though I would see the *now saving* message on my not-so-smartphone screen. It's a *mysterium* technology doesn't like to think it shares with faith. Mina disclaimed any responsibility for it. Initially, I suspected foul play by spirit people who didn't want recordings made for reasons that made sense to them, or else I just bungled it each and every time. Instead, Gabriel—reflecting Mina's aversion to modern, spiritually destructive electronics—was the culprit here, though, at other times, 'random people' did the deed. Technology was innocent . . . this time.

"Dad," said El, "their whole *family* is here."

I shoved eyebrows to receded hairline. "Angels have families?"

"Oh. My. *God*," she said after a flurry of questions. "They're *brothers*!" A thermonuclear love triangle, then. "And they have two sisters!" She paused, solemn. "Their parents are here." I was still stuck on family and siblings. "Wow, Dad, the whole house is filling up." She looked around, maybe straightened her posture, and then announced with pleasure and gravity, "Mother's here." Her face lit with the supernal glow I'd seen yesterday afternoon when we'd first met her. She crooned, "*Hi*, Mother!"

"What's the feeling in the house?" I felt a little left out with only my prickly chills for company.

"Everybody's crying and hugging. *Ohmigod*, Dad, the joy and happiness feels so strong, I want to cry, too!" Her timbre indeed was weepy.

I reeled off a checklist of status requests. Mina let us know that Gabriel, Lucifer, and Michael are brothers in that order with bookend sisters.[26] It wasn't just Michael and Lucifer reconciling, but their siblings, too. Their family reconciled with other angelic families,

---

26. Fraternal twins to Gabriel and Michael, plus twixt Gabriel and Lucifer (playing into his drama).

who then reconciled with others, who paid it forward. With that earlier-mentioned 'mental layer' now dispersed, Mina could and did 'broadcast' the Big Reveal and Reconciliation to all of spirit humanity.[27] On its heels, The Corruption's debunking shock-waved through the universe. As that *jupitérien* mob of angels departed, vast spirit crowds—about 60% from *other* worlds—streamed into our home's environs including all of history's religious leaders who'd been paying shocked attention to our bursting their bubbles.

Then El plopped a real wonderment in my lap. "Creator's saying you're the most famous person in the universe right now, Dad."

"Me!? Umm. . ." *Shit?*

"*Everybody* knows your name."

I plopped my head against the chairback. "Not sure I want that."

"Well, could've left it alone."

"Thanks. I'll stick that on my tombstone."

As I ruminated on ethereal *Cheers*-style fame, Michael's newly bestowed infamy had quite naturally cut out for him a less-than-attractive 'ninth-step' effort[28] that would take him through eight Earth months of penance before the aggrieved petered out. After some preliminary meetings with all three angels over the next week or so regarding my writing *The Story of Life*, we didn't see much of Michael for some time.

"Creator is *soooo* happy somebody's finally exposed the whole situation in a way everybody in spirit world gets. But now. . ." She wandered a few seconds. "Now I'm feeling such huge joy and excitement and. . .um. . .like, pure delight? at what's happening. It's just so intense, Dad. Dang, I wish you were feeling it."

"Humph."

"It's so lit!" she said. "The energy's off the charts."

It certainly was. And just like that we went from seeming to break the universe to healing it, all in about seventeen hours. My head spun to make Linda Blair jealous.

---

27. Your own spirit self got the message, too, but since your brain doesn't fully integrate mind owing to The Corruption's effects, this is news to your physical self (*SOL* § 1.2.2:253).

28. From the 12-step program created by Alcoholics Anonymous in 1935.

And here, Mina dropped his biggest bombshell yet. Humanity's chief obstacle (that 'stultifying mental layer') to throwing off The Corruption and psychically healing[29] had ceased to exist. El vibrated with Mother and Mina's giddy exhilaration at this hoped-for, yet not entirely certain, blossoming of a new world as it now shifted to Game Over for the crusty old.[30]

1.2 THE NEGATIVE COLLECTIVE CONSCIOUSNESS

What was this obstacle, this 'stultifying mental layer'? Why did it disappear with Michael and Lucifer's Reconciliation? What makes *their* conflict so special in a peevish universe fit to bust? And just how does it affect you? We spell it out in THE CORRUPTION (*SOL* CH. 24:361), but here's the nutshell.

Humanity is not fallen[31] nor stuck with a selfish gene.[32] We aren't shorn of an original sacred nature nor even had one. No magical salvific to remedy a situation beyond our control—or, per Alan Watts, "grimly to face" (1951, 22) the ineluctable suckage of life— is of any use. We are not in a state of irremediable sin because sin isn't real. It's a human delusion, an artifact of The Corruption and Michael's Lie.[33] Though we want to reconcile the self-winding contradictions in life's ineffable struggle and our way of being with some diaphanous higher, better, divine self, it's a deficient analysis and anyhow Mina rejects the characterization. Rather, our forebears birthed *unconditionally free*[30] and, therefore, free to love—and we do!—whether we're civilized or savage about it. No existent nature or divine law circumscribes us. Besides pain and suffering, there's nothing wrong with, and no contradiction in, the human psyche.[31] We aren't "wired for perversity and prone to do evil" (Venema et al. 2017, 195) to thus "fall short of the glory of God" (Rom. 3:23), nor enslaved to our unevolved, mad reptilian brain.

---

29. In this context, a catchall term for salvation, liberation, forgiveness, 'divine' assimilation and ascension, enlightenment, restoration; whatever you call it in your faith language.

30. Take a moment; sit back, close your eyes, and truly unpack *unconditionally free*.

31. Erroneously *human nature* in psychology and *fallen nature* in religion, but *way of habit* is more fitting.

So why is life so unremittingly unloving, inertial, and destructive if it isn't profane by nature or God's own creative intent, or the imprecision of Darwin's random, ruthless evolution? The short answer is that we're exactly how we choose to be, as we are consummately free. *We habituated* life exactly as it is. That's problematic because we Corrupted ourselves by choosing a Corrupt baseline—say, Accountability over freedom, or consideration *from* others over consideration *for* others—and, ants to honey, our unhappy *astī* followed.[32] Our *choice* ever brings suffering. Change our choice, change our state of being. There is no Satan, Devil, anti-God, yin–yang darkness, biological determinism or biogram,[34] natural evil, or even acts of evil or evil persons—howsoever harmful—nor any moral state of being. Morality itself is a delusion, and one of Accountability's many thugs. Habit alone self-coerces us to be as we are. Our pain and suffering powers the cycle of violence. Any ultimate deity or idea that's a perfect standard of good is illusory. Becoming aware of reality is how we free ourselves from delusion to heal and thus achieve a happier outcome.

That now-defunct 'mental layer' (we call it a *noosphere* for an academic twist)[35] formed from our individual mindsets as a collective force of habit. El termed it the Negative Collective Consciousness (NCC, i.e., Ultraculture; SOL § 4.1:291).[36] Physical humanity imbibed The Corruption and Michael's Lie from its very *noogenesis*[37] via the angels and, more so than them, we took it on the chin. Spirit and physical humanity's Corrupt self-coercion got so powerful it severed Mina from his creation,[38] literally from his own family.[39] Premised as it was on The Corruption, merely shattering Michael's Lie could only do so much. Lucifer's reaction, which Michael so feared, was the fulcrum. Their utter rejections of Accountableism embodied in their apotheosis of forgiveness and reconciliation knocked the legs out from under The Corruption's premise itself, and every story of life it ever engendered in our collective mind. The combination swept through humanity's collective consciousness like a cleansing tornado. It was a one-two punch and the NCC folded. This was

---

32. Persian: 'is-ness' (for Ibn Sina: *momken-al-wujud*, ممکن الوجود; FN 23:33).

glaringly obvious in spirit world, and the people there jolted from it like a bad dream.

The important take-away is that, having self-manifested our mess, we aren't helpless. Now the NCC is gone, neither will our still-habitual[40] but eventually-quenched Accountableist mindset bring it back. Its dissolution is permanent, says Mina, because its genesis is undone and rendered inert. From here on, freedom rooted in Mina's original premise will only expand, so long as enough of humanity wants it to, because . . . freedom. Free of the NCC, Mina flashed the Reconciliation throughout spirit humanity, which underwent an unprecedented sea change. Shockwaves roiled it (and less obviously, physical humanity) for months. Mina, keen to help and now permitted the tools, moved on the healing opportunity immediately (*below*). This was hard to take in. It's taken me a year just to write this much of it, and I think it's only a crude outline. Mina calls it "more a 'limited expression' of reality."

1.3 THE MEANING OF THE BIG HEALING

There in my bedroom that Friday morning, we felt our comfortably flowing rivers of belief and knowledge abruptly divert off a cliff. Ayako had plunged over the night before,[41] cried through it overnight, and now slept it off beyond the wall behind where I sat, first under Michael's watchful eye and then amidst his Reconciliation with Lucifer. El's façade of cheery imperturbability held steady, but her flitty eyes reminded me of a starling at the hawk's distant shriek. She'd process this like her sister later, absolutely. I could've just left it alone, chalked it up to, "it's interesting, aye, but not really my cuppa," and this morning's event would've aborted. Except it *was* my cuppa. I couldn't not know any more than I couldn't not breathe. I chewed on which made me the bigger idiot, but figured only time or someone wiser would know that.

Then my turn to face an Ayako-style inconvenient truth arrived with Mother. She let us know Michael and Lucifer's Reconciliation mooted last night's 'war' tomfoolery along with her (hard-nosed, to Ayako's mind) prescription regarding Ayako's future.

"Everything's changed?" I said. "In the whole universe?"

Yes.

Here's one of this book's fundamental messages of hope and liberation: the NCC's dissipation removed every block on Mina acting in the universe. From now on, he'll be healing wholesale everyone in the physical and spirit worlds of its deleterious effects, irrevocably healing humanity of the NCC and freeing us to change our Corruption habit and, to the degree each is ready and willing, of any traumas, trapped emotions, and the like as well. We consciously or unconsciously need merely express our desire. Through Michael and Lucifer's meme-busting choices, humanity nascently restored its pre-Corruption, pre-Lie awareness and annihilated the facticity of The Corruption and Michael's Lie as any sort of legitimate epistemology and archetypal, ontic *Dasein*.[33] Mina predicted a week to complete the Big Healing.[42]

I said, "So, everyone can be healed? No exceptions?"

Yes.

"What if they don't want to be healed," El wondered. I thought, *why would you imagine that?* "Will you still heal them?"

No.

"No?" I said. "Because you can't violate a person's freedom?"

Yes.

El said, "So, a person only needs to want to be healed, or ask to be healed, and you'll heal them?"

No.

"You mean there's a *condition*?" I practically gasped.

Yes.

Well, huh. I fixed El with a hard, oh-sure-there's-always-a-string-attached look.

She held my eyes in return. "I know what it is, Dad," she said. "They may not want to be healed in their subconscious,[34] even

---

33. German: from *Da-sein*, 'there-being/here-being' and ontologically prior to the one who asks the question of Being as a "being-in-the-world"—*Im-der-Welt-sein*—person (Heidegger 1962).

34. The subconscious as traditionally understood is not the subconscious we reference here (*SOL* § 2.1:393).

if they consciously ask to be healed. Everything happens in the subconscious."

Ah. "Makes sense," I said, thinking about the concept of self-sabotage and cognitive dissonance.[43] "We might want to be healed, Creator, but if something in our mind or heart is refusing, that's the condition?"

Yes.

"Can you do anything about that?"

No.

Hmm. We'd discovered the same thing in our earlier foray into Emotion Code with Ms. Medium, hadn't we, when people resisted healing or weren't ready to release their trauma, either because we hadn't dug deep enough to find its source, or their innermost self just wasn't ready to give it up.

I said to Mina, "So, your condition is people must want healing, not superficially but genuinely?"

Yes.

"It's not really a condition, Dad," said El. "More like, just reality."

Yes.

"And when it's in what we've always called our subconscious, then it's genuine," I said.

Yes.

"Because," she added, "how's he gonna heal you of whatever you really don't want healed?"

Yes.

I said, "Then a person just needs to figure out why, on a subconscious level, they may not want to be healed if they ask you to heal them but don't feel healed."[44]

Yes.

"Can you help them want to be healed?"

Maybe... no.

"It's up to them, Dad. Everything's up to each of us."

Yes.

As one of my other darling daughters is fond of opining, 'You may not think it be like it is but it do.' *Well, you love freedom*, I consoled myself. Apparently, we're free to be what we don't necessarily want to be but actually are. The story of hapless humanity.

I said, "Seems like there's gonna be a lot of people who don't get healed, though. All that negative universal energy gone and it won't make a difference—"

"He's saying no, Dad."

Ah, jeez. "But you said you won't heal anybody who doesn't want it or isn't ready anyhow to be healed. If that's the case—" But El was shaking her head. I said, "That's not the case?"

No.

"That 'no' means it's *not* the case, right?"

Yes.

I sighed. Yeah, a little petulantly, too. These sorts of contradictions and grammatical quirks are a common struggle with this mode of communication owing to its intrinsic limitations and our tendency to misconstrue. It'd be so much easier if we could get 'why' answers. I racked my brain for a scenario in which both his statements could be true. El and I pitched possibilities back and forth to a steady beat of *no.*

"Maybe he just can't heal everybody of the negative consciousness thing plus all their personal problems," El finally offered.

Hmm. "So…you can heal everybody of whatever ails their psyche, right?"

Yes.

"But if they're unwilling or not ready or whatever, then you can't."

Yes. I can't.

"And that's because you can't wave away problems people created themselves? I mean, you can't just change their heart, right? If they're resentful, let's say, then they're resentful. Unless a person wants out of that, you can't do anything, correct?"

Yes.

"So…"

"Creator," El said, "are we responsible for how the Negative Collective Consciousness affects us?"

No.

Ohhh. Nice work, El.

She continued, "That means it doesn't matter if they're willing or not? The negative collec—it isn't a problem of their own making?"

No.

"Ahh..."

"Ok, I get it," I said. "You'll heal everyone in the universe of the Negative Collective Consciousness. I mean, uh, how it's affected them?"

Yes.

"Ha!" I said with a gloat. "So, everybody gets healed of the nega-tive...*that*, but not their own personally-built problems if they're unwilling, or not ready, to give them up. Do we have it, now?"

Yes.

"Bingo!" I said, "Contradiction solved."

El grinned at me. "Yep. Nice work, Dad."

"*Danke*, you were pretty goo—"

She doubled over in a rowdy fit of hilarity, palms out, thumbs cradling her chin, but not with my German lingo sopped up from my dad. "I'm. *Weak*. They want you to write a book!"

My jaw dropped. That inconvenient truth I mentioned just said, "Hello, sucker!"

1.3.1 WEDNESDAY–THURSDAY, OCTOBER 11–12, 2017 CA. MIDNIGHT

I thought back a couple of nights to when we'd healed *Obāsan*. We'd moved from my bedroom to the main room as we got to know her and her family when all hell (figuratively) broke loose over their cheeky opinion that revising my 1998 book spiritually analyzing American race history, a new edition of which I'd been slaving over the last six months toward real publication, was a waste of time. That I should toss it. Move on. But to me, renewed racial conflict and Donald Trump promoting to inner city black youth their right to the American Dream got me to thinking that now would be the perfect time to re-issue my book. I'd spent January through April 2017 catching up with it, pleased to find that, twenty years later, it still made sense. In May, I settled into updating and revising it, using the vast research now available at Internet-accessible libraries unavailable to my itchy fingers two decades ago. Now, here it was October. I'd hoped to have it ready in just a few more months. My daughters knew the book was important to me. After all, I'd been "tirelessly torturing" them with my copious endnoted research and analyses for months.

Affronted by those give-up ancestors, I'd fired off a logically fallacious call to authority. "Do you think it's a waste of time, Creator?" Because, who'd know better and could shut them up?

No.

Whew. "So, it's important? I should get it published?"

Yes and *yes*. I figured out later he was being kind. What we'd learn writing *The Story of Life* would make that one redundant.

"Ha, in your face!" I crowed.

My girls howled. That ended those ancestors' uninformed slander of my book. It probably didn't change their opinion any, I had to admit. Oh, well. You take your victories where you find them. But then it was *Obāsan*'s turn to be affronted, thinking me pretty rude when I commented a little too bluntly on her family's early twentieth-century social passing from Ryukyu island bumpkins to upstanding Japanese elites. It took some humble pie to quell her vexation, but then she laughed for the first time.

"*Obāsan* says you're not half the ass she thought you were, Dad," Ayako outrageously said with more cheek than her new ancestors. The girls were uproarious.

1.4 Friday ca. 10 am: Our Commission to Write 'Story of Life'

But now, Mina was saying he'd rather I shelve that work of stupendous social significance for a new book dishing the full monty on what had just ensued. I was *shook*. His earlier, solid shutdown of those craven ancestors had left me not only unprepared for his sudden change of focus but frankly unwilling, too. It felt a bit like Ayako's scenario with Mother last night. Hoisting my jaw from the floor was getting to be a comedy routine. El's chuckling eye from her spot riveted twixt my bed and master bath got me wondering if she'd spied a silver lining in Mina's wrench in my works.

"Can I write it after I finish my book?" I pleaded.

No.

"Maybe I can do them both at the same time."

Maybe . . . no. Not really. Come on, get a grip.

"So you definitely want me to write this new book?"

Yes.

"Right now?"

Yes.

El piped in her two cents. "*Duh,* Dad. You don't *have* to do anything. Creator won't judge you because you don't write it, you know that. He told us so."

Yes.

Fine. True enough. We'd extensively combed through his total rejection of judgment, punishment, and coercion[35] last night whilst possibly a little too merrily disemboweling religion and philosophy

---

35. Spirit people are far less fastidious than Mina about engaging in these sorts of behaviors. Nothing's beyond the pale for some of them in their private pursuits of accountability.

as we illuminated the real creator and our real relationship. So, he wasn't *exactly* issuing marching orders, then.

"He'll just find somebody else," El impishly added. "That's what he always has to do anyhow."

Wait. How could some poser write it without *our* life-quaking experience? Would Michael and Lucifer stage an instant replay? Just because it sounds like there's reverse psychology going on doesn't invalidate the point. My daughters sure weren't inclined to write it, that went without saying. The Reconciliation was a once-in-eternity moment born out of our curiosity and newfound energy testing along with Michael and Lucifer's own 'present-in-the-world' and 'potential-in-the-world' psyches. El was a mensch energy testing all my whining with Mina. I cycled through the five stages of grief seven ways from Sunday before at last penciling in his precious book.

I finally croaked, "Can I finish my racism book after I write this one, then? I mean, cripes! Will it even still be relevant or meaningful after all this?" I had to wonder as I finally caught on that no Adam and Eve meant no Cain and Abel.[45]

Yes, yes.

"He can still write a book with footnotes?" said El, thinking of the book's academic chops, I supposed . . . or more likely all my prideful boasting in my endnoted research and, too, that some semblance of academia would pique my interest so I could be more happily dragged onboard this train. I wondered, though, what I could possibly analyze or cite in a revelatory work. This was my first revelation. I hadn't the foggiest how to proceed. Wouldn't I just be writing a mouthpiece? "Because," she added with an incisory look at me, "he really loves his footnotes." Okay, stop.

Yes.

Just because Mina doesn't coerce (or guilt) people to do or be anything doesn't mean our own sense of moral duty or plain old people pleasing is absent. I reasoned this event was big news. I mean, BIG. NEWS. Not sharing it would be poking a sharp stick in humanity's eye, which (in the physical world, anyway) largely disagrees with life and the creator who made it, and is always combing the grass for pleasanter alternatives. But I considered how spirit people might react when I inevitably relocated to spirit world . . . or, probably more salient, its less restrained coterie even before I rested in peace beneath Shady Acres.[46] And, honestly, this was hardly an impossible situation. Unlike your traditional revelation which, let's face it, most of us take with a grain of salt, this one comes with a means to verify it for yourself directly with Mina and spirit persons; even more, if you're really curious and develop your skill. You needn't believe any of this off the shelf, you can just energy test it.

I said, "Well, fine, then. But, hmmm . . ."—a little jauntier now— "I wonder how it'll sell? You know, these kinds of books can really—"

"Hold on, Dad," said El, conversing with Mina amidst a blooming smirk. "You can't charge for it. He doesn't want people forced to pay for healing."

"What?!" My jaw was getting tired of this routine.

"He wants a story that's healing. I totally agree. It's terrible—"

"Sure, sure, but how am I supposed to print and distribute it?"

"He says you'll find a way. I mean, it's not like you're dumb, Dad,"—*Thanks?*—"and, like he said before, charging money to heal and teach the truth about him is wrong."

"I thought we were free," I sulked.

"Your book is." She grinned, and quite evilly.

"Har-dee-har—"

"Remember what Aya said, Dad: 'It's our birthright.' "

"Pshaw! Nobody will take it seriously if they don't have to put out any dough for it. Even the most worthless books on Amazon or Smashwords or—"

"Obviously, you can charge if you want, but he can't be happy with that. You know how he feels."

"—in the bargain bin cost at least something."

Isn't there a word for that? But watching El's face was like seeing Mina's own. Ah, anyhow I agreed with his scruples, dammit! I'd even said so last night.

I said (sniveling like a real victim, I'm sure), "All right, what the heck, what's one more impossible task for an old Moonie? The book will be free. I'll figure out the logistics. But I'm gonna need a sugar daddy if you really want this book all over the world."

El grinned, less evilly. "Or, three."

That settled, I spent a week persuading myself I'd made the right decision while polishing off my racism book's in-process manuscript work which the last hectic, ground-shifting seven days had interrupted (CH. 5:57). With everything we'd learned in just two days, my multi-year manuscript now read like semi-fiction anyway. A serious re-think was in its future. So much for holding up to the flow of history, I complained apropos of nobody. More sighs. Finally, with a last longing look at the pile of research material scattered across my desk and floor, I loaded forty-plus mewling books into bags to cart them home to their libraries, closed all documents on my computer, and cleared my Einsteinian desk for action.

Mina then asked me to hold off for thirty days to pump barbells on my spiritual sensitivity. Intuitive leaps would be important in this work, he said, and I needed to muscle-up. Like most un-jaded clergy, I'd cultivated a strong link to my Christian–Unificationist God through work, study, and prayer. I've briefly seen and talked with spirit persons and angels a number of times over the years, but it always seemed random and accidental, like a dollop of grace or maybe a flight of fancy. I'd never nurtured any mediumistic spiritual abilities because I never thought I had the aptitude and, well, who really needed it? Not sensible clergy, certainly. But I did now. My three middle children are all mediums to one degree or another, casually seeing or talking with spirit persons since they were old enough to tell me about it. I've progressed since October 2017, astonished to discover I've been an empath and undeveloped medium all along. . .which might explain a lot about my personality, emotions, and dubious choices over the years. Spiritual boot camp for thirty days or not, I'd be starting *The Story of Life* relying on intuition and energy testing—and my daughters, naturally. As a resource, they're a couple of Godiva chocolate bunnies.

By now, morning was closing on noon. We already felt worn out. El had missed out on all the sleep she'd tetchily coveted, but the excitement she'd finally caught had made up for that. If I weren't a teetotaler, I'd be swilling something bracing, neat. Mina, Lucifer, Gabriel, and the multitudes went off to heal the universe and maybe Monday-morning quarterback. Michael moved out on his ninth-step rounds that he was looking forward to like an overdue dental visit where he still owed fees. Mother headed out on her own business in her own universe[36] until she returned a bit later to help a tired Mina (healing a universe takes energy). And Ayako was now up and about. Over lunch, we shared with her our dramatic scoop, especially that, as a result of this morning's events, Mother and Mina had rescinded their Ayako Providence formulated in last night's rough waters. She seemed decidedly underwhelmed.

"I'm emotionally drained, Dad," she said, slumping on a counter stool. "Don't wanna talk about it."

"Fair enough."

---

36. The multiverse is real but not how science or fiction imagines it (*soz* Table 12:312).

Our Six-day Prolegomenon

Friday October 13, 2017 ca. 10:30 am

Following all that and before we lunched with a newly risen Ayako, Mina was sharing his dim views on a franchise known as ThetaHealing[37] and the damaging energy it produces in place of any connection to a healing 'Source' energy, in part because it demands money to heal and teach spiritual so-called truths, a practice Mina "loathes." He asked us to pass his uncompromising message to the certified instructor—*ThetaHealer*, Ms. Medium's very own daughter—conducting the ThetaHealing Advanced DNA workshop that kicked off this very evening way up in Maryland. Ms. Medium had earlier captured my tentative agreement to consider attending with Ayako but, honestly, after getting Mina's lowdown on the story of life last night and this morning, another

---

37. An 'energy' healing modality promoted by Vianna Stibal of Bigfork, Montana to discern, remove, and replace limiting beliefs, blocks, and traumas trapping emotional energies leading to mental or physical disease and dysfunction.

turgid $880 spent on that was for the birds. Still, a verbal *no thank you* did seem in order.

1.1   SHARING THE NEWS WITH MS. MEDIUM ...

After this morning's Reconciliation and while Ayako was still sleeping off last night's trauma, El and I got Ms. Medium on speakerphone ostensibly to convey Mina's message in lieu of a drive up to Maryland. First tentatively, then with greater assurance, we outlined everything we'd just learned, though the part about not charging money for healing got stuck in my throat. She absorbed all we said in silence. Uttering our last word, naught but the proverbial hiss lit up the line.

"I want to be you when I grow up," she jested with El, who'd done most of the explaining after I'd faltered. Kneeling against my bed and propped on her elbows, El raised a speculative challenge to me under an impeaching brow. "And I believe you," Ms. Medium continued with conviction, her voice suave and alluring. "I believe everything you've just said."

Wow, didn't see that coming. That's because it wasn't news to her. Michael had confided the truth to her years before but she'd reacted, well, let's just say, poorly.

Before we managed a comeback, she added, "Are you coming to the workshop? I think you'll really—"

Didn't she just say she believed what we'd only just told her? *We're talking to* God, *lady. What's your* workshop *got?* "Um, I don't think there's any point after, you know, all we've learned."

"It'll be a really great workshop. I know you and Ayako will get a lot out of it."

Like what? I asked myself, eyes rolling for El's benefit. Anyway, how would she know we'd get a lot out of it? Maybe that's just how mediums talk when they're on the economic hustings.

"She shouldn't charge money for what she's doing," El whispered, impatient with my kid gloves treatment. "Don't forget, Dad."

"Well, Ms. Medium," I hemmed and hawed; El bored holes in me and willed the right words to flow, "it's kind of like this: Creator wants us to . . ." Yeah. *Dang*. This didn't feel like a message I could blurt over the phone and expect to impart productively. Sure, it was easy for her to believe our woo-woo over the phone . . . until it sewed her pocketbook shut. If I wanted a shot at her responding positively, maybe in-person was the way to go. And it was a persuasive reason to procrastinate. I might have something in common with Michael, there. "Ayako's still sleeping," I concluded. "When she's up we'll decide."

El curled her face at me like she'd shoveled soggy cornflakes into her mouth, then hustled from the room for the real thing. *Meh*. I rang off with Ms. Medium.

Following lunch, the three of us resolved to trek the hundred miles north to unload on ThetaHealer in person what we'd handed to Ms. Medium over the phone as a way to grease Mina's no-charging-money-to-heal message. Then, we'd decline to attend the Advanced DNA all in one fell swoop. For me, just voicing it seemed aggressively confrontational. It almost felt like proselytizing, never my métier ironically enough. Believe me, we weren't looking forward to the conversation even if—maybe because?—it was a revelatory message. In all likelihood, we'd simply be Muhammad preaching up Mecca's unamused merchants. If there's one area where people blank on God, it's being deprived of money they figure is or should be theirs. Hadn't Luke quoted the Big Man himself dictating "the worker deserves his wages" (Lk. 10:7)? Already, we'd be throwing their bible out the window. I daresay it wouldn't be the first time I did something inane. At least I'd have my kids for a shield.

"Hilarious, Dad," Ayako said to that. *Yeah*.

1.2 EXACTLY ONE WEEK EARLIER . . .

As we entered Friday the 13th's afternoon, we were coming full circle in a seven-day spiritual whirlwind that had started last Friday (the 6th) when Ms. Medium had persuaded me to attend ThetaHealing's Basic DNA weekend workshop following an Emotion Code healing session with her several Sundays back. Emotion Code had struck some inscrutable chord in me which, overall, intrigued me.[47] I thought ThetaHealing's thing might be a good means to socially connect my unhappy older daughter with Ms. Medium the Happy Healer.

"Trust me," I said with all my fatherly panache. "You'll love it."

"Hm."

Ayako is spiritually sensitive and aware, having already studied in her school years chakras, auras, emotions, pendulums, clair senses, paranormalism, spiritualism, mediumism, and the rest of the psychic barnyard. I'd hoped she'd hit it off with the motherly Ms. Medium because, if my kids lacked anything, it was a helpful mother figure. She demurred to the last minute, then broke her reclusive mold to sign up. That was a game changer because it's what incited El's leading question that fateful Thursday evening the twelfth.

I coolly smiled at her unexpected "Ok, Dad, I'll go," but, inside, I was *hot-diggity-dog!* It was a major step and I felt terrific for her. Surely, something good would come from her new behavior. I'd been trying for months to get her into an Emotion Code healing session with Ms. Medium to see if any trapped emotions and traumas underlay her depression and maybe restore her zest for life. But she'd brutally resisted; out of angsty shyness, was my take. Her anxiety, depression, and mild agoraphobia increasingly, if not a little despairingly, worried me like the growing roar of water from up a canyon. "But I'm not going it alone," she added.

My cool smile faltered at the low-low price of only $440 each (generously including Vianna's voluminous page-turner, *ThetaHealing: Introducing an Extraordinary Energy Healing Modality*), but I sucked it up so she'd team up. I was betting real skin something peachy keen would pop loose in her. Little did I know. I turned expectantly to El and opened my mouth.

"No thanks!" she barked in one of history's greater ironies. "I have no interest in that stuff at all! You can just go without me."

I blew a laugh at her independence rally in the run-up to her presently four-days-away eighteenth birthday. I said, "Suit yourself, big girl. Food's in the pantry. Have fun."

"Hmmmph."

1.2.1 Friday–Sunday, Oct. 6–8, 2017: ThetaHealing Workshop

Emotion Code uses pendulum and some muscle testing modalities to identify trapped negative emotional energy and 'heart walls' in a person, the causes of which can be addressed and cleared to pave the way for the psyche thus body to self-heal. ThetaHealing, in contrast, attempts to use meditation and prayer to achieve a theta-wave brain state to enable the body-sway test—using the body itself as a pendulum—to identify core limiting subconscious beliefs and traumas so they can be cleared, replaced, and psyche and body can self (or, according to Vianna, instantly and miraculously) heal. Ayako was immediately taken with sway testing, and got some real world practice working on her co-participants. I realized I'd encountered it myself a couple years earlier. Having tried it on my own with little practical result, I'd forgot all about it. Seeing it in action with a roomful of practitioners at the Basic DNA workshop re-whetted my appetite. Maybe it wasn't as offbeat or as difficult as I'd thought, I persuaded myself. Yet, I couldn't seem to do it. I didn't see Creator's 'white light' that Vianna said we were supposed to zoom toward in meditation in order to 'connect' to 'Source' energy's theta-wave state. Nor did I see the various colors that acted as signposts on the way through the "seven planes of existence." [48]

Ayako saw it all and then some. Success following her own style, however, tipped her to the monkey business in Vianna's theories even as I fancied it at face value. Instead of seeing and entering the Vianna-approved white light that connects to the "Creator of All That Is" (Stibal 2011, *ix*) to enable sway testing, Ayako saw only yellows and purples that, in her experience, shook out as higher order energy. So, right away, she saw B-O-G-U-S type itself across her mind's eye in a clattery teletype from Common Sense. Mina later told us Ms. Medium and ThetaHealer had sensed Ayako was spiritually "more powerful" than they, which got their attention.

Meanwhile, Ayako noticed Archangel Michael hanging with her during the workshop and her ancient, highly respected guardian angels keeping out of sight to avoid tipping our discerning mother–daughter duo to Ayako as someone worth, as it were, possessing.

Mina noted how they saw and sensed Michael at the workshop but said nothing. Instead, they siphoned Ayako's energy to the point she could hardly move, lift a limb, or open her eyes.

"Just paralyzed in my sofa seat," she recalled.

Mina said they funneled it from all of us at the workshop, though I don't recall feeling especially tired. Bone-weary is my standard operating procedure, so they'd really have to open the tap to get my attention. *They aren't malicious,* Mina monished us, *just inadvertent; the result of connecting to Vianna's negative energy source.*

We learned Ayako's energy vibration is very high, just below angels. At home, lower-vibration spirit people avoided her proximity because her energy field was too strong, hence, uncomfortable for them. Hidé, for instance, retreated to the far side of the basement whenever she'd shower next to El's bedroom just to avoid her "too intense" energy envelope. He couldn't even pass by the door to the stairs because it was too close, and her energy rattled and "burned" him.[38] All that discomfort passed, however, when his energy strengthened in the Big Healing. Michael later opined (and Mina agreed) that Ayako eventually would've tumbled to Mina and energy testing even without attending ThetaHealer's workshop, but I have my doubts. Ayako chose to keep her misgivings about

---

38. Hidé found it uncomfortable passing incorporeally through walls and floors on the 'physical plane,' preferring to move around as if physically alive. Taiji was the opposite.

ThetaHealing from us—from *me*—until after the Big Healing, when suspicions over inexplicably spoiled food and sickened health on the heels of our new awareness finally crowded into all our minds and she'd put the pieces together.

In any case, Ms. Medium's thirtyish son very kindly helped me for hours to identify and heal trapped emotional energies and limiting beliefs. At last, *finally*, spiritual energy fluttered through my body when quering my subconscious,[39] pushing me forward and back quite independent of my own will—certainly not from losing my balance, which I strove to hold as sternly as a rooted tree.

Following the workshop's Sunday evening (October 8th) end, we gravitated to Ms. Medium's roomy, split-level ranch-style tract house for home-cooked burgers,[40] sway test practice, more poop on ThetaHealing, and to play cards. Whilst the workshop briefly mentioned chakras, I didn't really grasp at this point that sway testing necessitated them being open. Our modicum of training failed to do the trick for me. Reliably getting me 'online' (seeming so obstinately shuttered, a category-5 hurricane wouldn't have pried them open; afterward Mina directly taught Ayako and she taught me) bordered on the miraculous. While Ms. Medium cooked our hunger's salvation, her son grimly drilled into my trapped emotions, limiting beliefs, and past traumas with messianic determination. At last, my grudging chakras cracked their lids and I began consistently sway testing with faint conviction. Around midnight's far side, we shared parting hugs on the stoop with our new besties, then reluctantly motored the two hours to our rural Virginia home and, for me, a 4 AM date with my alarm clock.

1.2.2 Monday–Tuesday, October 9–10, 2017: Refuel 1 and 2

On ninety minutes of sleep, I hustled two fun hours to Lynchburg, Virginia. Swanked out in my Army blues, I was all squared away for Monday's PREFUEL event for chaplains at Jonathan Falwell's

---

39. As the traditional concept of the subconscious doesn't jive with reality, Emotion Code and ThetaHealing practitioners are, quite unawares, actually sway testing the responses of whomever most energetically replies: their client's own spirit self, family, or random spirit individuals. At the time, of course, we didn't know this, either.

three-day REFUEL conference for pastors at Liberty University.[50] Aside from a congenital aversion to pop-Christian emotionalism, PREFUEL passed innocuously enough. Mingling with uniformed chaplains from all the services brought me contentment and a sense of belonging I'd missed from decades of local Unification Church leaders ostracizing me from my spiritual alma mater.[40] I returned around 8 PM to a home spiritually quiet but a temporal cacophony of Japanese alt-rock ripping through YouTube on our big-screen overlaid with my wailing daughters hopping and skittering to its beat across our room-sized Persian rug. They regarded me with faces firmly believing no news is good news. After a couple hours thriftily schmoozing anyway over my glorious PREFUEL without neglecting their alt-rock ipseity, I slipped into my welcoming, non-judgmental bed for tomorrow's 4 AM dash to REFUEL's Day Two.

While I sang my heart out at Tuesday's REFUEL, my daughters got up to high shenanigans at home. The previous day, Ayako had quietly inducted I'm-not-interested-in-that-stuff El into Theta-Healing's wondrous world of sway testing, substituting her own methods for Vianna's disagreeable trek through jelly-filled barriers to the white light and dodgy creator hiding out on the back forty of the "seventh plane" (Stibal 2011, 26). El had picked it up like a natural, but didn't take off full speed until today. She'd blithely deep-sixed her earlier "no thanks" declamation after the two of them recognized sway testing's possibilities for communicating with *people* instead of their boring subconscious. She flew off the blocks in a sprint. In a Monday afternoon phone call, the girls deliriously recounted their adventures delving into family and ethnicity with Mina—addressed pre-Big Healing as "Creator" in deference to Emotion Code—which, in roundabout fashion, led them to meeting their two favorite Japanese superstars, Hideto Matsumoto (d. 1998) and Taiji Sawada (d. 2011). Both, according to them, murdered.[51]

"How'd you even know to use it for that?" I'd said, startled.

Pungently, El said, "We have a book, Dad."

"So, we opened it," Ayako said.

---

40. From a reluctance to commit to mindless obedience and thoughtless Divine Principle study.

Ach! I'd forgot all about Vianna's 337-page how-to in Ayako's hands because ThetaHealer ran out of copies at the workshop and mine was still clawing through the postal system. "But the manual says *nothing* about using sway testing to talk to spirit world!"

"We improvised," she deadpanned.

Did they ever. Seven straight hours sway testing with Taiji.

"Hidé dipped after twenty minutes from all our death talk and didn't come back till midnight," Ayako later lamented with a giggle. "He still can't really face his murder. It gets him so mad."

Having now met Taiji and Hidé and brimming with excitement, they were dying to investigate their Asian pedigree. They've been obsessed by all things Japanese, Korean, and Chinese since wee sprouts. Goaded by maternal family rumors of a Chinese great-grandmother (apparent evidence to the contrary) supercharging their imaginations, not to mention Unificationism's built-in Asia worship, they've always *felt* Asian, specifically, Japanese.

"Where," I wondered in dubious strain, "could Asian genes be in your mom's obvious Africanity?"

"It's there, Dad. Just look at us. *Duh*."

Learning the sway test ropes with Taiji and Hidé emboldened them to leap into the mystical realm of The Ancestors, but the answers they got jolted them. For days afterward, they unrelentingly reproved me with, "When you've been lied to your whole life, *Dad*, about who you are . . ."[52]

In riposte, I said, "Just be glad you know your mom and I are your real parents."

Now, Tuesday morning, I was experimentally hand testing with Mina along the two-lane winding through the countryside, Ayako having taught me during our schmooze last night so I could try it out while driving. Which I did. In spades. After transitioning to the four-lane south of Charlottesville, my 'conversation' segued to my dad when I sensed he'd joined me in the car. He practically K.O.'d me with a stunning revelation about his wartime service.[53]

My 4 AM start dragged into a late dinner with my chaplain colleagues at some mediocre chain hashery. I finally reverse putt-putted my Prius into the double garage of our blazingly lit, night-defying prefabbed log house going on midnight. In my haste to rest my vengefully screaming fingertips-to-elbows—a lingering 2007 nerve injury still maddened by handling steering wheels—I snagged the side-view mirror on the garage door frame and, but for its handy foldability, would've snapped it clean off at the neck. Tired as I was, with sleep crowding out all else, I needed a few breaths of perspective before facing my Ancestors-intoxicated children and finding out— reminiscent of a certain biblical God strolling through his garden one fateful afternoon—what their uppity day had, in due course, wrought. I was surprised to find the Japanese alt-rock silenced like a former BFF (best friend forever) and the house tomblike. I'd only just shucked off my uniform for home clothes when my daughters poured breathless into my room.

"Dad!" El led off. "We found our ancestors!"

Was that a baleful eye I turned to them? I hated to think so, let alone make my tongue a party to it, so I said, "That right? Which ancestors?"

"On mom's side. And," she squealed in explosive excitement, "we're *Japanese!*"

I quirked a Spockian brow.

"Actually," her rather steadier sister said, "we're only part Japanese, the other part is Chinese with a smidge of Korean."

"And we found our great-great-grandmother!" El bubbled on. "I think she's from the *Amami* islands, in the Ryukyus."

"Okinawa?" My other brow joined its kin.

"*Nooo.*" El gazed on me like the mentally challenged. "*Amami.* It's its own ethnicity. We need your help to figure out her name and which island because you know Japanese. We're all confused."

Ah, jeez.

1.2.2.1 MEETING OBĀSAN . . .

I took a rib-bursting, see-ya-later-sleep breath. Loudly blew it off. It seemed a tall order. Wasn't I as much the noob? They expecting a miracle? I hadn't even brewed a midrats' tea. All the same, and in spite of my diffident self, I scrabbled up avid pen and paper and plopped onto my spurned bed. My daughters hovered across from me near the master bath's door. Ayako did the testing, as her responses, unlike El's and mine, were by now practically instantaneous. She'd spent the day really burning up the wires with Taiji. Despite exhaustion, she was in no mood to quit. Her skill made the conversational aspect of our communication a lot more sociable. I'd already enviously asked how she did it, but she'd shrugged it off as axiomatic. I took that with something less than a stiff upper lip.

It was an hour-plus getting their maternal great-great-grandma's story.[54] Fortunately, spirit world comes with a built-in universal translator, so we didn't have to rely on my rusty Japanese after all.[41] It wasn't so useful placing her in a historical, physical world context, either. We'd got a false start when I had her spell her family name in Japanese characters only for El to realize she'd given us her ethnic Amami, rather than her Japanese, surname.[42] A studious adoration of *Samurai Champloo* (anime; Fuji TV 2004–05) is what kick-started El's curiosity in Amami language, culture, and history, and now it paid a nifty dividend. But the girls were certain we'd need her Japanese surname to track down her extant family, Amami apparently being as moribund as Gaelic, or maybe grammatical English. For their part, they'd instantly bonded with their great-great, and El asked if she'd mind us calling her *Obāsan*.

She strongly assented, said El, with "a huge feeling of joy and happiness to finally connect with us. Apparently, she's watched over us since before we were born."

I slumped back at that one, ruminating on their mom's pregnancies and the girls' childhoods. That brought to mind their mom's announcement one day in the mid-1990s that she'd seen a silver-haired "old white lady" in a dream who said she'd been watching over the two of us and the girls' infant older brother but was "pretty damned unhappy" with our constant quarrelling. When I'd asked

---

41. Unless physically awake speaking voice-to-voice, in which case one does need a common lingo.

42. It later turned out she'd actually given us a family codeword, not her Amami surname, so the girls would have bonafides when they inevitably reached out to living family in the Ryukyus.

their mom to describe this old lady, out popped my own scary Irish-Texan paternal grandmother! The very same who would shortly be helping my dad protect me during Lucifer's upcoming melee with Michael. *Obāsan* seemed a different kettle of fish from my grandmother, but I quashed any extended-family comparisons to keep a neutral interest in the proceedings.

Sometime after 1 AM we'd learned all we could and healed *Obāsan* and her cantankerous family of their grief, sorrow, rage, guilt, and so forth using an egg salad of Emotion Code and ThetaHealing techniques. That's what happens when amateurs go unsupervised. We ignored our doctrinal deviations because there is no doctrine. If a person's wants it, Mina heals them.

We drifted into the main room of our house with *Obāsan* and her large, formerly reviled family in tow. I took to opining on how interesting it was that bumpkins from the Ryukyus (a conquered, colonized, contemptible set of islands to the Japanese) had managed to gain a Japanese surname and pass into its elites—so far as to work in a pre-war capacity for Emperor Hirohito—the way American blacks passed for white to sneak into WASP society. That went down like sour milk with *Obāsan*. She scolded me for being rude and obnoxious (and possibly stupid; the girls sometimes edited for my ego, bless their little lying hearts). I backed off fast. I'd taken an instant liking to *Obāsan* and preferred her good side. No telling what she could do if properly incited, and I didn't want to find out. I explained my western view of Japan–Ryukyu history but she swished that aside. The more I discussed my thinking, though, the more she caught my heart until pronouncing me "a good man" whom she liked, and we all had a laugh. Well, I tittered through beaded sweat. The girls whooped a few we-don't-know-this-guy yowls while *Obāsan* maybe nodded along to memories of her own Chinese-hating politician father helping govern WWII Japan's own Ryukyus-cannon-fodder policy.55 Yep. It can be like that.

My made-in-Korea wind-up mantel clock had long-since bonged away a drowsy 2 AM. I used a lull with *Obāsan* to say my goodnights. Ayako and El chittered undaunted beyond my bedroom door as I lay down and snapped off like a blown bulb.

1.2.3 WEDNESDAY, OCTOBER 11, 2017: REFUEL 3

Wednesday's third and final REFUEL convened at a brunchy 9 AM, but The Ancestors had dashed my plans for extra sleep. A paltry three-hour head start is all my alarm got before jangling me awake. When I fell out of bed at five-thirty, my daughters were only just saying their goodnights and staggering off to their bedrooms. In the boiling shower, I dwelled on *Obāsan* and who-all-else my girls might have dredged up overnight. What surprises were in store for me when they awoke this time?[43][56]

Zipping down the county road to the conference with my usual scalding *masala* tea in hand, I chatted up Mina and built my hand testing skills. This was so convenient, I thought admiringly. No more one way babbling to a figment God maybe shooting pool than listening to *me*. Now I could babble in response to *answers*. Inevitably, this led me to consider if he'd be willing to ask Jesus and Sun-myung to give me a few minutes of their time. He was, they did, and we small-talked around my unexpectedly well-tied tongue. Nothing faith shattering like later in the week, though. Baby steps. That's all you can expect with a frog pulling your tongue down your dry throat.

Day three of the conference surprised me. Now, I abhor Christian pop music with the best of atheists and have since before I was born (don't judge me). Even so, throughout the conference I'd noticed the music pleasantly uplifted me even as I choked on many of the lyrics.[44] During the 'praise' sessions between typecast speakers, I felt so spiritually energized that I raised my hands along with everyone else, something I'd never done. I didn't even feel stupid or self-conscious. I just belted out the songs, hands in the air, sappy lyrics be damned. Or I recast them on the fly when lyrically nimble enough. The emotional atmosphere triggered it, naturally, but I couldn't

---

43. The suspense wouldn't last long. El ecstatically reported by phone they'd connected to yet another Japanese music sensation (still alive, so his pseudonym will be Akiō) who turned out to be family, too.

44. Harsh, I know. I apologize to all its great melody-producing artists. On the other hand, 'dislike' is far too milquetoast to convey Mina's revulsion at its heartbreaking Jesus-death worship, magical God, and dystopic, lickspittle, domestic-violence themes rampant in this genre's lyrics that reflect modern Christianity generally.

help but think God's spirit was laying it on me right thick. And why not? Wasn't I a fervent believer just like this in-the-clouds crowd, even if my bohemian faith clashed over a few measly details?

On breaks in the crowded coffee courts, I surreptitiously communed with Mina and Sun-myung about the REFUEL conference and Jesus on his perspective. It made me weigh how folks might react if they'd had any inkling he was standing right there with a jaundiced eye. I couldn't get enough of this new access to heaven's wise heavyweights, and that's an understatement. I tucked into Jesus' feelings generated by his eponymous faith and Sun-myung's on his own church's rowdy postmortem schism. It didn't occur to me to ask the really pointed questions until El kicked open that door later in the week, which right now was still a day away.

But *today*, Divine Principle riding o'er the Bible like Windows over DOS still soothed my soul and ordered my world. I'm surprised how, in most ways, I just accepted things as they were, that maybe I wasn't as critical a thinker as I back-patted myself. Looking back, it seems all my theological *sturm und drang* keeping me in hot Unificationist water really only tweaked the baseline. When Sun-myung's unexpected 2012 demise crashed the Unification Church with the shock and awe of Bear Stearns' hedge funds going belly up, I'd scrabbled through 2015 before working out that Mrs. Hak-ja Han Moon had checked herself and her freshly-wrested dead husband's religion into *l'hôtel des délires*. Only now, under Mina's tutelage, was I toying with truly radical, faith-bending inklings. And then Jesus casually said on break that he'd washed his hands of Christianity a long time ago.₅₇ *Damn.* I'd been on the wrong track. Stuff like that needed time to soak in. El was sure ahead of me there.

There was no getting around *sans*-Jesus REFUEL's results, though. I was *pumped*. Energized and spiritually replenished after several draining years a chaplain surrounded by brainy psychoanalytic types devoid of spiritual fervor and Godly solutions to soldiers' problems else their cups running over with magical but empty Goditis not to mention the dry-boned pastors and institutional leaders of my church and, overall, Christianity's generally defunct *élan vital*. If I hadn't already put feelers across Michelangelo's finger chasm and discovered Mina, I'd have thought Traditional God Himself was riding my shoulders at the conference. REFUEL was what I'd been looking for! It bookended my idea of a chaplain: spiritized like those four WWII heroes who'd given up their lifejackets to go down with their ship, *The Longest Day*'s (1962) padre so determined to rescue his underwater communion kit so nobody would go without the sacraments that he paid no mind to enemy fire whipping by, or even those who quietly recognized the spiritual genesis of apparently psychological dysfunctions like PTSD.

I attended a tasty post-conference buffet into the evening with Jonathan Falwell and friends, then highwayed home. I took a few minutes to once more badger my dad to let me share his WWII whopper with his grandkids but no dice. He was taking what felt like a C-note burning a hole in my jeans to eternity.

1.3 SIX-DAY JOURNEY'S END . . .

At home Wednesday night, I babbled on about the "amazing" RE-FUEL conference while the girls labored like stevedores to push the conversation back to their new BFFs *Obāsan*, Hidé,[58] Taiji, their new-found Chinese great-great-grandfather they call *Yéyé*,[45] still-living megastar cousin Akiō, spirit visitors, and the Japanese side of our family now using our house like an earthbound timeshare. The girls laser-focused on *Obāsan* and her illicit China-born daughter (their great-grandmother) who so implausibly ended up in St. Vincent and the Grenadines in the early 1950s to bear their grandmother Martina, whom I personally know and which, at last, hooked me up real-time to the girls' historical revelations.[59]

I was thoroughly wound down by this preludial six-day odyssey—Friday's ThetaHealing start through Wednesday's REFUEL end followed by tomorrow's lead-up to the Big Event—when yet another midnight-plus rolled around and I hit the rack. My indefatigable daughters plugged away, learning what they could or chatting up

---

45. Less formal Mandarin (爷爷): *maternal grandfather*. He tolerates their preference for *yéyé*, but favors the correct Cantonese paternal (阿公) *ah-gung*. Ayako obliged him but now my ear prefers *yéyé*.

common interests far into the nether gloom. It was a great social game for them which Ayako realized is key to mastering energy testing competency, whereupon Mina asked that she teach it to the world as a social skill. Near noon the following day, the girls dragged themselves from bed weary as the world to run family errands with me. It was now Thursday noon, October 12, 2017, some five hours before El would unleash her fateful opening salvo on our world of wishful thinking.

In the Hurricane's Eye

Thursday October 12, 2017 Noonish

Midday Thursday arrived calm and collected. The wild energies of ThetaHealing's Basic DNA weekend workshop, Monday–Wednesday's REFUEL conference, and their hand killing road tripping were behind me. Energy testing was giving us a wee touch of the spirit, aye, but it was small potatoes, nothing to work us into a lather. For me, God lounged all empyrean and hermitic in some magical, enigmatic corner of spacetime. For the present, we focused on acquainting ourselves with new personalities and tying down ethnicity. I wasn't so all-fired curious to see how well-grounded my Irish muttness might or might not be, although . . . African?

"Sure, why not?" I told myself. "The fam comes from America's South anyway. I'd be naïve to be surprised."[60] But, nope. I'd rather treasured our Gaelic-Nordic-Gallic-Germanic heritage before it occurred to me that, as we're primarily spirit than biological beings, ethnicity is utterly irrelevant, immaterial, and archaic, more a fun intramural sport than a fact of any consequence. Even Mina had ethnicity.[61] Now he's whatever he wants. Shorn of biology, he—like everyone in spirit world—is free to be how he wants to be. Now that was something I could get into. The girls, on the other hand, were sliding into their new Asianity with a little more gusto than purely which gens is scrawled on their ancestral sheepskin, settling into lost Eastern family lands after a long sojourn in the West.

As we set out for errands, our wheels thumped off the uneven lip of the garage sitting six inches off the eroded, graveled earth. For me, the spinal jolt was part and parcel of a serene foray into life's mundanity we'd made a million times, and that's all I'd envisaged today. I fast discovered the oddities of our new reality along for the ride. Ayako and El prattled non-stop with Hidé, Taiji, *Obāsan*, even me when I managed to shoehorn my comments in. And then we discovered one of my best friends hiding out *inside* me like a squatter in an abandoned tenement, except I wasn't exactly vacant; in spades, it turned out.[62]

1.1 RE-MEETING A BEST FRIEND . . .

What happened was, I'd street-parked alongside University of Mary Washington's Fredericksburg campus and hiked to its library to return a stack of reference materials from my soon-to-be-postponed racism book. Ambling back to my daughters waiting in the car, it hit me just how utterly depleted I felt. I stuttered along fatigued of every morsel of energy wholly untethered to spirit, all but zombified like some unlucky Haitian.[63] I wasn't exactly unused to bone weariness. Chronic pain from multitudinous injuries normalized an unnatural lassitude over the years. Sapped to flat-out prostrate was often my daily carousel. Yet, today, right now, felt strangely different. Calling me lethargic would be an insult to lethargy. If my eyeball showed a systems readout, I'd be seeing the *Batt* icon flashing red: *recharge now or shutdown, buddy*. I groped for the car door handle verging on collapse, then promptly did so into the driver's seat.

"Maybe it's everything you've been doing, Dad," Ayako not so helpfully said from the passenger side.

Not on your life, wobbled my head. "I need toothpicks to keep my eyelids open," I said, sounding whiny, I'm sure, but really just exasperated with my body. "I feel drained . . . like, vampire-drained, except this one's sucking energy."

That rang a bell with her. "Sounds like somebody hanging around you, then."

"You mean a spirit person?" Her head bobbed. "Like who?"

"I don't know. Somebody you were close to, maybe, who'd want to hang around you."

I snorted. "Nobody wants to hang around me."

"Don't be negative, Dad," El scolded from the backseat. "You just make it true."

Ah, je . . . "Why would anyone who even liked me that much want to be slurping out my energy like *The Mummy* movie mummy?"

Ayako said, "People have issues."

"Issues! That's it?"

She merely raised her what-do-you-expect? palms.

Gah. Fine, then. I plunked my head back on the headrest and stared at the sun visor. I murmured, "Who do I know like that who's dead . . . who'd plug into me like their own personal General Electric?" I made a few stabs at it. Ayako tested each one negative. I groaned.

Then El blurted, "It's Miss Helen!"[46]

I corkscrewed round to catch her eye. "How do you know that?"

She snapped a shrug. "It just came to me."

"You mean it popped into your head outta nowhere?"

"Yeah. Like that."

You know, there's times it's helpful to have kids crazier than you. "Helen Smith," I said a little tremulously as I asked probably the oddest question of my life, and in front of my kids to boot, "are you, uhhh . . . here, in the car?"

Yes, Ayako hand tested.

Ah, quit being squeamish. "Are you *in* me?"

Yes.

Damn! I stared slack-jawed at Ayako next to me as she tested Helen's responses to all my questions. Violated was certainly one emotion I was feeling. I mean, *shit!* Was nothing sacred? A whole host of images of my private life patently shared with Helen banged through my mind like cops on a warrant. Still, as they like to say before whipping out the handcuffs, points for honesty. I shook off my creepy-crawlies.

"You mean, right now?" I said.

No.

Well, that sounded better.

Ayako said, "But until just now?"

Yes.

Oh. Not that much better. I said, "Since you died?"

No.

"Within six months of dying?"

No.

"Within a year?"

Yes.

"Was it more or less one year after you died?"

Yes.

"But . . . but, why?"

"Dad," said El, "you can't—"

---

46. Totally not her real name (she picked it after all our dead-end suggestions) or personal details.

"Is it because," Ayako jumped in, "you found yourself in a low or dark place in spirit world?"

Yes!

"But she's a Blessed Moonie!" I said, aghast.[47]

"Forget about position, Dad," said El.

"Yeah," Ayako said equably. "It's just your energy vibrations. That's what matters in spirit world. Well . . . intention defines your energy, but, yeah."

"And why would you even be surprised?" my twisting screwdriver El said. "It's the Unification Church."

Ignoring her as a pastorally prudent parent ought, I said to Helen, "You were shocked and terrified where you ended up"—*Yes*—"and looked for a way out and eventually found me"—*Yes*—"and I was spiritually bright enough so that you felt safe and protected and comforted"—*Yes*—"like a home away from home?"

Yes!

"Really, really big yes," Ayako said, feeling Helen's energy.

"Boy . . . any harbor in a storm, I guess . . ."

Yes.

"Well, fuuu—rick."

"It is what it is, Dad."

"You just have to deal with it."

When did my kids get so adoringly philosophical?

As Helen transitioned to spirit world, she'd been frightfully upset. She wasn't ready. Tasks beckoned. People needed her. For all her faith, terror gripped her as she'd expired. She'd tried migrating to higher, brighter levels, but their potent energies pained her. Instead of putting up with her rubbish spirit accommodations, she'd retroverted to Earth for the comfort and normalcy of family and friends, but then she'd felt a vagrant. As a follower of Sun-myung's Divine Principle that teaches he's the second coming of Christ,[64] Helen, like any Moonie, absolutely anticipated a spiritually bright and happy residence for the persecuted faithful in spirit world. And why wouldn't she? She'd worked hard for the church, obeyed her

---

47. A Unification Church Blessing of Marriage participant, a salvific in that faith.

leaders, got Blessed, raised a Blessed child,[65] and studied a little Divine Principle on the side. Just your average, conflicted child of God trying to live right. Like all the faithful.

"Not a bad person a'tall, in my book," I told the girls. "She never harmed anybody, really."

In the same way that intention manifests our reality here—an impoverished mind begets an impoverished life, let's say—even more so does our thought define our situation in spirit world. Every facet of our being combines to create an overall life-intention often at variance with our conscious desire or our own self-image, such as seeking love while stubbornly holding onto hate or else pining for a lost lover, or at the very least not giving up on the fixation that "it's all about me."

It dismayed Helen that she'd gravitated to a land of "darkness and dread" peopled with the incompatible despite her own compatible energy. Naturally, she'd looked for an out. Then she had a lightbulb moment and came a-calling on me.[66] And there I was, all bright but not too shiny, energetically peaceful, and painless enough for a safe haven, and she'd clung fast. The upside was, she needn't stay put in her unhappy spirit world billet nor wander the Earth a vagabond to avoid it. The downside was...well, none, for her. The invasion of privacy and her contribution to my occasional death knell of fatigue she could live with; putting up with the intimate experience of me, too, I supposed, but I wisely didn't ask about that. She'd turned a blind eye anyway. I didn't see much of an upside for me, though. This news triggered long-forgotten memories of Korean *ansu* sessions where we'd evict just these sorts of wastrels through repeated beatings of our *own* body until they were convinced it wasn't *their* home.[67]

"So, are you the reason I'm feeling so washed-out right now?"

Yes. Sorry about that.

"Are you the *only* reason?"

No.

"You mean there's even more in there?" *Ansu* flooded my mind. "Like, a lot more?"

Yes, and *yes.*

1.2 Cleaning Out Spirit Squatters

This, I begrudged the universe, is how it was for virtually everyone prior to the Big Healing.[68] I shot hunted eyes over to Ayako, our spiritualist expert and, right now, my only steady oar in this uncharted sea. Under her astute queries, Helen clarified that thousands of spirit people 'infested' me, hiding in or clinging to me and, both purposefully and inadvertently, draining away my energy to greater or lesser degrees like those smart, furtive rats tapping power lines in the 1982 film, *The Secret of NIMH*. House-party physics would've made the energy loss inevitable in any case. There's no malice on their part—just trying to relieve their suffering—but that hardly comforted me.[69] We didn't know why this afternoon it had left me so knackered. Later, we found out that opening my chakras to dial up Mina's direct line had spiked my energy into beacon status that drew thousands more freeloaders to me who'd overwhelmed my already slaphappy generator.

"Is that right, Creator?" I said. "What Helen just said?"

Yes.

"How many are there?"

"Come on, Dad," El reminded me, "you can't ask a 'how many' question."

"When you're more together than your dad," I bellyached in frustration, but Ayako lit me up with a warm glow of real sympathy. "Are there hundreds, Creator?"

Yes.

"Thousands?"

Yes.

Gulp. "Tens of thousands?"

No.

"Well, thank God for small favors! Uh, you know what I mean."

"He says 'yeah,'" said Ayako.

After some trial and error, we arrived at a number of "about ten thousand." I needed a cleanout like nobody's business, but not with *ansu*. That sadistic ship burnt long ago to its waterline.

"Creator, can you—are you able—to remove them, clear them out of me?"

Yes.

"Wow! Really?"

Ayako got a high-energy response and laughed. "*Big* yes, Dad."

"Can you do it, like, right now?" Mind you, we were still sitting in the car parked at the curb, Ayako energetically hand testing in the front passenger seat. At least the windows were tinted.

Yes.

Using Emotion Code's methodology, I intoned, "Creator, it is commanded all the—"

"Wait, Dad!" said El. "You don't want to throw out Miss Helen, do you?"

Well, *yeah*. I mean, uhh, no . . . I guess? It seemed to El that I was heartlessly whirling Helen off into the dark bowels of her just desserts. Maybe I was being cruel. I wasn't feeling all that objective much less charitable at the moment.

"Miss Helen, do you want to be healed of any trapped emotions, traumas or limiting beliefs so you can change your situation? Cuz, we'd like you to."

Yes.

"Is there anything we need to deal with before you're ready to be healed?" El continued, her Emotion Code down pat.

No.

"So you're ready to be healed right now?"

"Big, *big* yes," Ayako said with a lilting laugh.

I cycled through the mixed salad we'd used on *Obāsan* and her family to ask Mina's healing.[48] Through welling tears, El monologued on Helen's energy change and its effect inside the car. My skin rippled with shivers scalp to seat then back again. I was getting real practice with goosebumps.

"She's in the back seat with me now, Dad."

---

48. Since the Big Healing, modalities like Emotion Code and ThetaHealing, along with their intoning jargon, are redundant. Mina heals automatically as soon as one's ready and permissive. Indeed, he's healing everyone right now upon entering spirit world post-death, as well as you in your spirit embodiment while awake or asleep according to your desire.

"You can feel her there?" I twisted round to look, wishing I could see spirit people like a real medium, the way one of our pastors' wives (avowedly) turns it on and off like a pair of Google glasses. I imagined Helen sitting beside El as she appeared in her vernal funeral photo.

"Yeah," said El. "I can feel her energy right up against me."

"Well, right, then. Creator, it is commanded all the spirit people who are in or clinging to me and the girls, except Helen"—just in case, right?—"be removed from us permanently and that we are protected from any further, um, 'infestation.'" I didn't know to where'd they go, but frankly didn't care. *Just get out!* was the long echo of my mind. My gaze roved across the rearview. Would Helen be sending me a glare for that "infestation" crack? I wondered how she felt being caught piggybacking off my life. On reflection, that felt stupid. She'd just directly experienced God flooding her with healing energy, loving her like the queen of the world. Wasn't she a different person now? Dishwater, drainpipe, right?

"Creator," Ayako said, "did it work?"

Yes.

"We're completely free of spirit people in us?" I said.

Yes.

I fist pumped. "Yes!"[49]

But how would I know? It's not like I felt emptier or my stolen energy surged back into me. I guessed I'd have to wait and see how I bounced back in the next few days... if I did. This spirit clearing-out didn't affect Hidé and Taiji or anyone else we'd met because they were hanging around *outside* us as guests, or at least acquaintances, and not *inside* like parasites. I didn't really like applying *parasite* to Helen, whom I still loved as a best friend. But it was what it was, no sense whitewashing it. And now, it was over.

This was all exploratory for us. I, for one, didn't really understand at all what we were getting into. That would come in the slow-mo

---

49. It dawned on me much later that we should've asked Mina to heal them all just like Helen instead of giving them the boot. When I sheepishly raised the issue, Mina said of course he didn't "throw them back into their suffering situations!" He'd healed them all. They'd then left naturally, voluntarily, *happily* for better digs.

thunderclap tonight and tomorrow. Contemplating the visceral reality of spirit world is old hat for serious Unificationists, and anyhow, this wasn't my first woo-woo rodeo. I've seen angels and spirit persons before, and even conversed with some of them. Yet, those times seemed so random that I'd felt disconnected from each moment as though watching another person. Our experience the last few days was firmly in our control and much more immediate, even intimate. It wasn't me watching me, it was me *being* me, and finding thousands of spirit people so entwined with my body, my existential singularity, that they degraded my energy and health. It shook to the core my placid, ontic *Dasein*. It was one thing to suffer Korean spiritualists jabbering on about spirit infestations bred by desperation to escape anguish only to callously whack them out of us during those long, painful *ansu* sessions for a bargain basement $1,000 fee, which we'd instead just instantly accomplished through a simple, painless, free request. It was quite another, indeed, to talk to and feel the heart of—to actually know!—someone giving me the business for real. Not a stranger or acquaintance, either, but a best friend. There were a million things I wanted to say to Helen. I couldn't think of a single one.

"Creator, can they come back?" El wondered.[70]

No.

Now that *was* good news. I cast back over my shoulder. "And you're good, Helen?"

"*Very* big yes," Ayako said, feeling Helen's deeply happy, extra energetic response. She must've been ecstatic: she joined my one spirit guide the next day to form a team, a 24–7–365 largely thankless on-call service.[71] Very humbling, that. What do you say to such a friend? *Thank you* seems awful paltry.

So far, you could say we'd gone through a few minor life updates leading into Thursday's Genesitic cool-of-the-day full upgrade. Our reality had expanded, yes, but honestly, not all *that* much. Discovering The Ancestors was a jump into a cool, dawn plunge pool for my daughters. But now they were catching their shocked breath. Hak-ja Han's goofy Moonism revamp and Helen's stage-left entrance withal, my Principle lifeview oddly enough only settled deeper in my mind like bones in a soupy seabed. I noted the incongruity as we nattered on about all we'd learned, yet unsure what to make of it. Then our errands wrapped up as daylight thought about packing its bags, and we traversed the narrow, winding roads home to El's inadvertent, total upheaval of our reality.

Doom Ride

Friday October 13, 2017 Mid-afternoon

Fast forward through Thursday night's Big Shake-up and Friday morning's Reconciliation and Big Healing, and it was now Friday mid-afternoon after lunch. We were on Virginia's schizophrenic Interstate 95 struggling north into Maryland to bunt Mina's in-your-face memo into ThetaHealer and her mom, Ms. Medium's, ballpark. For each of us, this task seemed an epochal showdown like hoving guns out round the headland. With each dying mile, our guts knotted a little tighter. The reason was more than just Ayako's and my aversion to handing people adverse news. It was Mina hitting us—undeterred by our fierce (maybe inanely curious) skepticism—with intel that Ms. Medium had forged Michael's seminal Angel Code story.

She accurately conveyed Gabriel's portion, he said, *but doesn't like Michael.* As soon as she'd realized Michael speaking—piously lampooning him for "push[ing] Gabriel out of the way so he could get the healing faster" when, actually, Gabriel had kindly yielded the floor—she'd begun dissembling. Not misinterpreting or mistaking this for that. Not confusing things, or shocked by something so bizarre she couldn't accurately convey it. Not even because she might've been a fake medium. Nope. *Lied.* She'd even wept conveying her ginned-up messages in these proceedings. Here's why.

1.1 Ms. Medium Betrays Michael . . .

Thirteen years before we'd fired up the Angel Code, Michael had quietly knocked on Ms. Medium's door to confide in her his hatchet job on Lucifer. Her advanced clair senses and devotion to Unificationism's Restoration[50] had caught his interest. Sun-myung taught her to not only love Lucifer-cum-Satan, but that he'd surrendered to God in 1999 because of Sun-myung's unconditional, death-defying, Principled love for him. That suggested to Michael that her Satan-hating days would be over, that she'd comprehend Lucifer in his new, *never*-Satan togs. Michael thus calculated she'd be conducive to helping him rebuild his burnt bridges, a sort of Swiss mission to his older brother.

She leaned that way, sure. But devotion aside, she didn't bend all that far toward unconditional love. That wasn't uncommon. Unificationists warmly embracing Sun-myung's rapturous *Satan surrendered, y'all!* coldly couldn't care less for the devil who'd put them in their toils. *What's it mean for me?* was the first concern on many a lip. Anyhow, wasn't his surrender really somebody else's mile marker on their own road to glory? Even less willing to friendlily backslap a Restored Lucifer than suspicious Christians an evangelized Saul, Unificationists left him in the firmament of evil like spoiled eggs forgotten in the pantry but smelling up the house. If pressed on why they continued heaping blame on Satan, they'd explain that *Satan* really meant his newly promoted minions now that Lucifer had (supposedly) gone legit. According to Sun-myung, *they* hadn't surrendered a thing. But this collective Satan redux had

---

50. Unificationist salvific term that denotes fallen nature's eradication and restoration of God's sovereignty on Earth.

nonetheless learned its evil ways at Lucifer's odious knee. Wasn't it thusly Lucifer's ultimate doing that the Unification Church still bled members like a pickled hemophiliac? Why its members, to varying degrees, cheated on their spouses, beat their children, abused their fellows, ignored Divine Principle, generally sinned with religious abandon, trod on Sun-myung's still-fresh grave and, worse, couldn't even manage to make a difference in the world? And look, they reasoned, we can even use the same pet name *Satan* for the vomitous lot of them.

The average Moonie mind could never manage to shear Lucifer of his opprobrium any more than world-weary Soviets could separate Rudolph Hess from Nazism four decades after *not* participating in Russia's immolation, or Americans Benedict Arnold twenty decades after switching horses midstream. If post-1999 their no-hoper foibles and providential failures persisted, it could only mean that Satan remained at large or, in any case, at fault. Who but the former *arch*angel, the Great Deceiver, had the moxie to spurn the Messiah's naïve love and pull off such a gangsterish sleight of hand? That Moonies are their own satanic saboteur is for them a distinction without a difference.

In this general frame of mind, Ms. Medium wasn't ready for the venerated Archangel Michael to say something along the lines of, "So, here's the thing: the Fall, Adam and Eve, and Satan aren't real. I made it all up to frame Lucifer. The unhappy rest sort of, well, just happened. But now I want to fix it."

She took it, Mina said, *pretty badly.*

I said, "Because Michael's perfidy stomped her heart?"

No. But perfidy's the key word, here.

Michael sticking it to his brother and seeding a weedy take on reality rightly shocked Ms. Medium. Moreover, she thought he should tell Lucifer without delay, then bit her tongue; she couldn't hide her growing contempt for him. But she counter-shocked him by wanting his help to rise up through ThetaHealing's constellation to superstardom. Its new and creative modality was mining hitherto untapped wallets with ease. And it worked . . . at least, so long as customers thought it did, and that was good enough. Ms. Medium's healer aspirations, plus Unificationism's close-held suite of sanative moneymakers, was adding up to a big fat zero for her and it wasn't fair. Being psychic, though, she'd already suspected ThetaHealing wasn't a benign curative, and then Michael made plain it was "dangerous and caused more harm than good, even killing people."

Yet, after his shocking revelation, she'd rejected his warning even as she'd believed it. Anyhow, *caveat emptor*.[51] She had kids to feed. Michael recoiled at the very idea. When he then had the gall to "full-on judge her cracked moral compass," Ayako told us, she'd played virtuous Stalin to Hitler's 1941 dupery after carving up Poland like BFFs, and offered him the blackmailer's option: "Help me or I blab your secret."[52]

She'd be lying for money as Michael had lied for revenge. What was the difference, really? In the bigger scheme, wouldn't her minor moral deviance pale beside his devastating fit of pique? Surely, in return for its money—though, unlike biblical tax collectors, by 2017 she'd reaped only poverty, misery, and anonymity for her dishonesty against Michael's beloved albeit undeserved angelic status—she'd help a few suffering souls. All without putting innocents in the frame or stitching up a fake deity like a certain somebody had. *Two wrongs don't make a right? Tell it to Michael!* He'd rejected her by refusing to help dredge up trusting sufferers using ThetaHealing's dark mire. Then he'd judged her as wanting. *What a hypocrite!* She couldn't appreciate the burden of alienation Michael's misdeed had brought him. How could she, when abandoning her own profession of faith had blinded her to her own? To top it all off, his penitent self-exposure only made her feel outrageously outed. Ms. Medium despised Michael for what he did to (and wouldn't do for) her. She branded him satanic for her own, and the world's, lied-to misery very much how she'd always blamed Lucifer, who *now*, according to Michael, wasn't even blameworthy. And wasn't her guilt for that

---

51. Latin: 'let the buyer beware.'

52. Paraphrased, of course; maybe the world's first 'deal with the angel.'

Michael's fault, too? After all her trust and sacrifice . . . how could life—*how could Michael!*—do this to her?

Michael had pricked her bubble of faith, but it didn't bring her any of the happy relief it had us. Why would it, when she'd invested in its polar opposite? Now she'd lumped him in with Satan. Who cared what Rev. Moon said about Lucifer? He'd reaped billions promising his followers honor, glory, even a pension. All they'd ever harvested was ridicule and penury. What did he know? Once dead, his own wife might bulldoze his grave given half the chance. And at the end of the day, what had she actually heard about Lucifer's surrender? Not a psychic thing.[53] Her hearty conditioning that Lucifer was Satan and Satan was hateful didn't flinch an inch. So, she'd rejected Michael and innocent Lucifer with him. She tried coming right out with the seamy truth to spiritualist friends and others to make good her blackmail, but came off a crackpot—except to one medium who'd believed her but (in different words) told her, "If you want to make money as a psychic, shut up about Michael." Well, turnabout was fair play. With luck, she could certainly dirty the phony's coattails.

Notwithstanding Michael's fury—"I still don't regret it, either"—with Ms. Medium's God-fearing willingness to risk harm to others for ThetaHealing money and his shock at her chutzpah, her contempt had scalpeled him to the nub. Ayako couldn't find words to convey how betrayed and hurt he'd felt. I struggled to empathize, even after he'd shared it with me. This was exactly the abhorrence he'd dreaded but had paralyzingly expected Lucifer—everyone!—to pile on him without pity. Even so, avoiding such an Accountableist outcome formed a motivating intention for him. People had a right to be steamed; he got it. But his target was Lucifer, not humanity. Mina says Michael didn't foresee nor intend its fallout. The larger human disaster unfolded from the already-Corrupted minds of every person who uncritically bought into Michael's Lie and then, ofttimes embellished, passed it on through living up to it. Michael wasn't and isn't the 'real' Satan. That said, he did have to get his

---

53. Naturally. Satan doesn't exist, so no surrender could've happened.

mess out. The irony was harsh and brutal. Unwittingly stuck in his own Accountableist mindset, he'd stymied himself in finding a way. Mina hovered helpfully in the wings quite ignored. Michael never thought he actually *knew* but was only guessing.[72] "I don't know what you're talking about" had been his uniform response.

Gabriel didn't know the truth, either, but knew his brother was troubled and grieving over something; probably just Mnèèptē, and he was past due getting that horse pastured out. For whatever reason, Michael wanted to work with humans and Gabriel humored him. Accordingly, he'd gone to Moth Man's angel fanatic friend to arrange another go but, at Michael's request, he'd stressed he not engage Ms. Medium at all. Yet, as soon as Moth Man's friend shuddered up from his glorious dream around two in the morning, he rang her up purely out of reflex. Life's just a basket of variables. Michael was cornered. After Gabriel went to all that trouble, what reason could Michael possibly give for now pulling out? No, he was pinned as a bug to a board. He'd made a valiant attempt with Ms. Medium, but it was a foregone conclusion. Pulling her in meant he'd get the kibosh, and so he had. His effort to come clean with some dignity and control was in a shambles. He fell back to reassess, only to be then swept up in our breaking adventure.

At the time, we knew very little more than that Ms. Medium's Angel Code 'readings' were lies. Discovering she'd also 'poisoned' us energetically via touch, proximity, food, and who knows what else, our relationship sundered mid-bud all on its own. Altogether it bulled the girls into taking Mina at his word that she'd actually lied. I lamented in doubt for months even as I made a slow peace with the facts on the ground.[73]

1.1.1 MICHAEL'S FURY AT MS. MEDIUM'S LIES . . .

I wasn't the only one with a coping deficiency. Michael lost his marbles over Ms. Medium's double-dealing. While Ayako and El chatted happily ping-ponging downstairs at Moth Man's suburban Maryland home back in August 2017, our third and doubly-attended

Angel Code meeting—a whole new client base taking shape right before Ms. Medium's all-seeing eyes!—séanced over their heads. Then mid-swing in the girls' game, "dizzying bursts of energy" skull-slammed them both in ball-meets-paddle fashion, and horse-kick headaches bloomed from nothing to the Big Bang. Uneasy eyes on the ceiling, they fretted over what no-good pot the 'grownups' had just daftly stirred.

None of us knew at the time that Michael had got so worked up over Ms. Medium's bodacious lying to all of us around Moth Man's dining room table that his livid energy surged EMP-like through the house and anyone sensitive to it. This was the meeting at which Ms. Medium channeled Michael's supposed hurt, terror, and self-loathing at "Lucifer's bullying after the fall" that he'd so cowardly failed to confront, where I'd felt my heart literally crushing itself beneath my ribs as if Michael's wounded psyche was my own. I could've cried with grief believing Michael's feelings were mine. Addressing Ms. Medium, I'd even apologized to Michael like a ringleader for my mere sliver of a part enabling Lucifer-cum-Satan. Witless me. It was Michael's EMP-like fury, anguish, sadness, sorrow, and exasperation with Ms. Medium's determined fabrications that was working me over every bit as good as it was my ping-ponging daughters downstairs.

"Michael knew exactly what she was doing," Ayako later revealed prior to us teasing out the whole saga. "He just couldn't believe a life-long Unificationist, with a spirit-world aware lifestyle and the Moonie desire to help humanity, plus her ability to actually see him . . . that she'd do that."

Man, was he ever the optimist. I said, "She literally saw, heard, and experienced him? *Knew* what he was really saying to all of us?"[54]

"Yet, could still lie. Michael was beside himself!" Ayako clapped a hand to her forehead. "And we suffered for it!"

Absently, I massaged my breastbone. "Surely, she felt all that wild energy. Didn't she at least get a—"

---

54. According to Mina, Ms. Medium isn't clairaudient but clairvoyant and claircognizant; hence, she still understands.

Ayako just waggled her chin. "Who cares about reactions when you're lying? Besides, she has control of her senses and can turn 'em off whenever."

"You're saying she just switched him off and ad-libbed?"

"I'm not saying it. Michael's saying it."

I guess that's a handy option we might now sometimes appreciate ourselves but . . . ad-libbed? That was some Oscar-level talent. Unbeknownst to me, the energy coming off many of those physically attending that session had to varying—"and creepy," according to Ayako—degrees repulsed my daughters. Both instinctually wanted to keep their distance and rejected out of hand my invitations to join in. I'd no idea how unappreciated it was when, months later, I'd tried setting up a friendship between Ms. Medium and Ayako via Emotion Code and ThetaHealing. Boy, howdy.

These Angel Code meetings bowled over all of us who'd so trustingly participated. Really, Ms. Medium's duplicity was fantastically challenging to accept—more for me than the girls, by far—even with Michael's attestation of Lucifer's innocence right there in front of us. Ms. Medium's tearful imagery never strayed from the biblical, bolstered by helpful Unificationist and new-agey overtones. That should've rung our oddity bell straight off. When "[a]ll genuine revelations are revelations of mystery" (Ward 2002, 238) or seamlessly jibe with extant belief, a giant snapping flag tends to run up the mast for me. Observation repeatedly demonstrates how unlikely it ever is that what we think we know is what's actually so until demonstrated. Expectation, meanwhile, expends all its energy reining in what we know to keep it tightly bound to what we believe. It wasn't that the angels' energy-tested stories were at total odds with Ms. Medium's own. Unlike the theological conundrums implicit in her Christocentric imagery, theirs possessed logic, consistency, universality, *and simplicity*. Occam's Razor is a compelling guide.

Honestly, such human frailties notwithstanding, we liked our (to all appearances) friendly, kind, and considerate Ms. Medium. Over our ThetaHealing Basic DNA weekend, it seemed to me that she and Ayako had built the beginnings of a sisterhood. I couldn't have been happier for my dystopic daughter. Really, Mina's pronouncement of lying was the worst news. Oh, we'd asked for it, aye. We could've stopped, ignored this elephant in the room. Or we could've brushed off any of the faith-eating news making up *The Story of Life*. Isn't that humanity's Machiavellian way with inconvenient truth? How hard could it be? Hadn't Ms. Medium accomplished it? Yet, turning a blind eye wasn't only uncharacteristic for us but seemed unhelpful and, considering her energy 'poisoning,' downright foolhardy, too. So we'd plowed on furrow after curious furrow until we looked up to behold ourselves on an endless plain of upturned reality. Well, you can't un-till a field.

Respectable reasons for why Ms. Medium's Michael and Gabriel stories diverged so dramatically from ours eventually ran dry. We abjectly accepted the only explanation still standing. Her betrayal of our trust ground on our nerves. More than that, the effect on our physical health as well as our food from ThetaHealing's mordant energy and Ms. Medium's own venom that permeated her till she was off-gassing it like a volcanic plume struck us even more incredulously. Never mind its effect on fragile intangibles like chakras and spiritual well-being.[74]

1.2 HE SAID SHE SAID: CLAIRVOYANCE *VS.* ENERGY TESTING

These vulturous thoughts gathered even more dread to our minds as we now trekked north up Interstate 95 for our closeup with Ms. Medium and her family. Only El appeared ready, if not disturbingly eager, to take the bit in teeth and do what needed doing. Maybe it was her 'never say die' boundless optimism that militaries find ever so attractive in recruits. She waves the comparison aside, but I see in her a little United States Marine Corps eyeing somebody's beach.

This naturally brings up the prickly issue of how one distinguishes what's true, credible, and sensible when confronted by critical discrepancies between (supposed) spiritual experiences. Why should we believe our energy testing and clair senses over Ms. Medium's experienced and not unconvincing (apparent) clairvoyance and claircognizance?[75] One reason is that, separately or together, we three consistently tested the same or similar answers and intuited more or less the same energy and feeling. Discrepancies and corrections to each other's energy testing errors only brought out a fuller understanding. Whether with Mina, the archangels, Hidé and Taiji, *Obāsan*, Sun-myung and Jesus, Helen, my dad, and others, we developed not just trusting relationships but could distinguish them intuitively or by their personalities and vibes from the way each one energy tests. The girls perceived all this more than I did. However, I often felt Lucifer cozy up close (especially to read this manuscript over my shoulder when he wasn't listening to it in my conscious thoughts) because sometimes he's so intense his energy translates to heat.[55] Besides, the things Ms. Medium attributed to Michael and Gabriel at our Angel Code get-togethers raised grave logic and consistency dilemmas in my mind.[76]

Between our direct, corporeal experiences and Ms. Medium's unverifiable 'readings,' there seemed no contest whom to believe. But it hurt having to choose. And here's the real problem with mediums: one can't validate their claims. They're either fake in whole or part, or they willfully, negligently, or innocently confuse local truths gleaned from their very narrow entrée into spirit realms with universal truths of spirit world, God, or our universe as a whole. "We tend to generalize on the basis of our given experience of how things are and then believe that we hooked up with the fundamental level of reality. This is how world-views are generated and they are always provincial" (Markus, par. 6). As they say in the apparently real spirit world city of Uversa, "All finite knowledge and creature understanding are *relative*."[77]

It might seem no more than a he-said-she-said spiritualist quarrel, something a provident person laughs off. You might be chuckling out a little sensible humor right now. But we didn't actually care what Ms. Medium *did* say in these meetings. We'd just had our own direct spiritual experience, and that was enough for us. Ms. Medium's chutzpah sorely chafed Michael and Gabriel, it did. Even so, they came off gracious about the whole thing. Neither Mina

---

55. I know! Right? Ironic, given his undeserved association with fiery hell.

nor angels compel or judge a person into doing anything,[78] even if humans hardly shy from it.[79] When humans whom Mina and angels engage end up veering off a cliff, they neatly move on to the next in line. People are too fickle to get worked up each time one flubs no matter what's at stake (don't conclude one is then a failure, hence rejected, judged, and booked for punishment by Mina; that would be false). No, we cared what Ms. Medium *didn't* say: the truth, the real story of life. We have to remember that once we're done with our physical bodies we continue living just as we are, only, *sans* biology. Whatever happens in our physical life, whatever we do, however we're traumatized—dead *in utero*, shot, bludgeoned, crucified, or deceased from a long, happy life of trials and tribulations— we heal. Nor are the disasters that befall civilization permanent.[56] Collectively, we get through them. There's nothing like eternity to make the long view the only view.

A more troubling corollary to Ms. Medium's nefarious conduct vis-à-vis Michael was Mina's remark that ThetaHealing, to which she was joined hip-to-socket, is a lie, too.[80] Ayako and I'd just gone through a $440-per-person *Weekend at Bernie's* (1989) that left us, if not spiritually dead, then so clogged by sticky wrong energy that we both felt *half* dead when almost any food Ayako ate left her nauseated.[81] And then a 'cold' hit us all.[82] Ayako fared worse than El and me, having spent two nights during the Basic DNA workshop in Ms. Medium's energy-contaminated home, eating energy-contaminated food, and participating two-plus days in an energy-contaminated program that drained her like a pre-dinner chicken strung up by the ankles. I was lucky bunking elsewhere. While it took El less than a week and me a couple more to shake the spiritual 'cold' and get Mina's nod that its negative energy had cleared, Ayako took closer to seven weeks. She was spiritually fitter than I was, so, in spite of the heavier dose of ill will, she endured far less interruption to her more muscular chakras than did I. In these early days, my chakras regularly stumbled and knocked me spiritually 'offline' like some crummy motel Wi-Fi outside Reno.[83]

---

56. An unhappy semi-exception is covered in EARTH'S HUMAN HISTORY (*SOL* CH. 32:531).

1.3 FRIDAY, OCTOBER 13, 2017 CA. 4 PM

Just when I thought a two-to-four-hour road trip up the sludge pipe to DC's Metro area couldn't get more interesting than its drab scenery, I proved myself wrong. Our new car-normal was my daughters hand testing animated convos with their new BFFs Hidé, Taiji, *Obāsan*, and anyone discovered entering our vehicle.[84] In the mix, our old-normal, window-glass-flexing singalongs to Bollywood epics competed with newer heavy metal visual-*kei* faves X Japan, GazettE or Diaura, Japanese alt-rock Buck-Tick, and other alt-musicians the girls were crazy for. My "you're too serious, Dad" Q&A's with Mother, Mina, and the angel squad periodically "blowing up" the car with BIG NEWS barely pushed in from the edges.[85]

This particular Friday afternoon's menagerie included Hidé, Taiji, Helen, *Obāsan* and some family members, our spirit guides, guardian angels, Jesus, Sun-myung, my dad, and others who "popped and dipped" as our conversation caught or lost their fancy. Most interesting to me was Lucifer—instinctively, I liked him—who came and went to channel energy from us while helping Mina conduct the Big

Healing, now in full swing since morning.[57] The girls intuitively and energetically sensed these arrivals and departures with ease. More a spiritual laggard myself, I noticed Lucifer only because 10–20°F temperature spikes heralded his arrival. I'd drop the windows to pull in the sixtyish outdoors until his departure cooled the heat wave and then up they'd go. He explained Mina was healing *everyone* in the universe.[58] It took energy beyond even Lucifer's expectations. He had little time for chitchat but, with brevity between arriving and departing, kept us up on whatever we'd ask. Mina was busy enough over those twenty-four hours that, when we called on him, his response seemed more like a languid radio call from Mars.

Feeling the lag, we asked, "You too busy with the Big Healing?" *Yes.*

So, just to clarify: "We can't ask you anything, then?" *No.*

"But, later, right?"

Laaaag (possibly a sigh). *Yes.*

All righty, then. Still getting used to him after all, especially as he was nothing like we'd expected even if we could've articulated *what* we'd expected, which we couldn't beyond the Great and Powerful Oz or maybe *der Überführer*. We weren't even sure he'd continue communicating. Our self-esteem just hadn't anticipated hearing from the creator of our universe and was faltering in its mission.

Lucifer, in keeping with the sensitive personality we were coming to recognize, apologized for channeling so much energy from us every time he popped in, especially to my daughters who so keenly felt the draw. Besides the sapping, "skull-cracking" pressure Ayako found characteristic of Mother's excited interactions with us when she'd pitched-in hand-in-glove to help heal with Mina, Ayako had worn herself out energy testing virtually nonstop all day for days. She now complained of being even more enervated than "my new usual." Then her eyes rolled back and she slumped into her seat... at

---

57. See *SOL* PART II and III for the energy relationship between the physical and spirit universe, and physical humanity's role.

58. All living things as affected by the NCC, close to a quintillion persons.

which point a surge of energy jolted her awake as Lucifer, alarmed at her state, channeled energy back. Meanwhile, El gently cycled between lively awake and dead asleep with pulse-like regularity as our clavering waxed and waned.[86]

I could only look askance at all this hurtling north into DC Metro's rush-hour molasses. Maybe my implicit trust in Mina, Mother, and Lucifer's harmlessness to my children with these energy antics scandalizes the casual observer. But we wanted to give without reserve whatever extra energy we could muster for this extraordinary, pivotal event, even if it did exhaust us. Otherwise, we'd have felt pretty much out of the bigger, seemingly all-hands-on-deck, picture. It wasn't as if our energy wouldn't bounce back with a little rest. It seemed natural, even ordinary, to accept this energy channeling all in stride rather than, as some might be tempted to say, a demonic[59] harbinger or akin to ThetaHealing's vampiric entity. We weren't alone donating juice to the effort anyway. It was universal.[87]

"It doesn't seem like much of an energy pull to me," I said, airily kissing off their complaints.

"You're *driving*, genius," the ever-droll Lucifer droned through Ayako (now giving me The Look).

"We sure don't want *your* eyeballs rolling up white," El quipped to me while checking her sister over.

"Hmmph." Now I felt a little cheated.

We sure weren't going to employ any of Ms. Medium's crooked depictions of spirit world, so we were at a loss to envision how the NCC-freed *ultima mundi* was right now transforming under Mina's love-unsparing revivification. It was a good bet no horn-blowing angels were casting around Ms. Medium's gold-plated harps, though. More like *Obāsan*'s midnight healing writ large, we guessed.[60] We wondered if people around the world would even notice. To be truthful, we were feeling a little full of ourselves about now. Like a refund out of China, humility travels on a slow boat. It turned out some people did notice, if only anecdotally. They felt

---

59. There's no such thing as demons, it's a human fable loosely based on human behavior.

60. *Close enough*, Mina told us. *Obāsan*-level dramatic for humans, less so for angels.

'something' unusual, unburdening, healing, or in some way special to them.₈₈ No one we knew described seeing visions of God healing the uncountable masses *à la* Ms. Medium's vivid Angel Code imagery, but so what? Few mediums have a clue about spirit world beyond their micro-level perspectives anyway (EN 77:188). They're hardly the pundits to abide for what's going on there at the macro level.

"Yeah, but it's all a pretty fantastic tale," you might mumble.

"We couldn't agree more," I say.

Still and all, it's our sense experience. We have to roll with it till something legitimately discounts it. At least you can energy test to corroborate our tale or to write your own.[61] The extra-sensory perception behind psychics' and mediums' blowy pronouncements can't be validated except by an equal or better extra-sensory sensor— or a common sensor. That works surprisingly often, too.

---

61. Or not. Sometimes answers differ for various reasons. As late-night informercials disclaim, "Your results may vary."

Confrontation

Friday October 13, 2017 ca. 5 pm

After creeping through torpid traffic, we ghosted as only a hybrid can into a tree-shrouded driveway at the Maryland home hosting their $440-per-head Theta-Healing Advanced DNA weekend workshop. It was just now getting underway. Six or seven attendees comfortably lolled about the bay-windowed living room. Ms. Medium's thirtyish son—the chap I really liked, who'd selflessly helped me achieve energy testing capability at the Basic DNA workshop the previous weekend—smiled angelically through the window from his roost on a plush sofa. I prefer to think he was happy to see us, but he could've just been reflecting his ThetaHealer sister's joy at another near grand walking through the door. Either way, it didn't offset my daughters' perception that the family's youthful skin seemed aged, wrinkled, and grayed out from their exposure to ThetaHealing's negative energy as if withered by prolonged tobacco or alcohol use. Or maybe they chain-smoked through eighty-proof meals. I kept an open mind. Ayako assayed the energy washing through her.

"The whole group's a mess," she opined.

"It's just their Moonie vibe, Aya."

"Do we really need another cat in this bag, girls?"

Shaking off the interminable car ride, El quietly passed on to us that Lucifer was back to give moral support. Like the rest of us, he'd been a nervous Nellie about our plan to update ThetaHealer. On top of which, he avouched to Ayako, his conflict aversion and fear of rejection left him "super nervous" after earlier requesting she tell Ms. Medium that he wanted to talk afterward (prima facie evidence, I'd supposed, of Ms. Medium's bona fides).[89]

Lucifer's no slouch, though. Along with Gabriel and Michael, he'd evinced a real affinity for us. So, besides Ms. Medium's wonky ThetaHealing vibe and mishandling Michael's Angel Code messages, her change of heart since (or fakery during) our phone call this morning markedly agitated him to set things straight with her. What sort of response might he get? He wasn't too sanguine, considering Michael's salty Angel Code affair. It's not like he thrives on rejection. Lucifer stands nine feet and can come across, El might graciously say, *stern*. But relationships amongst spirit persons differ little from here regardless age, power, influence, or lack thereof. Any real medium would be looking up at our approach. We wondered how ours would react—if she did.

Not keen at all, I rapped on the door. Happy voices were a warm welcome justifiably mistaking us for paying customers. Ms. Medium and ThetaHealer trailed outside after pleasantries to discuss our attendance and for what I'd phrased as "an important message from Creator." I felt chilled despite the warmish mid-sixties air. Maybe it was fear. I'm not great at disappointing people. Simple disagreement sometimes looms over me a ferocious specter of past conflict. Not too unlike Lucifer, evidently. That's not what this was or for what we'd come, but a face-off is how it felt. Prescient I was, too. Our plan soured the instant we circled up in front of the house beyond the covered porch and I opened my mouth.

Ayako had latched herself to a white-painted porch support on my left to prop up her shaky, used-up body. By now, it felt to her more a shell than when sleeping 'neath this morning's big scene. Michael—"still angry, but more hurt, than anything," Ayako had said, by Ms. Medium's sniffy predilections—'portaled' in to quietly observe from the sidelines. He took up station to Ayako's left for strength in her knackered state and to deflect the negative energy spritzing from Ms. Medium and ThetaHealer. I faced the latter across the circle with El to my right and Ms. Medium to El's right and ThetaHealer's left. Lucifer seethed between them because she'd instantly snapped shut her spirit eyes like nosy-neighbor blinds to pretend she hadn't noticed him prowling her neighborhood. He'd got his answer, at any rate.

1.1.1   REFLECTING ON MS. MEDIUM IGNORING LUCIFER . . .

Afterward in the car, I said to Ayako, "She can close her senses just like that, and *poof!* he disappears?"

"Sure, why not? It's no different than closing your eyes so you don't have to acknowledge something."

"Ah. The way people stare at their feet . . . or look away as if you're not already in their face."

She laughed. "But more effective."

"She's a medium. What possible motivation could she have to ignore an angel? Isn't that, like, bad form or something?"

"She's trying to resurrect the Moonie passion for spirit world and healing people because she saw how much money you can make from it."

"How are those two things even connected?" Ayako looked at me like I'd asked her to explain why it's wet when raining. "So . . . what, she felt shamed seeing the Great Satan in Michael's easy company after all her talk about his fear of Lucifer the Bully? Like she'd been caught out?"

"Yeah," Ayako said with a bit of snigger. "I'm sure it was a very embarrassing moment for her unless she's that callous."

"El-oh-el," carped El in a dour monotone from the backseat.

1.2 Ms. Medium Reacts to the Angels ...

Michael, however, was interpreting Ms. Medium's fleeting but bracing eye-lock from across our loose circle as a pair of incoming stilettos. Meanwhile Lucifer, practically bumping shoulders with her, was reduced to a will-o'-the-wisp on the wrong side of her second sight.[90] Frankly, she seemed just on the edge of wild eyed. Probably the stress, I thought, though I hadn't seen her explicitly swing her eyes up to a nine-foot altitude. But would a medium have to do that?

On the other hand, our spirit bodies can manifest custom sizes (EN 84:191). Lucifer could've drawn up eye-to-eye or knee-high to a munchkin for all I knew at the time.[62] To a psychic medium, however, this couldn't have looked *less* like an ordinary conversation. El sensed Ms. Medium shrink into herself, just psychically step out of the meeting and retreat to the peanut gallery.

1.2.1 Ayako Opines About Lucifer ...

Talking it over driving home, Ayako said, "I started feeling really bad inside at that point, Dad. Everything just seemed wrong. I felt really upset on the inside."

"You're a pretty sensitive person, you know. I'm not surprised you felt—"

"No, no. It didn't feel like any type of reaction *I* would've had!"

Giving her the eye, I said, "What do you mean?"

"It turns out it was Lucifer's feelings of rejection and heartbreak, really super intense."

"Huh." He hadn't let on about that when we'd talked it over later, but Ayako well knew that wasn't his style. A quiet sufferer, he is, at least with us. "Ms. Medium's attitude must've been like one more blistering spike in his back, I reckon." My fingers lightly drummed the steering wheel as I considered her. "The deepest and hottest,

---

62. He prefers his natural height in all practical cases, even if feeling a need to stoop, but did sport angel wings paired with a dapper European sartorial cut to impress—humor and style balance his pathos—though not oxford wingtips; a missed opportunity, I opined.

maybe, since she now knows the truth, said she totally believed it, then backstabbed him anyway when he showed up. I mean, what the he—?"

"It's not like our church wants to forgive Lucifer," El chimed in, "even if Sun-myung did tell them true love had 'melted' his heart. Even if God himself..." She dropped to a doleful whisper. "Nothing but hate for the guy and he didn't even do anything."

Ayako sighed with a bit of song. "And everybody's guardian angels—especially mine!—losing their *ish* didn't help at all. Haha, no wonder she was looking crazy."

1.3 ThetaHealer Gives Us the Business...

Not ThetaHealer, though. She bellied up to the bar like an industry professional, suffering none of her mother's misgivings. According to Lucifer and later El, then finally Mina, ThetaHealer could see all the angels present (most sporting wings for effect) except for Ayako's who, like the archangels, are "ancient, advanced, and ooze a regal air."[91] They once more obscured their presence to avoid giving Family ThetaHealer any inclination that Ayako was more than she seemed, although it might not have mattered. Like her mother, ThetaHealer disregarded the angels, too.

"So, what is it you want to say?" ThetaHealer said, friendly yet cautious considering her wonderment at this impromptu ensemble. She stood easy on her heels, relaxed, open, confidently in charge and, from El's vantage, inclined to listen. Props for that. Yet, her fingers gently kneaded wrists at waist level like Chinese *Baoding* balls.

"Well," I drawled, "we decided—all of us—that we can't come to the workshop but wanted to tell you in person because we were also asked to give you a message about it."

"A message? From who?" I guessed she wasn't going to fight the loss of income but, judging by the face drama, her slightly bored antenna sure perked up.

"Yes, hmm, well, it's like this..." and, in very general terms, El and I laid out our experience with Mina: the no-Fall, The Corruption, Lucifer's frame-up and his Reconciliation with Michael, the Big

Healing, who God really is, and an elevator pitch framing the kernel of *The Story of Life*.

ThetaHealer looked round our group, and not a little incredulously, either. Who could blame her? All the same, I expected her, as a spiritualist, to give us the benefit of the doubt, if not sway test our claims on the spot since that was her shtick. In scurvy silence, Ms. Medium cast her eyes everywhere except upon her own daughter. We gradually realized she'd deleted our morning phone call from her brain log. ThetaHealer's tone was chary. "*Creator* said this?"

I nodded. El said "Yes!" and with quite some nerve, too, which left me shifting on my feet. Even so, her bald confidence was comforting. This was our first sally into the public square with our revelatory experience. We were all feeling warbly, perhaps me most of all. Sure, the First Amendment shielded us, something Martin Luther and Jesus—Joseph Smith, I suppose—would've appreciated. But my children swelled with the habitude of their youthful *dégagé* and their second-generation, scot-free, 'blessed child' status. Amongst politically complex Unificationists, that put them on equal spiritual footing with thirty-ish ThetaHealer despite their greater youth but a well-greased rung or two *above* her thrice older first-generation mother. It perforce left them feeling far less a pariah here than I. Ironically, Ms. Medium's kids inadvertently galvanized me when, debriefing, Ayako and then Mina clued me in they had indeed authenticated our story in real time, yet ignored it. Until then, I don't think I ever really appreciated the lengths to which people go to fool themselves.

"How are you receiving this information?" ThetaHealer's hard tone continued.

"Sway testing," El declared (*energy testing*; SOL PART V).

ThetaHealer's eyebrows hit the clouds. "Sway testing? You can't use the muscle test for that!"

"Well, we did," Ayako snapped out like gunfire.

"And it works!" El added.

I tossed my own two cents into the ring. "We've been having a shocking, unbelievable spiritual experience with it all week."

To ensure I couldn't give an encore performance of this morning's cowardly phone call, El said, "Creator wants—well, asked us to tell you—he doesn't want people charging money to teach about healing, or love, or doing healing. It's wrong. He doesn't like people doing it, he said."

Well, that was diplomatic. "That's really why we can't attend the workshop," I now admitted, and to back up my outspoken daughter. "Or don't want to, I guess, because, well, we agree with Creator."

ThetaHealer shifted to the balls of her feet, tense, brows beetled, and poised to sway test, debunking her chastising us for doing it. I could see the boxer in her winding up. She hit me with narrowed, laser eyes and the lazy voice of authority. "It sounds more like you're connecting with a dark, negative entity instead."

Yeah, *that* shoe's on the other foot, right enough. The thing is, she couldn't just say it wasn't possible to connect to spirit people through sway testing because, for starters, that would invalidate ThetaHealing's principal modality. Sway testing is sway testing. It accurately reads spiritual energy as a yes or no (or a maybe), or it doesn't. It connects to universal 'Source' energy of Creator of All That Is—God—and the subconscious, or it doesn't. Our reading the energy of identifiable spirit persons, including Mina and angels, was really just our advanced awareness as a variant of ThetaHealing's application.

Second, she couldn't tell us we were sway testing incorrectly. She'd not only trained us the previous weekend, but issued us certificates of competence in Basic DNA, as well. Besides, incorrect testing simply gives one a yes instead of a no or vice versa, or no response at all. It doesn't invalidate muscle testing itself.

Third, as for connecting to a negative entity instead of Creator, we relied not just on our sense of the energy, psychic imagery, sounds, touch, and other clair senses, but on logic, rationality, consistency, simplicity, and common sense to guide us. Just as ThetaHealer assumably does when connecting through jelly via the seven planes of existence to Vianna's white light she presumes is universal 'Source' energy and the subconscious.

Plainly, she wanted to shut us down on all three counts. Our wild, money-changers-in-the-temple talk certainly had to stop. What if her students were listening? They might want a refund. Perhaps she anticipated my gnarly daughters pouncing like wolf spiders if she'd tried to poo-poo our experience using any of the above. In the end, it left her with the logic of illogic. Her conundrum was real. It was only natural she'd get defensive and resort to her version of shrieking, "It's the Devil!"

I opened my mouth to reply but El—the material girl who'd said *No thanks! I have no interest in that stuff at all*—beat me to it, her voice tinged with choler. "No, we haven't connected to some dark entity! We've felt only the kindest, most loving, embracing, and positive energy! We're absolutely not talking to any sort of negative entity! That's Vianna's 'creator.'"

A little taken aback by El's furious snap back, though a tad so over-focused on El's scourging of philanthropic avarice that she'd missed her closing zinger, ThetaHealer said, "What's wrong with charging money for helping people with ThetaHealing?"

"It's not just ThetaHealing," said El. "It's everything."

"That's right," I said, "it's the problem of excluding people from understanding God or love or happiness or healing if they can't pay for it."

"Well, everybody charges. It's quite normal in the industry."

I said, "Yeah, it is normal, like crime is normal—"

"Funny you call healing people an 'industry,'" El slipped in.

"—but normality doesn't make something right, much less even desirable."

The *snick* of an unsheathing knife in her voice, ThetaHealer said, "We aren't doing anything criminal."

"I didn't mean that how it sounded," I said. Well, maybe: $440 was a lot of dough for what Vianna's $10 book already covered. "But I ran into this same problem with Leal Brown's Luv-One healing program. If you can't pay for her book or membership, or for her retreats and workshops that go for up to a thousand bucks, she isn't helping you. You're on your own." Yeah, yeah, I know, there's

YouTube and the public library; that wasn't my point. And to be fair, Leal is a caring woman who gives free teasers and sometimes scholarships the needy into her upper-middle class interventions. But the exception demonstrates the rule. It's a business.

She said, "That just proves my point. Her healing practice is obviously valuable."

"I guess, if you're teaching real estate or spirit animals or car repair. Dial for dollars all you want. But you're helping people find God and love, healing and happiness. I mean, it's a human need. People are desperate. It's easy taking advantage of them. Leal's program *is* valuable, but not monetarily. That's not why, as she says, God gave it to her."

"People get what they pay for, just like anything. They're more likely to get taken advan—"

"If they can't pay they just get to suffer? Charging money's exactly why Leal can't spread her healing, why it's anemic. Imagine church door-charges or priests' hands out over the communion plate."

She'd taken to hugging her arms. Feet apart, she needed only a Spartan shield to complete her defensive posture. This manifestly wasn't any sort of discussion. More like fighting a tuna in rough seas. Should I just put up my hands with a, "Well, that's all we wanted to say"? Hadn't we now done as Mina asked?

"You think churches don't charge for their so-called salvation?"

"I'm just saying, demanding money to heal discourages healing. It keeps people...well, it promotes exactly what it pretends it wants to fix."

She pushed out a hard "Pshaw!" and looked askance.

"I don't always charge," Ms. Medium piped up from the third tier, eyes swinging (through Lucifer) from El to me and back. "If people can't pay, it's no charge or a donation they can afford."

Being caught up in the moment, I didn't respond to that. But I had to hand it to her. She may harshly judge the penitent and leave the innocent scorned, lie about angels, invent fictitious spirit worlds to generate a psychic reputation and thereby customers and the admiration of her community, be sopped in Vianna's negative, life-sucking energy and besotted with her in general, and overall seep energetic 'poison' into us, but she was definitely on point with her fee-for-service flexibility. She'd only asked me to give a $20 donation for her Emotion Code healing a few months back, and I'd certainly appreciated her for it.

"How else do you help humanity," ThetaHealer challenged us, "without the money to help humanity?"

"How, exactly," I countered, "are you helping humanity when, without payment, you're not helping?"

"Answer: you're not helping," Ayako pelted out.

"I mean, you're really just selling a product you call 'help.'"

"That *helps* people," ThetaHealer said, now fondling the high ground yet sending each squirming hand back to wringing the other's neck.

"With an absolute spiritual necessity!" El said.

"So long as they pay first," Ayako added, conjuring in my mind an image of St. Peter saying to the faultless petitioner from under his craggy brow, "Yeah, but *then* you went and..."

El continued, "Creator doesn't like charging money for spiritual necessities because, like Dad mentioned, it excludes people. But what it really does is *create* suffering."

"And prolongs it," Ayako said.

"But not end it," said I.

"No. That's all wrong. You can't just give food away and that's a necessity. Somebody has to grow it. Nobody gives it away for free. People have to pay for their groceries."

"That's what gardens are for," snapped Ayako.

ThetaHealer gave her a hard, pitiless glare. The energy rocketed from tense to electric. She'd segued from her *Baoding* wrist massage to folded arms and then back to a meaner hand wrangle. A nervous tic, I supposed, arriving like an attentive lawyer as soon as scrutiny said hello to her cash cow. But now I had to ask myself if I was really seeing her hands doing what I thought they were doing. In one smooth motion, she'd shifted to stridently jackhammering her index finger in and out of her other circled index finger and thumb, perversely simulating with her *manus* the timeless affront of the *digitus impudicus.*

I wasn't sure if my mouth fell, but it felt so as my astounded eyes dropped to her hands, back up to her face, then again to her hands. Her finger enthusiastically humped its sister now parachuted from her waist, lingering squarely atop the fork in her road for the remainder of our accidental excursus. I couldn't be sure if she was doing it unconsciously in shame or maybe fury, or as a calculated retort she'd never utter in front of her mother. Fervid braziers seared Ayako then me from her impassive, tight-reined face.

Ms. Medium's trembling-bird eyes fleeted round our amoeba-shaped circle while ThetaHealer's younger brother eavesdropped from just inside the front door, expertly sway testing right along with Ayako and his slower sister who seemed stung Ayako sway tested more responsively than she.

1.3.1 Ayako Opines On Thetahealer . . .

"Honestly," Ayako said later, "she was so tight."

I said, "According to Mina, she really was consciously sway testing everything we were saying and coming up with the same results over and over."

"Told you."

I could only shake my head at sway testing speed as a contention. "Maybe it's like same-dress syndrome, or just plain old competitiveness." I didn't know, but marveled it lent all the more *oomph* to our controversy.

"People like that can't stand looking less to people," she said.

Mina later told us ThetaHealer's brother—spiritually more aware than she—instinctively knew our message was true even without sway testing it, but had elected to remain quiet to not rock the family boat in which he still dwelled, proving yet again that pragmatism usually trumps verity. But I could appreciate he didn't need any extra domestic squabbles. In any case, I didn't want the accusation I'd fomented any laid at my feet like some decapitated horse head beneath my sheets.

1.4 ThetaHealer Takes On Mina's Message . . .

"It's not wrong to charge people money for my services," Theta-Healer was saying. "I had to pay for my training—"

"We're not the ones to convince," I said, glancing at the girls. "We're not trying to put you on the spot anyhow. I totally understand where you're coming from. It's all very surprising and unexpected for us, too. We just thought you'd want to hear Creator's message—since, you know, you teach about him and all."

"And we agree, too," said El. "With his message, I mean."

"I don't set the price anyway. That's Vianna, she requires we charge for the workshop. I have no control over—"

"It *is* wrong to charge money, though," Ayako cut in, "because you're denying people healing, what they were born to, which is their birthright from God. You don't think that's wrong?"

"That's stupid. Money is just—"

"It's not stupid!" That was the wrong word and set Ayako aflame. She was acutely edgy, I thought. She could throw a pout with the best of them. But at home. In her *sanctum sanctorum*. I supposed it could've been the tensity of our extraordinary week. Or maybe she was feeling Michael's iconic sword waving alarmingly about. ThetaHealer could simply represent something Ayako despised. "It's wrong to charge money for healing, including *how* to be healed. Is it stupid to demand honesty just because everybody lies?"

"I. Don't. Lie."

"I'm just saying. Payment to heal is like denying people a right to life. That's—"

"What?! No one's—"

"—Creator's attitude."

"—denied any right to life just because they pay for training."

"You just said people have to pay for groceries. So, if they can't pay, they can't eat. Isn't that denying them a right to life?"

"That's—"

"But isn't it the same principle?"

I mumbled, "I guess gardening's looking a bit less irrelevant right about now."

"Plus, people are paying for something—like healing—they can easily do themselves." Ayako pointedly glanced Ms. Medium's way. "The fact you charge for that without telling them they can do it *is* deceitful."

Ms. Medium either didn't catch that, or chose the no-reply option. Possibly, she'd closed her senses to Ayako, too. But ThetaHealer bristled. "I'm not deceiving anybody, Ayako, and neither is Vianna." Her eyes set upon her unhelpful mother. "In any case, people can't heal themselves if they aren't shown how."

"Exactly," Ayako said. "Creator's original point."

ThetaHealer paused on the finger sex to spread her hands in triumph. "So, then, training people *is* the only way to better the world."

"You're trying to make a better world but you charge money for it?" Ayako snickered. "You're kidding."

Bloody hell, these girls are a couple of snapping turtles! Was I proud or aghast? I couldn't decide. I pondered how Mina was taking our performance. Was he egging us on or face palming? Were we giving him a bad rep or planting his flag? Was ThetaHealer's response a foregone conclusion and Ayako's mini-tirade merely her pushing a Sisyphean boulder up ThetaHealer's unwilling hill? Or, like sound resonance, would our effort only later reach the 'shatter frequency' of her mindset's formidable crags? I couldn't answer any of these riddles and tied a mental string to my finger to find out later.[92]

"I have to pay my expenses to fly here and pay for my needs, to have my life."

"You don't charge your mom or your brother," Ayako said, "so you're obviously okay with doing free healing and free workshops in principle."

"So long as it's for the right people," said El with a whiff of Groucho Marx.

ThetaHealer had been running a spastic, high-strung head wag cycling to Ayako's pontificating, but now cocked it puppy-like to one side. Congenial, she said to the girls, "You're both young. You don't understand everybody has to make a living regardless the field they choose. I chose to make my living helping people. What have you chosen to do?"

"That just means you chose to make a living off people's suffering, like a vampire," said Ayako. "Get another job and volunteer for this instead of making excuse after excuse to justify yourself."

If ThetaHealer was softening, Ayako just stiffened her spine. Her fingers leapt back into coitus and frantically banged away. Heck, they'd shifted into overdrive with Ayako's stinging slap. I'm sure thirtyish ThetaHealer didn't appreciate their young effrontery.

I had to admit—with a certain, perhaps shameful? glee—that these young ladies of mine could hold their own. I wasn't too sure about myself, though. I was white hot over ThetaHealer's rank hand gesture, but restrained a caustic mouth from provoking worse. We were only here delivering a simple message anyway—from God, *yeah*, but not as judge and jury. It sure wasn't our place to assault anyone's freedom. And anyway, didn't such Accountableism doom everything Mina held dear?

My legs trembled. Whether from anger, stress, the spiritual energy surging around and through us, disgusted angels, the 64-degree temps, or some combination of it all was hard to say. I could barely keep my feet. I was feeling how Ayako looked.

El caught me with a worried eye, wondering if my fear of Theta-Healer's aggression was getting the best of me—the way my kids felt I used to placate domestic violence—and could maybe leave them fending for themselves. I'd noticed a wood-slatted porch chair behind me and now scuttled over to it. Perched on its unyielding seat edge, my outstretched legs jumped under my skin with a frenetic will of their own.

Lucifer later chuckled, *Nah, you weren't shaking from any spiritual energy.* Yeah, I was probably just fuming. Conflict averse too, maybe, so, laugh-back, buddy.

To me, ThetaHealer said, "You said this comes from Creator?"

"Yes," El answered for me. "It hurts him seeing—"

"Hurts? Well, that's your clue right there you're not talking to the Creator of All That Is. He doesn't have feelings. He's not a *person*."

I blinked. "He's not a—?"

"He *is* a person!" said El, riled once more. I vaguely advised myself we might be unwisely entering the shouting phase, but wasn't really listening. I wondered if we three might've bonded with Mina more than your average 'revealee' bonds with their revelator. "He feels more deeply than any of us."

"No. Creator is just an energy source in the universe. *The* universal energy. 'Source' energy."

Ayako stiffened, astonished. El hugged herself against the onslaught of tumultuous, indignant angelic energy battering her from all quarters. Ms. Medium had raised ThetaHealer in a Moonie household, and Moonies are thoroughly wedded to a God of personhood who embodies a personality of unconditional love. We thought it bizarre she'd convert her childhood's parental God of love into a wall outlet. Then again, maybe in her household that God had got locked out. But to chalk up *our* spiritual experience to the manipulations of a negative entity because we broke the sway testing rulebook of *her* ThetaHealing practice? Okay, fine, let's be honest. We were challenging her business model along with her ethics and altruism. Who'd take that lying down?

"What kind of God is that?" I wondered aloud.

She said, "God is only here to serve people. He has no agenda, like religion or money. He's just an energy being, not a sentient person." Those ideas seemed primitive to us, a throwback to, I don't know, animism or shamanism, or something Neanderthal if not *Homo heidelbergensis*. She continued, "It's a dark entity you're connecting to, not Creator."

"We've felt Creator's love and his feelings," El said, "even *heard* them. He's told us how he feels!"

"And none of it is dark," pronounced Ayako.

"There *is* no God like you're talking about," ThetaHealer said. "Creator has no personality, no love, no feelings at all. Whoever you're talking to is not a Being of Light."

That sounded to me as irrational as an abuser crying their love while droppin' a whuppin.' Why not sway test it right now, I was thinking. Didn't she want to know? Was she afraid of the answer? Lack of curiosity is a mortal sin in my book. If sin was real, I mean. Which it isn't.

My children's faces reflected how appalling ThetaHealer sounded. I glanced at Ms. Medium for a reaction to her daughter's most un-Moonie belief system, but she wasn't coming down from the cheap seats. Maybe it was a long-lost argument at home. El edged nearer me as tears overflowed her lashes, which seemed a little over the top. I didn't realize that, after five days, she was approaching emotional overload.

It wasn't only El or us feeling this way. Our crew of disgusted angels, who mindfully prized today's Big Event and their stake in our effort, were boiling over. My daughters vibrated to their truculent energy like antennas in a high-wattage ether. And all the while, ThetaHealer's half-bent finger slithered in and out, in and out, all but touching her sex appeal. *Fuck. You.*

Ayako and El were oblivious to the finger action, but not to the energy. I watched El losing it and caught up to my own advice. It was time to cinch this conversation down. Michael, firm alongside Ayako—"the two level-headed ones," she later japed—beamed "a death stare" at her guardian angels now out from their 'bush' and raucously fomenting a verbal beat-down of ThetaHealer's own, who'd paraded their discomfort with their charge's attitude yet, nevertheless, had her back per their commitment. Gabriel now quietly parked himself on my right without flair, limiting himself to *Observing with Gravitas* to try curbing some of this angelic ardor.[63] Ours own, too, perchance. Ms. Medium seemed to wither under the spiritual tension what with "Michael's hard, knowing glare," in Ayako's words, lighting her up plus Lucifer's slighted energy pulsing at her side.

"Do you have any shamans in your family?" inquired Theta-Healer with a fair dose of scorn. *Not ready to quit, are you.*

"You mean dark arts people?" I mused. "Witches, or whatever?" But she'd focused herself on Ayako.

---

63. Freedom means there's no command authority to exert dominance. This is their norm.

"No!" belched Ayako. "We have nothing to do with shamanism!"

"Isn't that Vianna and her husband's thing?" El was quaky.

ThetaHealer glared, but her voice held steady. "It's most likely a malevolent spirit at work here. That's who's telling you all this."

"Why would a malevolent spirit even care about charging money?" I said, and wondered if her pounding finger wasn't itself operated by one even now spurning Mina's Big Healing.

"Seems it would want people charging even more money if it's really malevolent," Ayako cracked, wordfully slicing yet another *Z-for-Zorro* segment across ThetaHealer's knurled forehead.

Her cheeks flushed with our message—or delivery, if we're being fair—stacked over and above Ayako's superior sway testing caliber. She'd only think a thought and move with verve whereas ThetaHealer had to wait for a demonstrably weaker push. Well, in truth, I couldn't blame ThetaHealer for that. El and I felt similar frustrations at home wishing Ayako's energism energized us, too.

ThetaHealer did know our message was valid. She couldn't help her trained, sensitive medium's body moving to Mina—apparently not so busy healing he couldn't pay attention to this nicely hosed quagmire—responding to her thoughts and feelings with the same answers Ayako sway tested. Being a sway test practitioner, ThetaHealer could hardly discount a *no*-push when she told herself charging money to heal was okay or that her creator was nothing more than a universal Energizer bunny. Rather than accept this revelation, she ignored it to discredit the message. This whole conversation devolved into an exercise in futility as she rationalized contradicting her own sway testing experience.

1.4.1 Ayako Recalls ThetaHealer's Scrutiny ...

"She was so mad!" Ayako recalled as we later staggered home. I'd noticed very little of this covert catfight at the time, but Ayako had scrutinized ThetaHealer's body with gator eyes. "She knew all my sway testing was right on, Dad. She couldn't help but test the same as me, so she knew Creator was telling her the same thing!" She chortled. "Talk about stubborn."

1.5 OUR CONFAB WINDS DOWN ...

Right now, though, ThetaHealer looked to be wondering how Ayako could be so expertly, if not masterly, sway testing as good as her little brother with his thousands of hours of experience. Hadn't Ayako attended her Basic DNA workshop only the previous weekend and only just learned the technique? A sensible supposition. Who'd pay $440 to learn what they already knew? She recognized Ayako's psychic ability, but didn't know how experienced as an empath, psychic, and medium she was, having practiced a wide variety of spiritual disciplines including astral projection, and capable in degrees of all eight clair senses. Her sister and I are comparatively novices, one reason Mina asked her to take on Michael's role of Teacher in our wee threesome.[64] In certain key areas, she's dramatically more advanced than ThetaHealer and Ms. Medium. Certainly, more a medium than either had taken her for.

"Look," I said, "I appreciate your situation. We only came up to tell you what Creator said. Obviously, it's up to you to—"

"You can do what you want. I'm going to charge money, regardless." She looked around, then across her right shoulder at the house. "I have students waiting." She didn't have to say *who've paid*, but that came through loud and clear. "Thanks for coming."

"Sure. Thanks for listening." I was now satisfied a phone call was a poor substitute for this face-to-face, however sideways it went.

El, her posture slumped, turned for the Prius as ThetaHealer disappeared into the house. Ms. Medium reached out an unsure hand and said, "Are you okay, El? What's wrong?"

El's frazzled mind raced. *Are you kidding? You're asking that now? As soon as your daughter walks away, you break your vow of silence after telling us this morning you believed our every word? We thought you'd have our back.*

Ms. Medium shuffled forward to hug her, but Lucifer bodily blocked her so they couldn't touch. He was too in a boil himself to follow up his request to Ayako (who hadn't forgot) to ask Ms.

---

64. For us in these early days, Mina had asked El to take on Gabriel's Messenger role and me, Lucifer's Mediator role. She'd been a good messenger today, aye, but I'd felt no mediating skills at all.

Medium to talk with him when we'd finished. He gave it a go some days later, but all he managed was some shouting with her spirit self before abruptly turning on his stylish heel. They did talk later while she was awake, but she turned hard-hearted Barb'ry Allen's ear to him.[93] He 'portaled' away dejected by her shard-studded 'heart wall' not yet realizing, he surprised me by saying, that she wasn't actually hearing his words.

Lucifer spiritually took El in his arms, a towering nine-foot comforter El physically felt as she visibly trembled and wept. My arm wound round her and I pulled her into my chest. If Ms. Medium seemed overpowered by the furious energies, El was staggered. Ayako was already spent when we'd started but nonetheless had stood-to like a soldier.

The least spiritually aware of them all, I could almost appreciate Ms. Medium's query to El because, outwardly, our ten-minute conversation sounded benign. To the ear, no one's tone rose to lead a bystander to presume anyone was hot under the collar. Just folks conversing with a few jabs and barbs. It was under the hood and out of sight that our dust up's real engine roared, fumed, belched, and shuddered like a dark, unholy Monster Truck. Ms. Medium had closed her spirit senses and cut herself out of most of the real action. In our debriefing while driving home, the girls gave me a finer appreciation for the subtext and undercurrents that were at play and for what they'd just gone through on a level I'd noticed only in my trembling legs, intuitive leaps, disturbed vibes, and the cold mercury oozing through my skin.

1.5.1   OUR CONVALESCENT THOUGHTS . . .

Ostensibly, our meeting was to see about pulling Ms. Medium and ThetaHealer—spiritually powerful mediums and sway testers fully capable of all we were doing and vastly more—up from their crude, money-grubbing, toxic energy bath. Whatever Mina thinks of their attitudes, he feels no judgment or rejection for them. That's a truth worth accentuating. It harkens back to Catholicism's bromide to hate the sin but love the sinner except without the sin, or the hate. We're free to be free, but one isn't free when judged, rejected, and penalized by the freedom-giver for exercising it.

Regardless, our effort's fuller purpose lay in Mina hoping the three of us could publicly stand behind his story of life and leave the safety of our home to carry its illumination to others. We'd demonstrated the mojo to step up to the plate and swing the bat on humanity's birthright. Timorously running the bases would only make it an easy out, so we ran hard.

Once stuck in, Gabriel and Michael had encouraged our Angel Code meetings with stories to gauge Ms. Medium's reliability because, well, they didn't know. However unlikely, ThetaHealer One or Two or both could've embraced our message because breaching the NCC paved the way for the Big Healing and its irrevocable change of spirit world. As tough as it might be, Mina wanted us to publicize it and me to drop my prized book project for which I was well versed to write my iffy, obscure, serpentine, and possibly unwelcome account. Then, before my eyes could even roll up dollar signs, he'd nixed any remuneration and I'd thought, *ah, nuts!* And Family ThetaHealer now served as a barometer for all of it.

With a small sense of kismet, it seemed things had now come full circle since our Basic DNA beginnings last Friday. We'd built our own destiny now, hewing to our curiosity and honoring Mina's request to bring opportunity to Ms. Medium and her family. Given our personalities, could or would we have done it any different? It's hard to say.

Mina, too, is of a mind we'd eventually have stumbled across energy testing spirit people on our own. Ayako, anyway. To my way of thinking, the resonance between the three of us is what harvested this morning's spectacular results. I'd singly fumbled all that away in my half-assed muscle testing explorations a couple years earlier when I'd failed to make the leap from testing my 'subconscious' to testing its originator, which was already obvious—if unnoticed—in Divine Principle. Together, we'd fertilized each of our strengths, inquisitiveness, and willingness to transcend the obtuse physical for the esoteric spiritual as an objective reality we could show and tell. This is where I think free will and fate tend to get all mixed up.

1.6 DECAMPING WITH HEAVY HEARTS ...

With ThetaHealer departed and Lucifer holding Ms. Medium at bay, we bade our farewells. I said to Ms. Medium, "El's okay, just super tired and feeling overwhelmed."

"I'll talk with you later, then," she said, hovering behind a weak smile on the far side of Lucifer.

Not if we see you first, we all cautioned ourselves.

Honestly, I was feeling supremely disappointed with Ms. Medium at this point. My children now exuded the sort of affection for her that Americans reserve for Nazi doctors—or monkey brains, maybe. Their inclination for another conversation with her floated drowned in the deep end. Foremost in our minds was our experience being sickened from her negative energy and the way it had clung to us to wreck our foodstuffs a hundred miles away.[94] To whom else had we unwittingly carried it?

"You don't hang around a nuclear pile without a rad suit, do you?" I later explained to a less-than credulous Moth Man. "Keeping our distance from her seems the only healthy choice."

"Better you than me," he said. Alas.

Revival Ride

Friday October 13, 2017 ca. 6 pm

We plopped into the Prius then burbled backward down the driveway. Ms. Medium fruitlessly waved us on our way. I returned a polite hand and thumbed the knee-banger gear selector over to DRIVE and motored away. A collective sigh of relief swarmed the cabin. It hadn't even been that long of a conversation, yet zonked us like a daylong broadsword battle in heavy armor on the boot-sucking moors.

"Well, that's done," I said. "I hope Pro—"

"Thank God!" Ayako doubled over then pitched against her seatback. "That was just too much!"

Seated right behind me, El burst into full-blown hysterics. Tears streamed down her face onto her shirt. I wanted to stop and hold her, but she babbled Lucifer was doing that.

"Well, jeez, but . . . okay," I drawled, like I'd just been sacked.

"*God*, my chest hurts *really* badly," she sobbed. "I can hardly breathe. Nothing works."

Tears welled in my eyes. In my own chest detonated a kinder, gentler brand of Michael's earlier Angel Code EMP. I figured she'd built up a bunker load of emotional energy by now and it sorely needed venting. What's more efficacious than crying? I dropped the window for a cool breeze and hoped it soothed El, too. Ayako pulled some napkins from the glove box and passed them back to her sister whose grateful, sloppy-wet eyes registered their bonded love.

Ayako resettled herself and said, "Lucifer's *so* angry."

I glanced her way. "With ThetaHealer?"

"Ms. Medium. I mean, he's pretty unhappy with ThetaHealer, the way she's teaching people her junk that Protector"—how we now addressed him since last night—"is basically nobody, a thing."

"So weird," I said. "Not even a person, much less your traditional deity. He's ticked because she's misrepresenting him, but knows better?"

She did some quick hand tests. "Yes. But he's really furious with Ms. Medium"—another pause to test—"and he says she doesn't know any better about Protector and stuff, but she should. She's capable of knowing the truth."

"Mad, like Michael?"

"No, Michael's not angry. He's just really sorrowful—as usual." She cheeped a laugh. "He has a very calm spirit, overall. That's how I feel him when he shows up."

I nodded along as I drove, thinking he wasn't too calmly sorrowful with Ms. Medium at our EMP'd Angel Code session. His outrage had boomed through my girls' heads like the world's biggest gong. I guess everybody has their limits.

"But Lucifer was practically raging back there," Ayako continued.

"Raging? That's not doing his rep any—"

"You know what I mean, Dad. Ms. Medium knew he was there. She tuned him out, ignored him, and she let Michael just stew. I mean, all she had to do was recognize him there and give him an

'I'm sorry' look, or a thought, or just something, and they'd be fine with that."

"I was shaking like a leaf," I said, "like all that fiery energy was running through me. Felt like being low-voltage electrocuted."

"Low voltage? Ha! The angels were ready to start a big fight! Mine were practically out of control." She chuckled.

"I thought yours were this ancient, wise, married couple who never lost their cool, even hung on in The Fracas like troopers."

"Didn't I tell you I got new ones? My originals were spending too much time away calming spirit world after the fight. Anyway, they couldn't stop picking their own fight with ThetaHealer's guardian angels . . . saying things like, 'How can you let her talk like that?' and, 'Why are you sticking with her?' and, 'Can't you even deal with her?' And then her angels got furious, too!"

"With your angels? Well, it's not like they weren't being pretty provoca—"

"With ThetaHealer!" She bounced her skull off the headrest. "Oh-em-*gee*! With my guardian angels, too, yeah. With everybody." She gave me a cool, twinkly, self-conscious eye. "They were feeling pretty attacked, Dad."

"I bet!" I rested my own noggin on the headrest and rocked it gently to and fro as a comfort, eyeing the slightly unfocused road from beneath the rim of my eyeglasses. A smirk played along my lips at the image of all these fulminous angels versus their traditional sagacity . . . screwy all in itself, considering the monotheisms teach a third of the angels launched a civil war against God, the other two-thirds literally beat them into the dirt, then iced their cake with prodigious odium. More and more, the ancient Greeks and Hindus were looking pretty keyed-in to the lifestyles of the divine and celestial.

"Michael spent his time trying to defuse all that"—incredulity marked her face—"but everybody's angels were in an uproar. It was like a giant schoolyard riot!"

Lucifer's opinion and all that, I'm certain I was trembling from all that wild energy more than dread. I've never quaked like that before. Maybe in a real fight, I suppose. Ayako was an old hand with spiritual chaos. El and I were greenhorns riding hell for leather into a whole new, unimagined, mind-bending reality. So much still made so little sense to us. The reality of spirit world mixing it up with the physical one hit like a visceral one-two bowling ball to the chin. We needed a minute to catch ourselves, thank you. It might've all been obvious to my religious faith, but I'd never noticed with adequate thoughtfulness to make a difference. Ayako's inner coolness under this sort of fire was a blessing it took some time to appreciate— I guess because, at her age, I mostly incurred her outer snark.

I said, "So much uproar just over attitude? Seems excessive."

"Dad, angels are *intense*. They feel on a whole different level. They know how people are. We don't usually get under their skin. But when somebody for sure knows what's going on spiritually, then twists it all around anyway—especially for money!—that really gets them hot. Think about it. How would you feel?"

"A lot like the people I bet Michael's running into right about now on his ninth-step rounds."

"Come on, now, leave him alone."

"Okay . . . so, maybe they were feeling how The Corruption had grabbed 'em, if they ever think back on it."

"Why wouldn't they?" She felt no need to test it but did anyhow, pronouncing, "Of course they think about it."

"Alright, don't get all protective on me. Protector said they knew better, but went with it all the same and never even asked him for answers, all I'm saying."

"Um . . ."—test, test—"yeah. Especially now, it's all so insulting with the whole Reconciliation and healing that's going on."

"Like turning Protector into some faceless gnome," I griped.

"Like lying about the truth!" she said, still a little hot there, herself. "She sway tested my same answers over and over, but denied it all. *Lied* about it. I watched her! Is she a sway tester or not? Is sway testing real or not? She teaches it. She uses it to make money. But when it contradicts what she wants, she ignores it. Then she teaches all those lies to people who don't know any better . . ."

I sniggered. "But pay through the nose for it."

"Yeah! It's *just* like The Corruption."

From the back seat, a somewhat composed El growled through tears, "That makes *any* normal person mad, Dad!"

With that, she launched into 'fighting up' Ms. Medium ex post facto with Ayako helping to process her feelings. While they went hammer and tongs at ThetaHealer One and Two, I realized I needed to decompress a beat, myself. We'd lunched about six hours ago, but it seemed like days. We were starving dogs. It occurred to me to drop by Moth Man's not-too-distant castle to enjoy some welcoming company for a change. He was always up for the sort of woo-woo we were sitting on. Fancied himself its persecuted king in the local Unification Church. He'd gobble this stuff right up. I took a minute to jink off the roadway for a Google Maps consult, then navigated to Moth Man's while, backseat, El—Ayako frequently twisting round during our review to engage her little sister—worked at winding herself down, interjecting less emotional and more thoughtful counterarguments to Family ThetaHealers' perspective.

1.1 VISITING MY FRIEND MOTH MAN ...

The girls weren't too hip for a rest stop at Moth Man's, but graciously give their dad his due. Besides, they were hungry and Moth Man always stocked snacks galore. Sometimes his kitchen looks to us like a hole-in-the-wall corner store. They hung out quietly in his living room with one of his same-age sons sharing chips, dips, drinks, and happy talk. Trotting along behind my spiritual kin in his quest to complete his honey-do tasks, I spilled some of our beans on Mina and ThetaHealer. Disappointment hit a little hard that he didn't seem to catch much of it. In awe, I realized our woo-woo was too strong even for the master.

He said, "Angry angels? Lucifer framed, you say? God prefers we call him *Protector*? And he's got a freakin' *wife*?" His perplexity read like a tachometer in the red zone; it was all so far outside even his open-door gonzo box. Spirit animals and Unificationism's take-no-prisoners imperative to Restore The World at any cost pretty much pussy-whipped his day-to-day worldview into an eyes-down approach to life. Ms. Medium was his fellow traveler. I trod their thorny path only on tippy toes.

1.1.1 AYAKO AND EL OPINE ON MOTH MAN . . .

Ayako and El later had the same take. "Dad, he probably thinks you're just another Moonie psycho."

"Except I'm not a Moonie," I protested. "Not really, anymore." Not by most members' definition anyway, most of all Moth Man's.

"Once a Moonie psycho," said El, "always a Moo—"

"Whatever." We did show up for church a few times a month, mostly as a social call for the girls and their previous Maryland school chums. I looked forward to those visits like a parolee from the hermitage, ditching church and its insipid pastoral henpecking to pace the block talking Real God with Moth Man. Our 100-mile gesture just to get there was enough in their convert-hungry minds to see us all in the family who'd hopefully tithe though, in all honesty, they really saw us more the inbred cousins preferably bolted in the cellar when company called. "I think I'm now more a Sunnie than a Moonie," I added.[95]

"They're not going to like you any better, Dad," El said with wisdom beyond my years.

1.2 MOTH MAN PRONOUNCES SENTENCE . . .

Moth Man at last gave his predicted assessment: "You're officially crazier than I am, buddy."

"That's crazier than I want to be."

"They're gonna excommunicate you, brother."

I let go a belly laugh. "Like they haven't done that how many times already? Who cares, mate." Wasn't it since the Renaissance when rogue Christians snarled in religion's face, 'O, Excommunication, where is thy sting?'[96] Bring it on, ye posers!

He felt dubious of my breezy dismissal of folks appropriating God's wrath. "I'm talking the world, here, bro. You better be careful who you piss off."

"All things considered, I'm not sure how I'd go about doing that."

What we did do was head over to Boston Market in Riverdale, Maryland. We took a booth in the windowed corner with our chicken and vittles and Moth Man largely deflected my glad tidings of Mina. *Propheting 101*, I sourly groused.

He said, "What you really need is a marketing team."

"That's what the book's for."

"Yeah, but how're you gonna get the book in front of people?"

Well, he sure had me there. I leaned back. "I couldn't pay them, anyway. The book has to be free."

"Whaaa—?" He just stared at the crazy guy.

"I'm gonna need a sugar daddy."

"Or three!" El spluttered through a buttery corncob.

Moth Man drummed a finger ditty on the tabletop. A self-published author of little renown himself (*Drink Your Own Water: A Treatise on Urine Therapy* his best seller), he did know a thing or two of the publishing challenge I faced. He said, "Yeah, okay . . . you can work with that. Ebooks don't really cost anything once you set them up. Self publishing, eh? You can get it out to everybo—what?"

"Ahh. . ." I sounded pretty lame even to myself. "Protector doesn't really dig electronics. He wants a print book only."

His head was nodding but his forehead and Sicilian brows clawed heavenward, glazed eyeballs trying to follow but anchored to their sockets. His disbelief challenged each of my girls in turn.

Ayako said, "It has to do with energy fields and electronics radiation. Hurts the body, but really it closes your third-eye chakra."

"It does?"

"Yeah," she said agreeably. "If you're reading it as an ebook, then you're getting the opposite of what you want, because you want your third-eye open so you can sway test and intuit, or just be more spiritually aware in general."

He swung back to me with a chuckle while his head wagged no. "Print only? You're gonna need to marry Crœsus, buddy."

Everybody's a comedian. "Maybe I can change his mind."[65]

---

65. Well, I did. In 2019, he accepted an ebook so long as we included a disclaimer about chakras.

"There's that. Lot managed it in the Bible."

"And it went so well for him. Thanks."

 Dismissing my publishing param-eters, Moth Man regaled the girls with spirit animals, pronounc-ing Ayako's the eagle and El's the praying mantis. Ayako munched her chicken with the couldn't-care-less of the dead. El picked up on the mantis with a certain cool satisfaction that twitched up the corners of my mouth. Some while back, he'd introduced me to mine: the hawk. Apropos it was, too, as I'd grown up in the Rockies soaring in my imagination high on thermals and winging through clouds, though I'd seen myself more a majestically screamin' bald eagle than a puny, squawkin' hawk. I did hear they're smarter, so there's that. Funnily enough, Moth Man gets his spirit animal dope through muscle testing, what he also calls universal 'Source' energy. That made him a kindred spirit of sorts—I know, not unlike Ms. Medium and her family—but that's where we parted.

The girls were only half listening. They looked and felt washed out, utterly depleted and discharged like my dad-gutted Prius battery back in 2016 (EN 50:182). Finishing with dinner, their hollowed-out faces said, "Just get us home to our beds, Dad. *Puh-leeze.*"

Right. *Ugh.* Another hundred-mile cruise. I wasn't feeling too spirited myself. But then when the going gets tough, aren't even—especially!—faulty dads supposed to get going?

1.3 OUR RIDE HOME TAKES A DETOUR...

Except for Interstate 95's eternal stop-and-go pileup along northern Virginia's Woodbridge–Occoquan traffic disrupter where The Road of Good Intentions corsets five lanes of traffic into three with an on-ramp and incline thrown in for the challenge, we flowed south relatively freely now the evening rush hour had played out. Our car talk resumed its new-normal tenor as the girls, energized by their victuals and sense of safety in the family car, on and off engaged Taiji, Hidé, Helen, *Obāsan*, and others. Hidé and Taiji pointedly lightened the conversation to ease everyone's feelings. They are considerate that way.

At one point, I turned the discussion to Mother to find out how she'd produced her children and noted, "By the way, that's a lot of kids you had! What about their father? Same guy?"

That detour took us into one of those BIG NEWS moments I mentioned earlier, which got our car's spirit denizens clamoring, pulling in Jesus, Sun-myung, and others whom we never identified. Then Ayako sensed someone besides the usual crowd fielding her questions. After some investigation, it turned out that both of ThetaHealer's guardian angels had been apologizing to our guardian angels and everyone concerned for ThetaHealer's attitude and their own part in the earlier fray for a good forty minutes or so before we clued to their presence.

"But wait," I said, "aren't one of you supposed to be with your 'guardee' at all times?"

Yes.

"Then what're you both doing here, and for so long? You jail-breaking? Heh-heh."

Pause.

Ayako grinned. "Not getting an answer to that one, Dad...Wait. You don't want to go back?"

No.

"Let me get this straight," I said. "I was just joking but...you don't want to be her guardian angels anymore?"

Pause. I imagined them turning their faces toward each other, maybe sheepishly checking out all our guardian angels. *No.*

"*Boiii!*" squalled Ayako. "That sure created a shh—shtuff storm with the other angels!" After a minute, she added with a flash of teeth, "My angels chased them back to their job. Ha-ha! My new ones are real ancient too, Dad, top of the line. You sure don't mess with *them*."

"They were fighting?" I said.

"No, no, no. They just lectured them how they can't be away so long. It's very bad."

"They'll get in trouble, then?"

"That's not their reality. Nobody forces anybody."

"Unless you're some sad sack in the darker levels," I said, my thoughts running to Helen. "Before the Big Healing clears them all out, I guess." We still expected another six days for that job.

1.3.1 Side Trip: Our Discovery of Cosmo …

Speaking of guardian angels, some days later Ayako and I were chewing the spiritual fat in her bedroom with "the squad," as the girls were now wont to call our happy and growing covey of spirit folk which, for the moment, included Lucifer as CEO and chief bottle washer of Guardian Angels, Inc., or whatever. I was availing myself of Ayako's superior spiritual awareness, energism, and Teacher status among us. That means I was having her energy test for me. She lay stretched out lazily on her bed with her nose to the iPhone. I'd squeezed myself into the narrow strip of carpeted floor between her bed, stacks of laundry, musical instruments, and the closet. She'd picked the smallest room when we'd moved in, and small is being generous. It had a private half-bath half the bedroom's size that she'd seen as the perfect trade off. El's usual YouTube on the 70-inch flat-screen in the main room was entertaining her, but she leapt up with Mother's general burst of *yes* energy to my asking if she was a created being like Mina. Until then, see, we'd been imagining Mother as the *über* 'deity' of the multiverse, and it wasn't lost on me how *that* theological reversal would energize the when-God-created-man-She-was-only-kidding crowd.

Ayako sat bolt upright and said, "Oh-em-gee, Dad, the room's filling up with everybody! Sun-myung and Jesus are bouncing off the walls. I can feel people all over my bed!"

One of our bigger BIG NEWS moments. I often wondered how it was that, according to Mina, such titans as Jesus and curiosity hounds like Sun-myung or axial thinkers like Zoroaster or Plato or

Marx, or just anybody, hadn't already asked many of the questions we were now pulling out of our collective hat. I supposed I could sort of see it. We didn't imagine *this* question till our spontaneous conversation had sparked it just now. Yet, hadn't it been oh-so-obvious ever since we learned of Mina's mother? New concepts, like bread dough, just need time to rise. What we've learned of Mina and the universe falls so far outside our traditional thought matrix that follow-on query B to revelation A is very often less than self-evident until it is self-evident. But one needs to care and be curious, too; if you don't want to hunt, what is it you're going to catch? Besides, while angels already figured they knew all there was, Mina said a lot of these big-name doers and thinkers in life lost all their dash and wonder in spirit world because most of their existential angst resolved itself with death. What hangs on is swamped by how much more there is across the briny void to engage one's mind. And, too, people don't easily shed ingrained concepts. My dad and mom (d. 2018), for example, said they don't really talk to Mina themselves because they haven't shook off their grisly Catholic indoctrination even as they listen in on our conversations with him.

El flung open Ayako's door and smoked to a stop by her bed while I was trying to get a name for Mother's creator but missing the tendril. I bandied about such (not always serious) pseudonyms as Morpheus (*NO!*), Cosmos (*No*), Universe (*Hmm...*), Big Daddy (*Oh, please*), Optimus Prime (*Absolutely not*).

Full of hope casting back to when she'd met Mother, El said, "Can we meet him, Mother?"

No.

Her face fell into a moue. "Can I call him Mr. Universe?"

I barked an inadvertent "Haw!" at that steroidal image.

No.

Well, rats. And I liked it. What *were* we going to call him?

"He's an introvert, Dad," Ayako said, hand testing on the bed. "He created everything from the start (nope; FN 66:134) and travels universe to universe checking everything out, seeing how everybody's doing, just enjoying the life and being Mr. Anonymous."

"Talk about behind the scenes," I said, with grumpy air quotes. But even I wouldn't have suggested calling him Mr. Anonymous.

"He doesn't want to be known," she added. "He doesn't want to be *worshipped*."

Ah, yes, the danger one never seems to escape when it comes to people. Ayako tested that he has no prior creator.[66] *Yeah,* I thought dubiously, *but what'll we find out tomorrow?* Because, so far, this train had no brakes.

"He doesn't want to talk to us?" El said to Mother.

Ayako hand tested. "He's just not ready yet, El. He'll let us know."

"So the buck stops with him?" I said.

Yes.

"He created the first universe all the others are patterned off of?"

Yes. (FN 66; *SOL* § 1.2.1.1:338)

"And he is, as they say, timeless? Always existed?"

Maybe...yes.

I gasped. Ayako looked at me. "You don't know?"

No. Not exactly.

Perplexed faces all around but Jesus and Sun-myung were feeling charged up and maybe on the job, though that didn't help us. I gave a nod to disgruntlement that those two might use my brainstorm to springboard to a lot of awesome knowledge from Mina that I was dying to know (well, not *that* dying to know) with their Johnny-on-the-spot option. Boy, was I pining for clairvoyance. All I had in my toolbox was what I could think up to test and the intuition that helped it along. It's a lot, don't get me wrong, but you have to exercise it like a racehorse to muscle it up to contender status. And dang it, all that my brilliant insight had effectively accomplished was to find Creator Prime two degrees removed from where humanity always thought he was with all the same unanswered questions (now answered in *SOL* PARTS II–V) and on walkabout.

---

66. No, nor did he create everything from the start though he taught Mina to create our universe. He has no prior creator, as none of us do, since we're all emergent ℒife (*SOL* CH. 19:245). We hadn't yet learned to discern literal from nuanced responses nor *maybe, kind of, not exactly*, etc. at this early stage. Mother never inquired into his backstory and had inaccurate information. We later corrected it with Cosmo and Mina. See Cosmo's deets in *SOL* § 1.2.1.1:338.

"Philosophers are gonna laugh," I half-joked.

"Quit worrying about reactions, Dad." My homegrown therapist.

"Easy for you to say, El, you're not doing the book. Did you ever ask him this stuff, Protector?"

Maybe . . . no.

"Seriously?"

Yes.

"Because you didn't care?"

No.

"Then because . . . uhh . . ."—waiting for intuition to strike—"you already knew what you needed or wanted to know, so it wasn't pressing? I mean, um, you didn't *need* to know, so you just never thought about it? Am I right?"

Yes.

Far be it for me to say, but isn't that the definition of complacence? "You gonna ask him about it now?"

Yes. Ayako felt him laughing through the energy of his reply.

"Because you're suddenly curious?"

Yes.

Wow. We'd piqued his interest in something new. How'd I feel about that? *Shrug.* It was too exciting for much reflection. I was still riding cloud nine to the penthouse with a jolly swelled head.

In the ensuing discussion—we agreed to call our alleged *über* creator Universe but, after a few months, it was only confusing us during our cosmology dialogues; I made an executive decision to switch to *Cosmo*—Mina and Mother said they'd ask him about opening a conversation with us as well as permission to put him in the book.[67] Mina was inexorable, though: no permission, no inclusion. It took seven months to get Cosmo's green light.[97]

Then it slipped out that ThetaHealer's guardian angels had been in the car with us. Through El, Lucifer instantly put his oar in. *What! Both? For how long?*

"Aya?" said El.

---

67. We realized 20 months later that we'd mistested much of Cosmo's reality (*sol* § 1.2.1.1:338). This is why re-testing and validating responses is critical to accuracy.

Ayako bit her lip. "Umm..."

We collectively shrugged and looked at one another like schoolkids in the principal's office. I said, "All told, somewhere going on an hour, maybe? We're not sure before we noticed."

El tested. "He says that's seriously not allowed."

"Are they in trouble?"

"Whoa," said El. "He's gone. He said he'll be back."

We hadn't intended to put ThetaHealer's guardian angels under the gun—as we understood it, anyway. Our conversation ad interim on their fate touched on all the dystopic possibilities. Then Lucifer rejoined us and, naturally, we pestered him for the deets.

He only said (through El), *Don't worry. If they're going to be like that, they can change persons if they want. She's got a replacement.*[98] Three sets of eyes briefly touched, then we changed the subject.

1.4 IN THE CAR, EL SPIRITUALLY OPENS AND LUCIFER ARRIVES...

For the moment, our confab in the car thrumming down I-95 from Maryland revved across the span of our trip from idle to Ayako's "fire speed" and back. El was more a yoyo now than on the drive up. Her spiritual strength being "a little undeveloped," in Ayako's cool judgment, and with today's exhausting events sitting on most of a week's dearth of sleep, the potent spiritual energy and ardent individuals infusing the car cyclically overwhelmed her and tears would flow. Then she'd snooze a bit till narcoleptically heaving awake in a burst of chatter. Round and round she went. The closer to home and the later the evening, the more frequent her crying bouts. El's spiritual senses had now opened beyond anything she'd experienced. So many sensations flooded her. She felt zapped in and out of physical reality the way it feels when your spirit self begins giving your body the heave-ho at the start of astral projection,[99] or that whole fifth of 190 proof Everclear kicks in. As a spiritualist first-timer, this terribly shocked and unsettled her.

Between tears, she said, "I'm seeing colors, Dad."

I inspected her in the rearview. "What, you're dizzy or something?"

"No, in my mind. Not with my eyes."

"Your spirit eyes?"

"I don't know. They're in my head, but I'm seeing them."

"So . . ."

"Purples, blues, yellows, like that. Colors. It's everywhere." She paused, thinking . . . experiencing. "Ohmigod, I'm *hearing* them!"

"You're hearing colors?" I turned to Ayako. "Is that real? Can you do that?"

She nodded with vigor. "It's called synesthesia." This was a pretty sudden onset.

El said, "Dad, I'm hearing Protector!"

"You mean you're hearing him talk, his voice?"

"No, no, it's through the colors . . . and feelings."

"Whaaat?" Dad School never covered this kind of 'listening to your child.'

Through sniffles, she said, "Yeah, jeez, I can understand him. I just . . . I don't know! I understand what he means. I can feel how he's feeling." She thought about it while my eyes alternated between the spotlighted roadway, her sister beside me, and El's darting wonder in the rearview. "It's like soft ideas . . . and colors. Nothing vocal, nothing I'm, like, hearing with my ears." She paused again, her face tight with concentration. "It's more like *seeing* the convo and feeling it, you know what I mean?"

"Sure, easy-peasy, why not?" Ayako was nodding. Naturally.

El settled back in her seat, her view angled out the dark window but a little glazed as she focused within. Had this been a strange week? Oh, aye! The portents were that next week would be a step above. And then Lucifer slid into the backseat like a pro a few miles from home and I knew I'd been thinking too small.

"He's apologizing, Dad," El said after a minute of between-the-ears discussion. Her tears picked up their pace. "He's soooo, so sorry the way he scared us last night. He's saying he feels really, really terrible about it. I'm telling him it's okay, we understand now."

I said, "You're talking to him in your head?" and scanned her face in the rearview when I could.

"Yeah, it's crazy!" She giggled through mushrooming tears. "It's not words. It's just . . . God, *I don't know*!" Sobs muted her for a moment. "I just feel it. I sense it. I see colors, hear feelings . . . it's . . . I just know what it all means."

"Jesus . . ." I muttered.

She added, "He's right next to me, I—"

"Jesus?"

"What? No. Lucifer."

"Gotta keep up, Dad," Ayako said with her typical twinkle in the midst of someone else's drama.

Ah, jeez.

"I can feel him," El continued. "His body heat . . . I mean, his energy, I guess. It feels warm. He's, like, all cuddled up close, holding me. Lucifer"—more wet sobs—"is your hand on my head?"

Up front, Ayako contemplated her little sister with savvy eyes. "She's okay, Dad, just kind of overcome."

"She and me both," I grumbled.

My view toured the gloomy road to El's mirrored face to Ayako to El to the road and back. Besides my concern, I certainly envied her newfound abilities if not the hysterics. Later, I developed some of these spiritual sense skills myself along with their effects which my just-eighteen daughter was evidently transiting right now.[100]

Her week's experience had artificially jacked up her sensitivity until a giant raw nerve. Built-up spiritual energies, and now Lucifer infusing her with his own over-the-top energy and feelings as he embraced and comforted her, blasted through her fragile, unprepared psyche like the camel's last straw. Over the following weeks these energies calmed and her spiritual sensitivity and clair senses receded to near original levels. Having the chance to catch her breath, she began her real spiritual skills building from there.

Her breathless sobs subsided into weeping. She leaned in a collapsed heap in the corner where the car door meets the seatback, looking for all the world a spent soldier in the trenches. My heart flew to her. I could scarcely imagine giant Lucifer gently holding her tight.

Ayako said, "Lucifer didn't realize El couldn't handle his energy. Angels feel so much more intensely than we do."

"On account of being angels? Or just as spiritual beings?"

"Because they're born and raised on the spiritual plane. They just don't have their essential selves so heavily filtered by ignorant physicality like us."

Ahhh. I digress, but must say I detest our physical nature dissed. . . why it's so aggravating reading the plethora of spiritual poseurs on the best-seller list hating on our corporeality and preaching an amorphous divine celestiality that doesn't even exist as the only true and worthy pursuit although, in this case, disagreement came hard. We are terribly ignorant, but there's nothing wrong, illusory, mistaken, punitive, or base in our physicality. We can rectify ignorance with awareness, not rejection for a pie-in-the-sky spirituality.

I said, "So, El got it directly and couldn't handle it."

"He mixed his energy with hers." She saw my brows furrow. "I mean, he sort of extended his aura"—her turn of phrase; spirit persons have no aura—"around her, like, he enveloped her, you know? So El could feel his heart for her, his love. I mean, um . . . the heartistic comfort he was trying to project."

"Sounds a little Vulcan mind meld-ish."

"Ha-ha! No, he's expressing with energy. Feelings, I guess, instead of words or a simple hug. You know, he's basically invisible for physical us. A lot gets missed in that sort of communication."

"Not to her." I had to laugh. "What a joke! She was absolutely terrified of him last night. This morning probably more furious than anything. Now, they're cuddled up in back like best friends."

"That's how it is, Dad. Welcome to the Millennial Generation."

When your kid's saying you're not in Boomer Kansas anymore. "But how could he not know she couldn't handle his energy?"

She tested that. "Because he saw my energy and assumed El was the same."

"Okay . . . but why? He could see hers, too, right?"

Ayako gave me a shrug-face as if I was dense. "He didn't try to see her energy situation."

"So, you have to *look*-look for that? Seems a little amateurish for a guy like him to miss som—"

"Come on, he just didn't think he needed to look."

"I know, but . . . well, you know what they say when you assume."

She blew off a lungful. "I don't know, Dad. That's as far as I asked. He just didn't think he needed to look first. Maybe he was all caught up in the moment." Yeah, I could see that. Had to give him his humanity, didn't I? *Hmm*. Lucifer was starting to look an awful lot like a regular Joe. Michael, too, the little we knew of him. Even lesser-known Gabriel.

"So, Lucifer," I said into the blank rearview mirror, thinking back to his first unsettling stopover in our home, "you're welcome to visit our house anytime."

Ayako hand tested. "Wow, he's totally shocked, Dad."

"What? Why?"

"Uh . . . he's never been invited into anyone's home before."

"Never?" Ayako was shaking her head before I even finished, and never's a short word. "Come on. That sounds impossible! How many billions of years old is he?"[68]

"He says it's true. He's wondering if it's even allowed."

"Allowed?! By whom? It's my bloody house! I'll have anybody in it I want." I looked around the car at the riders I couldn't see. "That goes for the whole squad, too, by the way, including Protector and Mother, if you're listening in."

"Well, he was just wondering," said Ayako.

"What about before the Fall? I mean the no-Fall, that is, before Michael saddled him with The Corruption blame."

Again with her dissenting headshake. "Nope. He says he's always been kind of an outsider, kind of not wanted around."

"Seriously? Since the universe kicked off? He's an archangel, for crying out loud!"

"It's how he was raised, apparently. He was born to be an archangel, from archangel parents, and they raised him to be conscious of that. He never felt he fit in."

---

68. Not billions, only millions, and angels were born long after Mina built our universe.

"That's what he's saying?"

"Yep. I tested it."

"So, angels are born to their positions?"

"Um . . . Protector says no," she now said. "Just Lucifer, Michael, and Gabriel."

"There's just the three, then."

"Yeah, Protector says." (Actually seven; *SOL* § 2.2:522.) She hand tested. "Ha-ha! Lucifer says he's nothing special, no such thing as archangels. Whoever does the job best is who does it."[69]

"Well, that's not what—" Something swirled in the back of my mind. "Hmm. Didn't we already test that he took over from his parents, or at least one of them?"

"I think—"

"Wait!" Another swirl. "You said that he didn't feel he fit in?"

A bevy of hand tests as Ayako dug into the topic. We coasted up to the mailbox cluster at the end of the paved, state-maintained road. Ahead of us loomed the gloomy, tree-shrouded tunnel of our mile-long, rocky, rutted, potholed, gravelly-dirt road the girls loathed even to crunch their boots over, but which I associated with the joy

---

69. We didn't know Lucifer was born coeval with physical humanity. His parents groomed him to oversee guardian angels, raising him differently than Gabriel and Michael. There's no such thing as 'archangels,' but it took months of climbing out of our Judeo-Christian angelology to figure out that 'angels' are regular human beings born in the spirit, rather than the physical, world. Physical humanity calls them angels, but they're spirit-born persons (*SOL* § 1.1:520).

of peaceful, right, country living. At its hip-wrenching end, we'd slide into our doorless garage and home sweet blessed home after this incredible day. We pulled abreast our mailbox and I opened my window, then clicked on the map light to illuminate its dark maw. Hoping for no spiders (a bird once nested in the newspaper tube underneath), I slipped out the mail and passed it to Ayako while snapping the bent-up box door closed with my left hand and electrically gassing the Prius onto the graveled dirt for a total six-second pit stop. My window thumped shut about when the hybrid's gas motor rattled on. I edged our car as slow as possible across the rubbly track of the girls' nightmares because I wasn't ready to quit our conversation right yet.

"He says he spent his whole life sad," Ayako said. "No one invited him over, like he's the nerd nobody would be seen dead with."

"Angels are like that?"

"They're people, Dad. They feel everything we do. How do you think The Corruption happened, anyway?" Thanks, but I didn't need reminding it was *angels* who got suckered in the first place then "stupidly"—Mina's phrasing, all I'm saying—passed it on. She added, "Lucifer spent all that time feeling ostracized and, since The Corruption, hated and reviled."

"Man, who'd a thunk? This story just gets weirder and wilder. And then Michael's fake news is when it really took a turn."

El piped up in a cracked voice. "He's crying, Dad. He doesn't want to talk about any of this."

Oh. "Well, then, I'm sorry we—"

"Protector's saying no, absolutely not!" said Ayako.

"I didn't even finish!" *Typical.* Last night Mina got so excited that he was even having this conversation with us that he was responding faster than I could articulate my queries into conscious thought, much less words (before realizing we could just talk in our heads), especially when I struggled with a concept but he knew where I was headed with it. That led me to re-test each time so, at the very least, I knew what I was asking and could make sense of the answer. Irksome, then. Maybe funny in hindsight. "I just meant—"

"Protector says don't let him off," she went on. "Make him talk about his problems. He's kept it quiet long enough, and it needs healing. I guess this is all coming out for the first time, Dad."

"Yeah, been getting a lot of that."

A bit lippy she said, "Welcome to the Big Healing."

With a quavering laugh in her crackly voice, El said, "I bet he was bullied as a kid."

Ayako's hands were a blur. "Oh. Em. Geeee! That's right!"

"I was joking, Aya."

"I know, El, but it's true. Nobody wanted him around. Ever."

I couldn't help but scoff. "What, because he's *the* archangel?"

"Don't laugh, Dad," Ayako scolded me. "Protector wants him to get this out."

I gave her a side-glance. She wasn't kidding, with that draconian expression. "So, it *was* because he was born to be a top archangel? In a world of no special position?" I couldn't help the sarcasm, but it garnered more disapproval from Ayako.

"Wow, he *was* bullied," said El in wonderment.

I said, "How would you even bully—"

"His parents were—I mean, are—archangels," El continued. "He was born special out of all the angels. They expected—"

"But he was the middle child! What were Gabriel and Michael, chopped liver? That makes no freaking sense." That, of course, was my ruthlessly hierarchical, class-conscious, Korean Unificationist mindset talking smack.

"Exactly," Ayako said contrarily. "You never heard of middle child syndrome, Dad?"

No, actually. "My own middle child's schooling me on child dynamics, now?"

"If the shoe fits."

I snapped hard eyes at her and she met me head-on. *Dang.* These grown-up kids.

El ignored our banter. "He says his parents tried to raise him as normal, but still treated him kind of pretty strict . . . um, different, in a sense . . . like he was special."

"You're hearing this in your head?" She ignored me, or nodded and I missed it. A faint, half-lit moon-over-Japan in Virginia's rural blackness, Ayako's face bobbed with her sister's words.

"They put more responsibility on him. Trained him to, you know, *be* his position . . . that he wasn't like everybody else."

"He wasn't just like Gabriel and Michael? I don't get it."

"Other picked up on that," Ayako said, hand testing.

El said, "I think—well, he's not exactly saying it—but it's like they thought it was okay to treat him all aloof . . . I don't know, like, not one of them and everything, since that's how his parents were."

Ayako said, "Lucifer's really sad, Dad. I mean, really, really sad."

"Yeah, he's crying again," El added, "and now I'm—"

Sniffles told me she was empathizing with soft tears in the backseat, I presumed in synchronicity with Lucifer.[70] They were each feeling the same thoughts and emotions intermingled in a way I couldn't understand beyond my monochromatic intellect. Imagination failed me. I'd experienced similar feelings that got me swooning in a past love relationship, but nothing ever sent me into El's paroxysms. Honestly, I couldn't erase her vivid description of now-weeping, cuddlesome Lucifer blasting into our living room last night like an avenging god of war, angelic wings flared wide, blazing eyes firing Zeus-level thunderbolts as he beelined for Michael, Ayako melting into her chair and El cringing like a bug under a falling shoe. As Mina said, people do what they do from suffering.

1.4.1   Ayako Digs Into Lucifer's Motives . . .

Ayako later asked him about the wings. "Was it just to look good? Make an impression?"

Yes, and *yes*.

She stopped there, but this called for a little more peering into Lucifer's head, which we didn't get to until much later. When we did, the reality was that he'd "looked down" on Michael involving

---

70. When I dug into this late the following summer, Mina, too, began weeping—at one point so deeply that his energy left me wobbling in a jerky circle as I sway tested. He needed a minute as he relived the memories.

physical humans in his business—to Lucifer, it was an obvious play because, although he wasn't sure of Michael's reasons, why else would he be lying to us right in front of Mina?—especially ones as young as my daughters. Not only had he been in full bristling mode at suddenly recognizing that, somehow, Michael was up to his neck in his tethering to the whipping post since his youth but, as Mina affirmed, he also wanted to "scare off" the girls from dabbling in his business and maybe doing more harm than good.

The latter was his star aim for now so intensely apologizing to El. He said he'd changed his heart on that score following their Reconciliation for a number of reasons, each one having left him jarringly touched. First, he recognized that only the truth, and not constructing a self-satisfying narrative, impelled us. Second, he saw how murderously difficult it was for Michael to get the story out, and only Ayako's presence had provided him the courage. Third, El's bang-up job energy testing for me with her perceptive empathy was unique. Fourth, and last, was our lack of any outrage, hate, scorn, judgment, or rejection for any of them, including all the 'angels.' Even Protector.[71]

1.5 Home Sweet Home . . .

As we rumbled down the last grade before the house, Ayako said, "I don't think we're gonna get to the bottom of Lucifer's business tonight, Dad."[72]

"So, Lucifer," I said, closing the circle, "you *are* welcome to visit us anytime. Hang out with us. Stay over tonight, if you want."

"Lucifer's so deeply moved, Dad," El said weepily. "He feels so much love and acceptance from us, he can't help but cry."

I said, "Well, uh . . . I do have to say, my perspective's changed, somewhat."

"He's a regular shmegular, Dad," quipped Ayako. "Welcome . . ."

---

71. Because when one considers the problem of evil, who is its chief culprit?

72. Months later, we did. Mina couldn't tutor me when physically awake back then, but only respond to my questions, which were coming from my limited, not to mention inaccurate, Judeo-Christian awareness, comprehension, and intuition.

"Lucifer," said El, "you want me to make you a pallet to sleep on?" And, to assuage my unmentioned (though, instinctually, no less felt) concern, she added: "I'll make it in the family room."

"Yeah, he's up for that, El." To me, Ayako said, "Thank you."

Denouement

10

Friday October 13, 2017 ca. 10 pm

The prius coasted up to our weather-beaten, plywood-sided storage shed. I reversed through a half circle into the right-hand garage bay hand-in-glove, and shut down its wheezing motor with another couple hundred-some miles racked up on its long-suffering odometer. El had herself pulled together by now. Pretty fast after all that crying but, you know, young and resilient goes a long way. A sunnier disposition now undeniably animated her. Her face lit with excitement at the assembled spirit persons (including Lucifer) she now sensed all around her.

She all but sprinted to Ayako's half-bath, then banged down the stairs to the laundry room. Yanking bedclothes off the tiptoe-tall white wire shelves, she neatly spread two light-colored sheets and a dark blanket topped with a fluffy white-cased pillow over the sad-blue, short-napped, and meanly unpadded family room carpet a few feet from her bedroom door. I ambled down a few minutes later and gazed on her happy, contented effort in a sort of wonder, touched to my soul by her innocence and sweetness in the way she was reaching out to this previously terrifying and detested angel with whom she'd just shared a couple hours of cherished, comforting intimacy. Later in the night, he relaxed atop it for about ninety minutes and chatted, reclining Roman dining style, with Taiji, Hidé, Helen, my dad, his mom, *Obāsan*, several of her family, and whoever else crowded into the capacious room before he had to go.

"Yeah, he had stuff to do, but he was being courteous," Ayako later commented. "He'd never let El's effort go to waste."

Meanwhile, Ayako sedately fired up the television and brought up YouTube to share their favorite Japanese alt-music with our ever-growing squad. With El now back upstairs, and x Japan's music videos blasting through the television speakers, Ayako put out two pieces of box chocolate on the kitchen counter for Lucifer to enjoy. My sweet tooth noticed and got me wondering if anybody would beat him to it.[73]

"Dad, sit down and chill with us," Ayako said, snagging me trying to slip into my bedroom to collapse before sleep with a nice piece of witless fiction on my plush, king-sized antidote to car seatery. I froze mid-stride, your basic deer in headlights. "The whole squad wants you here."

"Yeah, Dad," echoed her sister, "don't be a loser in your empty room."

Ah, jeez. I really wanted to check out for the night and threw a covetous gander through my open bedroom door. Exhaustion was Arnold bench-pressing his weight whistling *Edelweiss* compared to how my body was registering on the ol' life-o-meter. One way or another, I can be as much an introvert as Mother and Mina had painted Cosmo when I'm beat just short of a puddle.

None of our experience was as literal to me as to my daughters, either. Sure, I felt and sensed and swayed. I intuited and caught

---

73. Taiji and Hidé did, but left a piece for him. Spirit people can taste and enjoy physical food because all things physical have a spirit existence (THE 'REFLECTIVE' ENVIRONMENT, *SOL* § 7.1.1.1:212) as long as they exist, and can be interacted with like any object. This is how we shared physical meals and drinks with the squad.

vibes. I had a persistent faith—"a conviction of things not seen," as (maybe) St. Paul put it in Hebrews (11:1, ASV)—that smoothed life's scalpel-edged undulations. The girls snatched actual glimpses, though. They felt energy. Perceived thoughts and emotions, even smelled and touched. El was hearing colors and seeing sounds, for Pete's sake. Ayako intuited like a whisper in the ear.[74] It all left me with a sense of being the old guy on a walker in a room full of wildly gyrating kids. Bed with a novel had seemed a fine hideout.

But doggone it, I thought. *She's right.*

I supposed I could stretch my senses, practice perception, tune my ear. Maybe it's like learning a language, I consoled myself, and

---

74. Some weeks later, she heard me raking leaves in the front yard beyond the living room windows, except I was standing right beside her. After some testing, she found it was bored Taiji cleaning the yard. The *wrong* yard. The *physical* leaves yet awaited *me*.

my two nimble younkers just have it over their cloddish old man. How often comes an opportunity like this in a dad's life anyhow, one shared equally with his children? These last few spiritually fierce days had rebooted us as individuals and as a family. It left us bonded as drum-tight as nearly half a lifetime raising them through the holy hell of domestic violence and its battle fatigue never had. I thought that pat old foxhole metaphor was, for sure, right on the money with what our last two days had brought us.

"Our family is fire," Ayako later happily put it.

Wasn't I well-nigh in Dad Heaven? What was my bedroom now but a self-imposed purgatory? *Weary?* What was I thinking? Where were my manners? I gratefully sank into the cushy-enough sofa and half-listened, half-watched my daughters' x Japan crushes. Formerly physical Taiji and Hidé pyrotechnically screamed out their alleged music onstage while thoughts, images, and feelings from the last week nickelodeoned through me.

Knowing I still couldn't tell them in their outlandish stage getups, the girls excitedly pointed them out. "There's Taiji, Dad...when he was alive, heh-heh," followed by, "He says ha-ha yourself, Aya," and, "Look at Hidé's gorgeous hair!" or, "See how he's glaring at Yoshiki? ...hey, Hidé, is that cuz you were mad?" X Japan was one of many bands and genres they cycled through for our guests' pleasure, which made me wonder about good manners all over again.

Standing behind the sofa, El was particular about locating everybody's place in the room at any given moment. Excited squeals and happy banter revealed this or that person's arrival, or the discovery they were hanging out: Mina (just a flyby),[101] Jesus, Sun-myung, Lucifer, Gabriel, our guardian angels, Taiji, Hidé, Helen, Daphne (formerly, 'Frenchie the Innominate' until I learned her name) and all our spirit guides, my dad, *Obāsan*, and other Japanese, Chinese, Carib, Irish, and European family, and many more whom we didn't know, or even know about, filled the space. Tired or not, spiritual dimbulb or not, I could feel the voltage and its reality.

"Ayyy...turns out Gabriel's a music lover, Dad!" Ayako said, energy testing while El took a break. "A total tunes connoisseur."

I said, "Is that right?" I couldn't avoid a blasé response—maybe on account of being all highwayed-out and, I admit, feeling a little drowned by revelation after shock after astonishment—but, in truth, I was pretty surprised. I tried to imagine Gabriel hanging around concerts, nightclubs, and finger-pickers by the campfire checking out Earth's global music scene top to bottom like some millennian roadie working up his musical acumen. "What about rap and hip-hop?"

"Yep, he listens to *everything*."

"Does he? We're not the only inhabited planet and he's been around awhile, so that's a lot of music."

El hopped off her counter stool to test this new development herself. She gushed, "That's, like, so lit! And he *loves* this genre!"

The screeching Blue Hearts? "Maybe he's just being polite."

"Aw, quit resisting, Dad," Ayako reproved like a mother. "He's being real."

I chuckled and spread my palms. "Okay, okay. Got to know my limitations, I reckon."

Still, if I had to vegetate on the sofa, something mildly melodious would go down a treat. When the girls relented and went digging for more appetizing fare, Gabriel, through Ayako's grinning sway test, "loudly objected." The girls weren't fooling around with their new pals, so it was back to the alt-music scene, the volume nicely cranked to the majority crowd's happy endorsement. Dad could just take a backseat.

Taking in the room's physical and spirit activities, I caught my small family blossoming before my eyes. Our lives would never be the same. How could we return to the spiritually dulled, corporeal-only reality we'd been living where, among other things, Lucifer the sensitive, caring brother was a murderous, Jack Nicholson-esque psychopath and Mina the all-caring, liberty-loving grandparent a pedantic, judgmental *paterfamilias* in a universe filled with punishment, darkness, and dread? I couldn't turn my back on any of what I'd learned. I knew my cavorting children could never jettison their new way of life nor the friends and family they were growing to love and their presence to cherish. More than simple revelation, more even than a rockin' spiritual experience, we'd discovered a whole 'nother reality that's as natural a part of our lives as loving. And who wants to cut love out of life's itinerary?

Something thinly called music jangled my ears and pulled me from my reverie. I looked around. What a house my home—or maybe what a home my house?—had become. Ah, well. Some of the music wasn't half-bad. Heck, a few I even still put in my ears all voluntary-like. And the full spectrum conversation was righteous. My daughters were as joyous and loved as I'd *ever* seen them. What's that worth?

Part II

Aftermath

A New Dawn

Whew! We felt bowled over by all we'd learned those first two flabbergasting days meeting 'Creator,' The Ancestors, my dearest friend Helen, and all the others. Everything was so different. The proverbial scales were fallen from our eyes. The world—our very existence!—now plonked in virgin territory. It was unsettling. At the same time, our sense of liberation from the psychic bondage of the God Hypothesis, the Moral Dilemma, the Science Conceit, and our naturally evolving embrace of the absolute freedom of life... well, it was indescribable. You'll just have to experience it for yourself.

The Next Day

We cracked our eyes Saturday morning, October 14, 2017 on what effectively was a new life. The challenge now before us, besides our own growth and development, was to write *The Story of Life*. To accomplish that as its principal author, I had to learn more than I ever dreamed in those early days. I didn't want to merely regurgitate 'revelations' about the 'right life'—let's be honest, who really cares about one more woo-woo convo with God dissing our physical human existence?—but to explain in detail the what, how, and why. Real knowledge. I certainly wanted it. How about you?

1.1   Our First Hurdle

As wild as The Big Event was, the nearly five years it took to get *The Story of Life* into the world was a cosmic-class roller-coaster. The first summit to surmount was how to winnow reality from fantasy and truth from just plain BS. For us, it came down to establishing trust in the process. It was incredibly helpful there were three of us. We could bounce our experience off each other to cut through our confusion and skepticism. The girls handled the transition fairly

well. By that, I mean quick: as natural empaths, psychics, and mediums who feel, see, hear, and otherwise directly experience a much richer involvement than I. And it didn't hurt that, after El blurted how the girls were his cousins, Japanese rock superstar Akiō—yep, using pseudonyms— came back a silent week later having, to our mutual astonishment, confirmed it with his still living, psychic grandmother (EN 54:184). If that wasn't some real-world validation of ET, we figured nothing was.

Yet, I looked on the obtuse bystander pervaded by a lifetime's enculturation that, despite my church experience, militated against this kind of balderdash and poppycock. I incessantly wondered *who in the heck am I talking to, really?* No persuasion by the girls could set my heart at ease. I was on my own. Eventually, I noted nuances in the intensity and flavor of the energy I felt from different spirit people with whom I energy tested. That, and El's spunky example, regularly inspired me to query respondents' feelings and attitudes. I simply got to know them. Each person turned up a different personality. If there's a master manipulator behind our ET, then he, she, or it is one bloody great performer! But considering the un-cozenish content, we decided the deception scenario was unreasonable. By summer 2018, I finally began developing my own trust in this newfangled ET methodology, although Mina jokes with Ayako how my skepticism seesawed like a sine wave still two years more. It's only trust that resolves the conundrums arising in drinking new wine from new wineskins. Trust in the methodology, the data, the conveyor, or in whatever does it for you.

1.2   OUR SECOND HURDLE

Our next obstacle to working with ET was our Brobdingnagian worldview. A person's philosophy of life, by definition, frames their self-identity.[102] In those first two days, I'd lost virtually all the pillars supporting my awareness of the world and my place in it. In time, it appeared we now possessed at least as good a source in ET to understand our existence as science and philosophy ever had to wring metaphysical truths from their micro observations and macro reasoning. . . except better.[103] The girls didn't need much persuasion to abandon the rubble of their nascent worldviews, but I did.

Even so, the hard truth dawned that philosophy and science provide no coherent, rational story of existence, the smoke and mirrors of their reasoned, reductive, and quantum observations notwithstanding. The outcome of this vacuum in real awareness has been ugly, too, fueling deranged ideas across the millennia that produced only unremitting suffering and unhappiness. Modern science's vaunted enlightenment has only doltishly superseded religion as humanity's most life-destroying foundational thought process. Sure, nobody planned it that way. But, like religion and philosophy, justifying the means is the ineludible practical outcome of being fixated on the ends (i.e., humans are only biology, life is material, existence is finite, coercion a positive good) regardless how enlightened one's technique in pursuing awareness.[104]

Confronting the Book

Mina wasn't kidding when he said *The Story of Life* would crowd the boundaries of my intuitive and intellectual faculties. I had to bone up my science and philosophy to meliorate my conceptual awareness to form pertinent queries and then cognize the answers in the context of the many fields of inquiry into which they led me. I oft tried backstopping his revelations with the relevant literature. "Resist the impulse!" was his rallying cry along with, "Keep it simple!" Well, my efforts were pointless. False realities box in science and philosophy's mindsets too much for them ever to lend credence to their unavoidable intuitive and revelatory doppelgänger. Instead, new theories and hypotheses need forming and experimental and logical tests devised, but *SOL*'s deadline just didn't allow for much of that. Developing ET into a credible mode of inquiry will take a while. Data as 'revelation' will have to do for now.

It's not for nothing that (even religious) people gravitate toward science over revelation. "The 'scientific worldview,'" Rupert Sheldrake seems to acknowledge rather grumpily in *Science Set Free,* "is immensely influential because the sciences have been so successful [transforming our world] by an immense expansion of knowledge" (2012, 6). Even so, humanity remains qualitatively unsatisfied with it because it just fails on some unquantifiable level to give us a sense that the reality science shows us is the full human reality that is. Even materialistic "scientists remain[ed] dualists, and continue[d] to use dualistic metaphors" (ibid, 34), because it "seems impossible to be a consistent materialist. Materialism depends on a lingering dualism, more or less thinly disguised" (ibid, 36). And "many scientists have philosophies or religious faiths that make this 'scientific worldview' seem limited, at best a half-truth" (ibid, 23). The inconsistency lies in our being not simply material bodies. Our minds aren't confined to our skulls. Our thoughts aren't the random outcome of electrochemical neuronal activity. People just *know* this, including materialists who can't imagine (while pridefully accepting their Nobel Prize) that their lauded creative brilliance is only the inevitability of mere random chemistry like a monkey clacking at a keyboard[105] and not the fruit of purposive, irreducible, trans-brain individual consciousness that noncomputationally *thinks.*[106]

When it comes to reality, people want to know essentially three things: where are we, what are we, and why are we? We expect the answers to these (on their face, fairly simple) questions will tell us what's going on and the optimal way to play the game of life to achieve ultimate satisfaction: happiness. Allied with the unquenchable need to live, this is humanity's basic survival drive.[107] The (ET) fact is, the natural and *supra*natural[75] are normative. As concepts go, however—despite using them here and in *SOL*—the traditional natural and supranatural are defunct, as too the model of a deitic God and a universe under His arrant control that even data-driven quantum mystics can't or won't refine out of their archaism.[108]

Well, our direct-experience ET ruthlessly crowbarred the girls and me out of our traditional modes of perception. Lo and behold, there we were in the same paradox as the upstart quantum crowd wondering how to reconcile our understanding of reality with the scandalous data. We adopted their solution: more observation and analysis to clear the static. Old school physicists couldn't deny the ever-accumulating quantum data. Its quirky reality finally did-in their spiritual model. The reality which ET exposed to us crushed my family's own standard model of existence and sunk much of what we thought of as reality. In time, it will similarly push through humanity's mythic mindset, although via spiritual energy to derive falsifiable data instead of theoretical equations... or unmitigated imagination.

Scientists and philosophers—with whom I callously lump spiritualists—are both after knowledge, or perhaps better put, awareness and comprehension, though in seemingly different domains and to differing degrees. Regardless, Mina's (God's) gripe is they both deindividualize the person. On the one hand, we get the simple materialistic human biological machine in a random, physical world. The other hands us the complex transcendent human moral machine in a controlled, ersatz-spiritualized world. Both dehumanize and

---

75. Synonymous with *super*natural but without the religious, mystical, and magical baggage.

lead to harm. When applied to existential reality, both approaches assume too much. For example, the "tenets of materialism are more accurately seen as metaphysical extrapolations based on some scientific findings" (Taylor 2017, 150) and leaves the person playing second fiddle to ruthless gene survival or moral supremacy. If there's a single thread that runs through Mina, it's that the individual—the person, the human consciousness, *you*—is the inviolable cornerstone of All Existence (i.e., all that infinitely is; *SOL* § 1:90). Even if we recognize All Existence as a complex system, the human aspect is an emergent reality wholistically transcending its complexity.[76]

Our writing method engages Query & Response (QR; sometimes informed by research of the relevant literature to the degree we are capable) to establish context and awareness, which we then validate with Mina. As the human person behind our physical embodiment, he's the authority on our universe. I ask if he agrees with what I wrote, if it is true and accurate of reality, and so forth. If his answer is *no*—I certainly get that often enough—I work it out to our mutual satisfaction. Sometimes, that means glumly jettisoning words, phrases, or whole trends of thought I thought clever and spot-on but ultimately didn't energy test as correct. This prevents me inserting my own fancy into the text and making the book just another highbrow work of fictional nonfiction. That said, however, text that later reliably tests as incorrect is on me alone for not vetting it as thoroughly as I thought I had.

The Story of Life—this book is a part—matters to Mina on the theory that awareness of reality leads to happier choices, thus a happier life. This is the fundamental truth in today's spirit world following the Big Healing October 13, 2017 as the reality about our creator, the universe, and life settled into humanity's shared mindset and, through Mina's healing, spurred the release of eons of ignorance and psychic trauma. Overall, every person in existence— starting with spirit humanity that's more amenable, and by that

---

76. In this book, *wholism* is the whole in and of itself. *Holism* is the parts as they interact to create the whole, and the relationship between the parts and whole. The distinction follows from the emergent type, which isn't greater than the sum of its parts so much as transcends the whole that was greater than the sum of *its* parts.

route working into physical humanity's more convoluted psyche—
is being gradually enlightened and uplifted to the degree that each is
willing to heal. Mina doesn't force the issue. For him, it's all about
healing. And we've now experienced it for ourselves, plenty.

Numerous spirit persons with axes to grind relentlessly assailed
me, for example, in a myriad of creative and shocking ways over
the course of writing *SOL*, from seizures and cognitive blindness to
grinding fatigue and pain, or sniped at me in less inimical or waspish
ways.[77] Ninety percent of these attacks weren't malicious, in Mina's
view. Often, they only wanted my attention to facilitate their healing
because they were unwilling or unable to approach Mina or my spirit
self directly. Still, it resulted in levels of harm, grief, aggravation, and
so on that I could've done quite nicely without and for which I
periodically wanted just a smidgeon of biblical vengeance. Mina
counseled me away from such feelings. Once I'd realize a problem
was a spiritual attack, my only sensible recourse was to identify and
converse with the person directly or indirectly through Mina or my
spirit self, and encourage them to accept healing. And they more
often than not did, because that's what they were initially (if not
eventually) after.

Because of our role in revealing The Corruption, Michael's Lie,
and publishing *Story of Life* books—Mina would forego them if it
made me happy not to write them; he'd find another way to accomplish his intent as he always has—vast crowds of spirit people come
to us for healing. Initially, we only facilitated it until we learned to
heal through Mina. It's quite sad that people lock themselves away
in their minds from reality and their deepest desire. Thankfully (in
spirit world, anyhow), it's a diminishing problem.[109]

Our information isn't revelation in the ordinary sense. It is a
presentation of supranatural data collected via ET (CH. 12:165). The
data isn't raw the way it would be from, say, a sociological or biological study. We don't interpret, analyze, or draw conclusions except
by verifying it via ET or empirically with observation. We derive

---

77. There are (formerly physical) people used to how spirit world was and not at all enamored of
the Big Healing's cosmic disruption to their personal fiefdoms and situations.

The Story of Life's data through querying spirit persons, primarily Mina. The information presented is the respondents' point of view, not ours. And since ET is a query-based mode of inquiry then a spirit person can't answer what's unasked.[78] That's why it can take a long time to build up sufficient data to achieve apprehension beyond some vague awareness. Investigators understand that queries flow from comprehension. Many queries just don't germinate until we develop the appropriate soil, although intuitive leaps make a handy shortcut. Our own habituated bias gets in the way, too, until our awareness expands and our bias updates.

ET is a skills-based mode of inquiry. Hence, one's testing can deviate from a respondent's answer for a variety of reasons. We might test a *no* when it should be a *yes* or some variant of *maybe*. Moreover, ET is *conversation*, not interrogation. It flows in the manner people converse including joking, teasing, or simply responding in a way to teach us to think and act for ourselves instead of depending on some deity or spirit sage for it all. This naturally differs in accord with whom one is ET conversing. It took us a bit to realize that some *yes* answers are people giving us the energy equivalent of a polite head nod or an "uh-huh," just as we all do in conversation to let the speaker know we haven't tuned them out for cat memes.

Then, what about fibbing, lying, and deception, isn't that normal conversation, too? Well, we've encountered it off and on in accord with whom we're conversing. Michael wasn't terribly forthcoming that first Friday, for sure. But in the end, he forthrightly implicated himself in a cosmic deception that put him in everybody's crosshairs. You simply need to be aware and get the straight dope from Mina if there's not a privacy issue.

We resolve contradictions that crop up in Mina's responses with better queries, more information, a greater comprehension, and verifying amongst one another. Besides intuition and validation, our crosscheck for these sorts of contradictions is logical consistency, rationality, reasonableness, and so forth.

---

78. Though, if we're standing, we get unsolicited responses just from talking or even thinking. We then dig into the details. It's a constant with Mina during any conversation with Ayako.

ET's credibility rests in the main less on knowing one is talking to the people one thinks they are than on the responses themselves. Anyone, with some effort, can identify to their satisfaction with whom they're conversing. But that doesn't mean that a person's responses are materially correct. That's the rub, isn't it? Responses can be empirically tested quickly like Akiō's living grandmother or over time as with Betelgeuse's supernova showing up in 2045 (*SOL* § 2:107). *The Story of Life* was ET's debut. It naturally awaits a larger validating pool to establish its bona fides. And that's where you, the interested reader, come in. The next chapter makes the case for ET as a mode of inquiry that produces data which leads to information, thence to knowledge.

ET as a Mode of Inquiry

The greatest challenge facing mankind is the challenge of distinguishing reality from fantasy... to decide which of our perceptions are genuine, and which are false...
—Michael Crichton[110]

The problem we have cognizing reality as it matters to us—who, what, why, and how we are—is that we can't readily observe much of it. The story of knowledge has been a tale of discovering how to witness and interpret what's unobserved, from germs and quarks, mind and will, to spirituality and a creator, and then build that into an understanding of reality we can comprehend. Science seeks to explain reality in *rationalistic natural* terms and found a method to uncover it. Philosophy seeks to explain the same reality in *humanistic supranatural* terms. Beyond its tools of reason, however, philosophy (especially its sub-discipline theology including religion and spiritualism focused on the *divine supranatural*) has failed to uncover any natural *or* supranatural reality at all. This puts us in a quandary. Science readily points to what it observes to exist (nature) and declares, "Reality!" Philosophy points to what it can't observe but only reason into existence (supranature) and posits, "Also reality!" The scientist scoffs at the philosopher as naught but a cerebral imagineer while ignoring our fuller reality for only its obvious parts the way a Mr. Magoo engineer, coming in through the only door, might myopically observe an underground home's aboveground furnace room *as* the house. See the forest-for-the-trees problem here?

Science and Philosophy

Science places great faith in the somatic senses. The thinking is that, if I can sense it outside my body then you can, too; it's objectively real and we can verify what we think we know with what actually is. Philosophy's faith is in the psychosomatic (rational) senses. Its problem is that, although I can sense something, you can't necessarily. People tend to accept, as an objective reality, that humans invisibly and inexplicably love, hate, conceive art, intuit, and use the power of thought—say, intention, often called a plan—to make things occur in observed reality. Pointing to objective data, science boils it down to neurons and chemistry whereas philosophy reasons a perhaps ineffable causation deduced from subjective data.

1.1 SCIENCE AND PHILOSOPHY'S EPIC FAIL

We're not so unlike the regressed society of Larry Niven's *Ringworld* (1970) that's ignorant of its artificial reality and psychologically quarantined from its inconvenient truth. For all of our intellectual progress, science and philosophy fail spectacularly to unveil who, what, where, how, and why we are. We need a means to experience the supranatural in a *repeatable* way that commutes our subjective experience to an objective one. That's energy testing (ET).

1.1.1 DATA'S DILEMMA

To understand how ET fits the repeatable experience paradigm, we need to understand what constitutes *data*. At its simplest, data is a collection of *datum*, a single piece of observation. It forms into data to establish a complete observation of which each datum is in some way a part. Data is raw, unorganized, unconsidered. It becomes *information* when we view it in a given context through analysis and derive *knowledge* by organizing, considering, and presenting it in such a way that it's useful.

1.1.1.1 EMPIRICAL AND RATIONAL DATA

Science collects data using the somatic senses allied with instruments to observe readily accessible nature. Anyone with the training, skill, and equipment can collect the same data, which is why folks consider it *objective*. It analyzes data into information, theory, and eventually knowledge. On the flipside, philosophy collects data using the mental senses (oft augmented by scientific data) to deductively observe humanistic supranature because it's been wholly inaccessible in any meaningful way. This limitation means it's not possible for any person even with the necessary training and skill to deduce the same observation, which is why folks consider it *subjective*. That seems to put the supranatural squarely out of reach for deriving information and knowledge. We can't repeat, measure, or test any of philosophy's observations, thus science tends to conclude the supranatural isn't real. At least, not objectively real like the world of matter.

Science is all about applying knowledge derived from observation to solving specific technical problems, from healing sickness to building transportation to lighting the darkness. Philosophy applies knowledge in the form of ideas to solving specific nonpareil human questions involving existence, freedom, and behavior as well as technical ones involving knowledge, value, beauty, and so on. The overall nature of experiential, data-driven science means it's limited in terms of what issues it can solve, particularly the metaphysical kind. On the other hand, the overall rationalist nature of philosophical inquiry—besides ill suited to solving real problems—means it can't answer the fundamental questions of life and reality, either.

Such limitations are an obstacle between these two classes of study and the common reality they seek. Each one attempts to derive meaning and comprehension of the larger world from data that's necessarily too limited for the task. False or misconstrued scientific *data* is correctible through repetition, *information* less so. Philosophy suffers generally from an incorrectability of information because we derive it from rational instead of experiential data. This is one reason why bad science goes away relatively quick while bad philosophy lingers like poor dental work. Without experiential data to keep it grounded, philosophy (like mathematics) is more likely than science to veer off to wherever the mind can rationally take it. And there's very little we can't rationalize when it suits us.

1.1.1.2 REVELATORY DATA

Religion, differing from general philosophy in seeking to explain the natural world in divine supranatural terms, tries to get around this metaphysical impasse via *revelation*, a substitute for experiential and rational observation that's limited to individuals and occasionally groups.[111] Theology is really philosophy working off revelatory instead of reasoned data. It therefore presents subjectively and is the reason Mina lumps it in with philosophy. Theologians verify revelation using philosophy's tools (if not calls to authority), but it never solves any human problems in the definitive manner science does. Nor does revelation advance beyond classical or modern philosophy to definitively solve any human or divine issues. Funnily enough, science scorning supranatural experience as imagination run wild or tricks of the subconscious, or that consciousness (non-evidentially) arises in matter—the brain—ironically itself relies upon the supranatural by definition: mind, which is invisible, non-natural, inexplicable, and only individually experiential.

1.2 SUPRANATURAL DATA'S EPIC REVIVAL

Mina lumps all types of inquiry under *Philosophy with a capital-P* as humanity's primary knowledge-seeking class of study. Yet, it's useful to recognize that the three primary modes of inquiry we use to acquire data (empiricism, rationalism, revelation) and their core subclasses of study from which we derive information (science, philosophy, theology) each interacts with and relies on the others. Even so, they're hamstrung producing real knowledge of our natural and supranatural reality. There's no getting around it.

The tendency in science and philosophy to scorn the supranatural as unworthy of study is simple bias that follows from a lack of ready tools to collect data, the presumption no tools exist, and broadly accepted explanations based on the most obvious and accessible: physical nature. That's a myopic perspective at best, a hydra raising another head each time a confounding observation posits a seemingly impossible or absurd new theory.

The real question here is, what method can repeatably collect supranatural data that presents objectively and resolves to objective information which veracity we can then repeatably establish? The answer is ᴇᴛ. In practice, it's revelation, so the question is, how can revelation transition to data? It's quite simple, really.

1.2.1 Energy Testing as Data

The functional value of data is that it's repeatably and independently collectible. Rationalism and revelation, which can never produce objective information, are therefore traditionally worthless tools for data collection. Data collection from the natural world only serves as data because anybody can access it. You might be surprised to know that anybody can access supranatural data, too, and ᴇᴛ is the tool for it. As with the natural world, anyone who learns the methodology taught in *soʟ* ᴘᴀʀᴛ ᴠ can, with the requisite training, skill, and their mind–body for equipment, collect for themselves any of the supranatural data we present in that book as well as this one. Of course, how one collects, reports, and analyzes natural data intrinsically is debatable, and it's no different with supranatural data. One can certainly err with ᴇᴛ as with other data collection methodologies. My daughters and I verify and re-verify each other's ᴇᴛ to clarify or correct our data and the information we derive from it. Ayako, El, and occasionally Moth Man (ꜰɴ 13:8; § 1.1:127) double-checked parts of my work as I wrote *The Story of Life*, and then I double-checked their corrections. Too, I double-check my own data continually when intuition, inconsistencies, or new data indicates it, or when Mina and others point out errors. The supranatural environment of our universe is as vibrant and dynamic as the natural. Nothing is static. It's a human environment after all. Even data that tests correctly can alter over time if conditions or one's awareness changes (*SOL* § 1.3:634).[79]

1.2.1.1 THE NONUTILITY OF REVELATION AS DATA

Revelation is defined loosely as information received from any *super*natural entity via communication by inexplicable, internal (spiritual) means. It is subjective, not repeatable, and unusable for hypothesizing about reality no matter how visceral or well reasoned. Even if revelation contains valid truth, it can't be verifed as knowledge. To consider it a theory in the scientific sense or a truth in the philosophical sense, one's bare option necessarily is faith (religion) or rational belief built up from logical analysis (e.g., Augustine, Aquinas). However, analysis can only verify a revelation's internal consistency, not its presumptive accuracy.[80] Yet, the whole point of collecting data is corroboration to establish its likelihood of accuracy. Shorn of that, revelation is just circular reasoning. It fails as an alternative to empirical and rational data.

1.2.1.2 THE UTILITY OF ENERGY TESTING AS DATA

ET is a third way. What it produces *is* data. It's not religion, metaphysical mumbo jumbo, enlightened soulspeak from the Summer Lands, or parlor tricks. It's a skills-based discipline. A direct, experiential, repeatable observation by the natural senses of a (seemingly) supranatural phenomenon producing information, knowledge, and wisdom. In collecting data from the supranatural, ET is classifiable as revelation but that's where the similarity ends. It's as different from traditional revelation as practice from theory. While traditional

---

79. During summer 2018, for instance, Mina explained spirit humanity's fear that he's a judgmental creator, Big Healing or no. Rechecking in February 2020, we found that fear mostly resolved.

80. More than science, philosophy (like mathematics) is chock-a-block with rational, internally consistent yet wrong ideas.

revelation is through inexplicable means, ᴇᴛ 'revelation' is via readily understood physical mechanisms: the sway (push; *sol* § 2.2.1:626) of one's body. One can explain, measure, test, and validate it. Its data comes via Query & Response (ǫʀ) as opposed to a mystical mind dump followed by rationalization. It's interactive; question follows answer until one is satisfied of an understanding. One checks it for internal consistency and overall logic as with traditional revelation and science. Crucially, however, one can winnow ᴇᴛ data in any direction until arriving at a datum capable of objective verification, say, air pressure in a car tire.₁₁₂ Other energy testers can test it.

Rather than revelation, ᴇᴛ is observation and experiment, and the resulting data is information. Revelation carries with it three problematic elements: 1) it links to an all-powerful God or vying brands of *Übermensch*;[81] 2) it is primarily personal; and 3) it is usually classified sacred and infallible thus unassailable, meaning, in the lingo of science, that it's unfalsifiable.₁₁₃ As that's not the case with ᴇᴛ, it's best to avoid promoting the misnomer. The bottom line is that traditional revelation isn't useful for discovering reality, supranatural or otherwise.

1.2.1.2.1 Eɴᴇʀɢʏ Tᴇsᴛɪɴɢ ɪs ᴀ Nᴇᴡ Cʟᴀss ᴏғ Sᴛᴜᴅʏ

Eᴛ isn't your grandmother's table knocking or any discipline arising in Philosophy with a capital-ᴘ. Whereas science, philosophy, and religion proceed upon oft-unfounded assumptions drawn from the other two, or that even negate one for the other, ᴇᴛ proceeds from a tabula rasa, its assumptions arising only from ǫʀ ᴇᴛ data. Of maximal gravity, ᴇᴛ is a direct line to our 'creator' from whom we can compile (toward empirically validating) any information.

Why ignore the supernatural just because we hitherto couldn't make head nor tails of it? Science hasn't a clue what to make of a quantum universe or consciousness or life, but that hasn't stopped it working the problem. Toward that end, people using ᴇᴛ will want

---

81. German: from *Thus Spake Zarathustra* (Nietzsche 1883–91), various translations rendering 'beyond-man' (Alexander Tille 1896), 'superman' (Thomas Common 1909), or 'overman' (Walter Kaufmann 1954).

to demonstrate, at least for themselves, that they're communicating with our 'creator' or with spirit persons they've identified by name and not Ming the Merciless or Joe Liar from the Outer Rim.

1.2.1.3 CONTEXTUALIZING AND DECONFLICTING ET DATA

Science never knows anything with a hundred percent certainty any more than law courts are ever a hundred percent certain of guilt or innocence. But we strive to use a preponderance of the evidence (however one defines evidence) to narrow the margin of error beyond a reasonable doubt. Like anything operated by humans, ET has a margin of error, too. My daughters and I slim it down using, for instance, alternative inquiries and an ET equivalent of the scientific control experiment to eliminate confounding variables. Acquiring and deconflicting ET data can sometimes be time intensive. It builds gradually into a reasonably coherent picture of reality amenable to classification, hypothesis, theory, and laws (in the scientific sense). When Mina contravenes established scientific theories, we apply to his explanations reason, logic, consistency, and—as William of Occam smartly advised in the 1320s—simplicity. That doesn't justify the data, it simply makes it worth pursuing further.

Energy Testing

We talked with spirit persons to write *The Story of Life* (of which this book is part) using energy testing as our medium augmented by clair senses, intuition, and our spirit eyes and ears. Quite simply, ET is chakra energy—not the popular version—interacting with the body's biological energy. Even if you have neither knowledge nor conscious awareness of ET, your physical body always responds to chakra energy which, if your chakras are sufficiently 'open,' sways your body to a greater or lesser degree.

When you query a spirit person, they choose to respond to you. You interpret this via your awareness–experience of it as 'movement' in your body. This is ET. Read *SOL* chapters 41 and 42 to learn all about energy testing in this context.

Thank you for reading our story! I'd appreciate so very much reading your comments on the bookseller's webpage. It means a lot to me and maybe other potential readers. I read all reviews to make my books better. Use the QR code or go to books2read.com/thebighealing.

Read all about...

... with figures, tables, Epilogue, Endnotes, Works Cited/Consulted, Index, plus ten spirit world testimonies from historical figures such as Jesus, Sun-myung Moon, Mohammad, Buddha, and Hitler

—in—

The Story of Life

Wherever books are sold.

Use your smartphone camera to follow the QR codes below to (L–R) visit the author at chrismckeon.com, visit toteppitpress.com for a *free* PDF with clickable cross-reference links, or purchase *The Story of Life* (or download *free* eBook). Thank you!

Notes

Chapter 1 – All Shook Up

1. [6] Moon 1996, 53–65. According to him, an illicit sexual relationship (symbolized by the "fruit" in Gen 3:1–13) between Lucifer and Eve is the original sin that separated us from God and brought about the violent, selfish world in which we live. His Divine Principle identifies Lucifer as Satan, the Devil, who consciously and willfully seduced Eve to steal Adam's place as God's son. At the same time, through 'owning' their love by converting Adam and Eve's hearts from God's originally intended unselfish lovingness to his new philosophy of selfish unlovingness, Lucifer dispossessed God and made himself god of this world (ibid, 68; Jn. 12:31, 2 Cor. 4:4).

2. [8] Emotion Code uses a pendulum or muscle test to communicate with the subconscious to identify trapped emotional energy in order to remove it so your body can heal its own disease and trauma. Dr. (of chiropractic) Bradley Nelson says he discovered it through prayer, study, and practice and popularized it in *The Emotion Code* (2007, 32, 91–2). In actuality, it energy tests the responses of any responding spirit person.

Chapter 2 – The Fracas

3. [18] Intense spiritual 'energy' expresses as heat one physically feels. My father later said they all endured pain in feeling 'burned,' though injury to the spirit body instantly heals via one's Intention (*SOL* § 3.2:282; *SOL* CH. 30:515). I didn't know at the time they were present much less bodyguarding me.

4. [19] Nigh on 76% of spirit humanity barged into our solar system wanting answers. They packed Earth, including its ocean surface, though not the sky. When room ran out, Mina said "the vast majority hung out in space" encircling our planet and on the moon, Mars, Neptune, some of Saturn's moons, and any space rock suitable, in their minds, upon which to congregate (all in the 'reflective' environment; *SOL* § 7.1.1.1:212).

5. [20] Ayako later said her original guardian angels—Gabriel's fraternal twin sister and her third-generation husband—left her immediately after the fight to help calm the situation in spirit world. They ended up needing to be away from her too long, so Lucifer—yes, he actually runs that 'department'!—replaced them with another ancient married couple of similar age, and friends with her original ones. For El, two boys her own age stepped up. In deference to my then-current infatuation with Scots-Irish redheads, Ayako announced he'd recruited "two hot redheads," which got plenty of laughs from my daughters and liberal red across my face.

6. [20] The Michael–Lucifer blow-up was so uproarious that ∼60% of all guardian 'angels' and ∼80% of all 'angels' came bodily to Earth to witness it, the remainder scrutinizing from afar. Of those who left their charges, some simply refused to continue being guardian 'angels' at all; others refused to go back to their current charges; still others said they'd go back when they felt the situation permitted but, right now, this issue ranked higher. The balance returned to their tasks as requested. Lucifer later told me he was "very sorry" his fight with Michael distracted so many 'angels' from their support task (*SOL* CH. 31:519). Once a guardian 'angel' leaves their post, his policy is they don't remain that same person's guardian. He's ultra serious about it because, prior to the Big Healing, he alone amongst the 'angels' understood that being born into the physical world in The Corruption's milieu is a significant (if brief) sacrifice as a critical component of the human spirit world. He didn't know its exact role until after the Big Healing, just that it was essential and we thereby endure a harsh, traumatic life and, accordingly, deserve guardians' very best.

7. [20] Mina later said El correctly read the volatile situation in spirit world but incorrectly placed it in a war context, being the only context in which we could envision such a disturbance. His *yes* answers acknowledged her questions and fear that "war is breaking out" while refraining from technically disagreeing via *no* answers in the midst of a drama that realistically would have only confused us in the midst of multiple shocks and limited mindsets. Unexpected answers confound us less now because of our growth and development.

8. [20] For example, one day Michael showed up "tired" and appeared not a little "stressed," sipping an alcoholic beverage he said he once discovered on another planet and enjoyed as part of his "relaxation regimen." He was in no mood to think about the world's bigger problems and deflected my "serious" questions for inconsequential chatting on account of two of his students getting into a "big fight," an "unusual situation" amongst 'angels.' The students had rejected his mediation because the shockwave of his Lucifer scam still reverberated and his reputation was in a bit of tatters. Talking it over later, I said, "The neighborhood finding the trusted-local-priest-doing-the-altar-boys-on-the-side sort of tatters?" Michael said if he'd been drinking when I put it that way, he'd have snorted it through his nose, but, *yes*. As it happened, Ayako's husband–wife guardian 'angels' were the parents of one of these students. Ayako went red for a laugh.

9. [21] In the Vedas and Sanskrit: Indra and Vritra, the *Devas* and *Asuras*, the *Ramayana* and *Mahabharata*; and biblically: Rev. 12:7–10, Isaiah 14:4–17, the Dead Sea Scrolls (War Scroll: 1QM, *Songs of the Sabbath Sacrifice* Scroll, Song 5: 4Q491–497, and perhaps the Melchizedek document 11Q13).

10. [21] Lucy (wife of British prime minister Stanley) Baldwin's vignette appears in the May 18, 1943 *Washington Post*, "Broadway Gazette" by Leonard Lyons, page 10, column 5, Washington, DC (https://quoteinvestigator.com/tag/pierre-daninos/ (accessed: 2018-06-25)). Mina felt Mother was trying to get Ayako to think and begin using her spirit mind in her physical life, and wouldn't actually have pressured her into their plan.

Chapter 3 – Michael's Reveal

11. [25] Yes for Sun-myung, who was spiritually strong, but of limited spiritual awareness. No for Jesus, who could fully interact with spirit world.

12. [27] We later realized that, in a general sense, this isn't always true. A number of times we thought Mina's viewpoint didn't work for us and defaulted to that of a person or 'angel.' For example, Gabriel vociferously insisted Ayako quit eating sugar. When she asked Mina about it, we understood his *yes* reply to mean, "if it makes you happy." One's happiness is everything to Mina. Until one clarifies their question isn't pursuing happiness per se but objective knowledge, he tends to accept how we view happiness as a default. If he didn't, he'd be intervening in our freedom without permission. Gabriel's attitude was, "Forget happy. It's at toxic levels, stop!" Ayako took Gabriel's advice. He kept at her for a couple months till she'd de-toxed. Thoughtlessly defaulting to Mina can be the logical fallacy of appealing to authority when it's better to query deeper or decide for oneself (*SOL* CH. 42:633).

13. [29] Gen. 32:22–31. Mina said this event never occurred, nor was Jacob (or Esau) a real person, although some stories credited to Jacob—twins struggling in the womb, bowing seven times, offering goods to a brother—are real.

14. [30] This book is revelatory, so it is what it is. 'Mitochondrial Eve' isn't the same concept (e.g., Ayala 1995; Learn 2016). Science and religion chase their tails on this. Religion myopically climbs into the morass of scriptural infallibility and gets stuck in abject adherence to ossified authority over dynamic, testable (or at least arguable) revelatory data or reasoning. It abandoned to querulous science the search for comprehension of the *bricolage* of life, which (regarding Adam and Eve) largely concludes: "[W]e can be confident that finding evidence that we were created independently of other animals or that we descend from only two people just isn't going to happen. Some ideas in science are so well supported that it is highly unlikely new evidence will substantially modify them, and these are among them . . . DNA evidence indicates that humans descend from a large population because we, as a species, are so genetically diverse in the present day that a large ancestral population is needed to transmit that diversity to us . . . every genetic analysis estimating ancestral population sizes has agreed that we descend from a population of thousands, not a single ancestral couple. Even though many of these methods are independent of each other, all methods employed to date agree that the human lineage has not dipped below several thousand individuals for the last three million years or more—long before our lineage was even remotely close to what we would call 'human.' Thus the hypothesis that humans descend solely from one ancestral couple has not yet found any experimental

support—and it is therefore not one that geneticists view as viable" (Venema et al. 2017, 55). This is inaccurate for the reasons described in EARTH'S HUMAN HISTORY (*SOL* CH. 32:531).

Scientific theories propose hypothetical mechanisms to explain data (observations). Specific consequences (predictions) of a proposition are developed. Scientists verify if the consequences (predictions) hold up. Energy (muscle; sway) testing opens a hitherto unknown mode of inquiry for gathering (spiritual; revelatory) data to propose previously unimagined hypotheses to which one can then apply empirical or logical analysis. While science says, "[y]ou simply cannot appeal to forces outside nature in the quest for understanding" (Ruse 2007, 285), energy testing pushes the boundary of "nature." Its data is akin to questioning a witness (making observations) from which one gathers testimony (data) to verify. One then empirically draws or reasons conclusions and consequences. We present energy-tested data herein as 'revelatory' because it's revealed, meaning energy tested. We expect the data will both increase and filter through humanity's reasoning faculties to eventually establish its empirical bonafides.

15. [30] She's from a different human-inhabited planet. Lucifer said the closest Earth language to spell its pronunciation is the Bantu language Gusii, centered on Kisii town in Kenya, Africa. Using the International Phonetic Alphabet (IPA), we initially spelled it mnɛɛptee, with each /ɛ/ pronounced as 'e' in 'dress' and drawn out, and the final /ee/ pronounced as in 'deep,' and short. I thought it sounded rather like ancient Egyptian as with Anck-Su-Namun in *The Mummy* (1999; film) or Nefertiti *The Mummy Returns* (2001), but Lucifer was all "Noooo, I don't think so."

16. [30] Mina didn't build our universe with any human–'angel' love prohibition although he didn't personally approve, either, because he viewed 'angels' as teachers and guides and, therefore, considered those *in that role* liaising with physical humans to be inappropriate. He reconsidered after observing Michael and Lucifer's gentlemanly behavior with Mnèèptē during her physical life and let it be known he had no problem with it. With The Corruption in play, however, his effort had little effect on the outcome of Michael's Lie.

17. [31] Michael was 18 years old at the time, Lucifer 22, Mnèèptē 24, and Gabriel 26. That was ca. 7.199MYA (Fig. 182:523).

18. [32] Lucifer and Mnèèptē consummated their relationship while she still lived in the physical world. Michael and other 'angels' knew about it because Lucifer didn't hide it. He had no reason to suppose their relationship was problematic—much less *wrong*—especially considering, in this early period of human history, Mnèèptē was two years "plus or minus one Earth month" older than Lucifer, thus 24 years old when their relationship kindled. Her planet orbits its sun comparatively faster than Earth, making her years shorter, hence her age somewhat younger than 24 as we reckon it.

19. [32] We're not *locked* in our physical body while alive. During sleep, our spirit self can 'detach' from our body to do whatever it likes until awakening pulls us back. Our vitiated spirit awareness means the time we spend on the 'spiritual plane' during sleep goes consciously unremembered except as dreams, déjà vu, intuitive feelings, and such like (*SOL* § 1.2.2.7:267).

20. [32] "St. Michael is one of the principal angels; his name was the war-cry of the good angels in the battle fought in heaven against the enemy and his followers" (https://www.catholic.org/encyclopedi a/view.php?id=7948 (accessed: 2021-11-23)).

21. [33] Beginning with simple spiritism, animism, and shamanism until people organized spirituality into religion.

22. [33] It took me through August 2018 to comprehend it in the version you're reading.

23. [33] From my autobiography *Victim to Victor* (2024). I usually found my out-of-the-box self careening the wrong way down the Unification Church's tightly-boxed one-way street.

24. [34] When Sun-myung proclaimed that Satan–Lucifer "surrendered" and returned to God owing to his unconditional love for him (Moon 1999, 11–12).

25. [34] They've had twelve children to date. Michael disclosed he'd never married, but later happily recounted his engagement to an Iroquois woman (d. 1875). Kir-el presumed they'd broken up when he later answered *no* to her query "Are you still engaged?" But his *no* was because they'd married by

then, so were, literally, no longer engaged. When I sang out "Congratulations, Michael!" he strongly pushed back a *no* response, surprisingly chiding me for thinking in the back of my thoughts that his wife was a "consolation prize," or that he'd "just picked anybody" to "level up" to Lucifer. I hadn't consciously noticed, and felt chastised. So, *ahem*. A good lesson to always dig into the what and why of energy test responses.

26. [34] Michael realized he was thoroughly in the wrong in 1999 when Lucifer reconciled with Mnèèptē and put everything behind him. His change of heart toward Michael, and Sun-myung declaring on January 13, 2001 "The Day of the Coronation of God's Kingship," his 2003 proclamation of the Nation of Cosmic Peace and Unity (Korean: "Cheonju Pyeonghwa Tongil Guk [천주 평화 톤길 국], or simply, *Cheon Il Guk* [천일국]; "The words Cheon Il refers to the singular reality encompassing both heaven and earth. Cheon Il Guk implies that two people unite and form a nation. (360-086, 2001.11.12)" in headline, "International President at the 2017 Mother's Day Hyojeong Culture Festival in Tokyo," May 14, 2017 (https://cheonilguk.blogspot.com/; accessed: 2021-12-03)), each predicated on his concept that unconditionally loving Lucifer–Satan had enabled his healing and repentance and resolved the human Fall, inspired Mother (P'najj; *SOL* § 1.2:336) to conceive her second son—Mina being the first—in March 2003, and physically born in December 2003. Sun-myung unknowingly followed this up with his proclamation of the "Age Before the Coming of Heaven" on May 5, 2004 (Moon, "Cheon Il Guk is the Ideal Heavenly Kingdom of Eternal Peace," June 13, 2006; http://www.unification.net/2006/20060613_1.html (accessed: 2022-01-30)). All these pronouncements celebrated, for him, the end of the Fall of Man's grip on humanity, the restoration in principle of God's relationship with us, and the imminence of the Kingdom of Heaven (the Ideal World).

Michael knew of Mother's second son but not when she'd conceived, because Mina only told him after the birth in a larger conversation about Lucifer's Sun-myung-inspired change and his own need to come clean about his Lie. Michael always came away from his series of conversations about this with Mina unwilling to admit to it and feeling judged, even though Mina obviously wasn't since he was loving him by respecting his autonomy and encouraging him to deal with it of his own volition without any looming punishment or judgment.

27. [34] Through the not-too-well-understood principles of reality that quantum entanglement (Parity; *SOL* § 6.11.3:197) only imperfectly describes, Mina is aware of and connected with everything in the universe such that every human being, including the spirit selves of the physically-alive, could 'receive' his 'broadcast' and 'know' the full details of what had just transpired in our house.

28. [36] Mediums hijacking messages from spirit persons for their own purposes is a common problem virtually impossible to detect unless one can smell BS. Healthy skepticism includes this book, of course, which admittedly is so far off the bell curve you'd be nuts to take it just on faith. Unlike a medium's 'mystery of faith,' we teach you in *SOL* PART V how to test it yourself to draw your own conclusions from your own experience instead of relying on ours.

Chapter 4 – The Big Healing

29. [41] Mina says El correctly used the word "apology" here but, at the same time, it's infused with many complex feelings and interpretations by Lucifer. Michael "apologizing" and Lucifer's remark did not imply any sort of Accountableism by either one.

30. [44] Mina said, "I expected the NCC would disappear, but wasn't sure till I was sure." I could say he can sure be enigmatic, but I intuited the quote to which he assented, so it could just be me.

31. [44] *Fallen* describes the universal human condition that promotes our ancient need to recognize our incomprehensible world as a place of the sacred and the profane—starting, perhaps, with the earliest human burial rituals, deitic carvings, and the like—and that humans in general became profane which, through interactions with the sacred, can restore their sacredness. Not all religions or cultures have a descent-from-original-nature myth as do most myths (Witzel 2012) and the three principal monotheisms. But all people have a theory of accountability, from explicating how that tree falling on Evil Bob was divine karmic judgment right down to promulgating why bad things happen to good people. Aside from spiritual experiences that independently lead toward a belief in gods, spirits, spirit

worlds, and the like, the demand for accountability in others serves up much of the energy behind the sense that human misbehavior results in—which natural disaster (or, failing that, Hell) delivers—divine justice (punishment). We can postulate, using conceptual frameworks like the archetypal psyche, "which is manifested in universal patterns and images such as are found in all the world's religions and mythologies" (Edinger 1992, 3; Witzel 2012), a "plausible psychological basis for the fall/salvation monomyth, that . . . corresponds to something very basic and important in the human condition, and is something universal. We would therefore expect it to find expression in myths and religions across cultures" (Uebersax 2018, par. 18).

32. [44] Such as Richard Dawkins' argument "that a predominant quality to be expected in a successful gene is ruthless selfishness. This gene selfishness will usually give rise to selfishness in individual behaviour" (Dawkins 1989, 2), a supposition that presumes causality in correlation.

33. [44] Religions, philosophies, and myths have their own views of the negative consequences of humanity separating itself from some original, paradisiacal existence. Even atheists and materialists advocating people being better than they are is just a roundabout secular way to reference sin. Most everyone knows that sin is (usually other people) simply not living as they should. Of course, when it comes to how one *ought* to live, the devil's in the details.

34. [45] As in sociobiology: originally proposed as 'hardwired' coding of the brain that begets social behavior, such as patterns of dominance and submission evolutionarily held over from early hominids' hunting life (Tiger et al. 1974).

35. [45] From Pierre Teilhard de Chardin (1959, 182) but somewhat recast in this book. The noosphere is not a collective identity, a collective consciousness, or even a "thinking layer" (ibid). It's a collective mental state or, more properly, a *way of being* (WOB; SOL § 2.2.1.1:234) although it's never moving to Teilhard's future "Omega point" evolutionary end state (ibid, 192, 259–60) because that's wishful thinking from blind conjecture.

36. [45] French sociologist Émile Durkheim (d. 1917) presaged this understanding with his observation that, "The totality of beliefs and sentiments common to the average members of a society forms a determinate system with a life of its own. It can be termed the collective or common consciousness [French: *conscience collective*; not to be confused with *conscience* in English] . . . By definition it is diffused over society as a whole, but nonetheless possesses specific characteristics that make it a distinctive reality . . . it is independent of the particular conditions in which individuals find themselves. Individuals pass on, but it abides . . . it does not change with every generation but . . . links successive generations to one another. Thus it is something totally different from the consciousnesses of individuals, although it is only realised in individuals" (1984, 38–9). Durkheim's concept "mediates conscious and unconscious religious factors within society" with "psychological implications" (Greenwood 1990, 485, 494) while Carl Jung's tenably more famous collective *un*conscious "mediates conscious and unconscious religious factors within the psyche" with "social implications" (ibid). Two sides to the same coin and both at least arguably derived from German philosopher Arthur Schopenhauer (d. 1860; ibid, 485, 494). This *negative* variant of the collective consciousness suffuses not merely a discrete collective—a physical world organization, culture, or society—but physical and spirit humanity in toto at once with a set of characteristics consistent with its negative impetus. The NCC expresses the mental state of the noosphere (SOL § 4.2:379).

37. [45] de Chardin 1959, 181. Noogenesis is unrelated to proto-humanity, arising in ♄uman development unrelated to a physical biosphere.

38. [45] "The NCC prevented Mina from healing people or working with humanity . . ." (McKeon 2017–19, 48). He could, however, work with 'angels' owing to their obvious spirit awareness although couldn't heal them. "He said it was virtually impossible for him to penetrate and thus his effort to help and guide humanity was always thwarted. Even if the NCC wasn't universal early on, it blocked him from anyone influenced by it. They simply wouldn't listen to or receive anything from Mina" (ibid). Perhaps trained that God is omnipotent (yet inexplicably powerless before human avarice), you might scoff at Mina's remark the NCC was so ingrained that he could exert barely any influence or healing. In counterpoint, consider reasoning with a person so utterly convinced of

their worldview they're immune to contrary evidence, such as believers in a flat Earth for whom contradictions are contrivances or distortions. What they accept, they insouciantly bend to fit their perspective (e.g., Natalie Wolchover, "Are Flat-Earthers Being Serious?" *Live Science*, May 30, 2017). How does one enlighten such a person when taking them into orbit necessarily involves 'trickery'? Similarly, the incriminatory story of life exclusively controlled and fostered through the ages via religion, philosophy, and culture, energized by the false reality of The Corruption and Michael's Lie, was an all-but insurmountable obstacle for Mina. This, not an indifferent, punitive, or testatious creator is the reason human history churns through its perverse bedlam generation to generation ad nauseam.

39. [45] The first 'angels' are Mina's own children with his spouse, Ag'poprje (*SOL* § 2.2:341). Those 'angels' then procreated the entire 'angelic,' or *spirit-born*, community that, in turn, sired the first physical-born humans, making us all Mina's descendant grandchildren (*SOL* § 1.1.3:533; *SOL* § 2.1.3:543).

40. [46] Neuroscientist Richard Burton remarks on habit: "The brain is only human; it, too, relies on established ways. As interneuronal connections increase, they become more difficult to overcome . . . habits, whether mental or physical, are exasperating examples of the power of these microscopic linkages. At the most personal level, most of us glumly acknowledge that we could abandon many of our failed self-improvement efforts if we could somehow painlessly alter these neural networks" (Burton 2008, 53). But habits, like psychiatrically diseased "[n]etworks aren't localized like a spot of rust on a fender. They aren't separable into their component parts any more than a cake can be reverse engineered into eggs, sugar, flour, water, and chocolate. These networks *are* the brain" (ibid, 54, 10; that said, the physical brain isn't the habituating bottleneck, it's the ethereal mind). We might think of the NCC as a neural network writ large built from our "skein of decisions" (Heffernan 2011, 20) multiplying in us mushroom-like across generations from the spore of Michael's Lie premised on The Corruption. We can productively understand all this through the lens of 'quantum entanglement' (Parity; *SOL* § 6.11.3:197) by which Mina is 'aware of all things' in the universe and can, within parameters, affect their states.

41. [46] Later in the day, after hearing of the Big Reveal and Big Healing, Ayako confided she'd felt abandoned the previous evening when El had run into my arms and we'd stood "safely" behind the kitchen counter while she'd felt pinned in her chair and "blowtorched" by the 'energy' of the 'angelic' fight; and then, even more primally, during our later prescriptive discussions with Mother and Mina following the tempest. Hearing that, having seen and heard her pain, I honestly felt a cad. Despite my faux pas, she announced on November 10, 2017 that her "clinical depression"—troubling her throughout childhood but especially since middle school—had simply "disappeared and is now totally gone." Her ongoing affect backed up her pronouncement.

42. [47] Contrary to our initial interpretation of Mina's one-week healing schedule, he finished the actual work in a day then took another six to recuperate and recharge. Likewise, as he continually heals the roughly 110 people who die every single minute just on Earth alone (158,116 per day; United Nations' *World Population Prospects*, 2011 (2010 Revised); mean figures for 2015–2020; https://www.un.org/e n/development/desa/population/publications/pdf/trends/WPP2010/WPP2010_Volume-I_Com prehensive-Tables.pdf (accessed 2020-04-20)), he's not getting the same downtime to recuperate and recharge and is drawing on 'energy' reserves from throughout the universe, including (he says) various specific, capable individuals.

43. [48] A quick read-up is Ellen Hendriksen, "Why Do We Self-Sabotage?" *Psychology Today*, October 10, 2017 (https://www.psychologytoday.com/us/blog/how-be-yourself/201710/why-do-we-self-sab otage (accessed: 2018-01-09)).

44. [48] In the car a few days before Christmas 2017, I felt a strong pressure-*cum*-pain around my left temple, usually one of several signals someone in spirit world is trying to get my attention or there's just an energetic conversation or activity going on around me. Ten minutes of hand testing later revealed my Uncle Joe (his real name; d. 2004) wanting to talk. I asked, "Did you get healed October 13th or afterwards?" *No.* Well, I'd forgot our experience between midnight and 2 AM October 11th when all my children's Japanese ancestors, except one, refused healing. As for my uncle, he'd refused it even after that day's momentous events (which he readily acknowledged he knew of) because he'd

felt angry with Mina on account of what turned out to be "the lies of the [Catholic] church." I said, "Why don't you come hang out at our house with everybody? You're totally welcome. It'll be fun." *No.* Some days later, he did ask Mina for healing but didn't feel it. "Yeah," I said, "something you don't want to let go is blocking it, which means you don't *really* want to be healed. You should look into that." He did let go his religious anger (and whatever else), so that, by July 2018 when I checked in with him, he now *felt* healed and was happily exploring infinite spirit world with a renewed interest in history.

45. [53] McKeon 1998. The book's argument builds off Unificationism's (now-deprecated) biblical Cain–Abel dynamic (Moon 1996, 190–2; Gen. 4).

46. [54] I got a taste of that in January 2018 when Mina let me know it was my wife's family in spirit world—wanting some accountability for their perception of how our marriage went—that provoked two back-to-back medically 'unprovoked' seizures, first during my mom's funeral mass, and then while tying my boots to check out of the emergency room. My face, ribs, back and all my torso muscles took a real beating from face planting in the floor and violently seizing in a grand mal twice in one day. Mina, Lucifer, my spirit guides, and guardian 'angels' were adamant they couldn't stop or even always successfully block such things ('ill-intention'—how things like this are done—is invisible even in spirit world) unless her family agreed to cease and desist. They didn't seem to particularly care they were disrupting Mina's work, either. I needed over three months' recovery to resume *The Story of Life*. So it was up to me. I got them on the horn so to speak and made peace with them; they agreed to leave me be. My new awareness of Mina, freedom, consideration, and doing no harm robbed me of any resentment I surely felt justified to manufacture over this incident. Instead, I found myself understanding how they were feeling and actually empathized—possibly on account of empathizing with my wife and stepdaughter's post-separation travails—and accepted this event the way I'd accept a little rain on my parade.

Chapter 5 – Our Six-day Prolegomenon

47. [59] I can't say with conviction that I felt particularly different after having various trapped emotional energies cleared from me. But Ms. Medium, a 'licensed' Emotion Code practitioner, said my great-great grandfather from Ireland was there with us since some of the emotional energy trapped in me originated in his experience dodging early 19th-century British justice. That experience stirred me to persuade Ayako to attend the ThetaHealing workshop, which arguably paved the way later on for El to pull the pin on her curiosity grenade.

48. [61] Stibal 2011, 143. "Visualize bringing up the energy through your feet, opening up all of your chakras as you go. Go up out of your crown, out to the Universe. Go beyond the Universe, past the white lights, past the dark light, past the white light, past the jelly-like substance that is the Laws, into a pearly, iridescent white light, into the Seventh Plane of Existence" (ibid, 224–33, "DNA Activation"). The seven planes are as follows. First, inorganic material. Second, organic material. Third, protein-based (human, animal) life, the purpose of which is to experience the challenge of emotion, instinct, and a physical body but which is an illusion, a figment of our minds. Fourth, spirit world, a "waiting room." Fifth, "Master's" penthouse after graduating from the fourth level: Jesus, Buddha, etc. and divided into multiple levels of "vibration and consciousness;" so, even in this rarefied world you're socially stratified by spiritual development. Sixth, Laws. And seventh, Creator of All That Is and 'Source' energy that powers the works. "This is the first time in the history of humanity that the planes of existence have been opened up simultaneously so that they can be understood and utilized as never before" (Stibal, "What Are the Seven Planes of Existence?" *Heal Your Life*, January 27, 2016; https://www.healyourlife.com/what-are-the-seven-planes-of-existence (accessed: 2018-08-23)). In reality, Mina and 'Source' energy have always been freely available to everyone. People simply tune it out for the reasons noted in *SOL*, although less so once in spirit world where physical life appears in its proper perspective. Mina says the physical–spirit universe exists in objective space. Whatever we create (even if only in our imagination), if we can interact with it then it's real.

49. [63] While I'd stayed overnight Friday and Saturday with friends, Ayako stayed with Ms. Medium, eating food from her backyard garden and getting, we later discovered, 'poisoned' by her toxic ('ill-

intentioned') spiritual energy that unbeknownst to us (including Ms. Medium) permeated her household. Her 'poison' took El and me 1–3 weeks and Ayako more like seven to flush out. We suffered flu-like symptoms that in Ayako's case simply wouldn't abate. New, unopened foods or those not prone to spoilage that we'd consumed trouble-free just days earlier now sickened us, particularly Ayako. We finally grew suspicious and queried Mina. He identified Ms. Medium and Vianna's negative, "ill-intentioned energy" as the culprits. There was nothing to do, he said, but "let it dissipate over time." In the meantime, "remove from your pantry Ms. Medium's garden vegetables and all the 'ill-intentionally' contaminated foods," which he identified. "Negative, dark spiritual energy is powerful stuff and best avoided," he told us. This led to a wider discussion on ThetaHealing and its founder, Vianna Stibal. Mina revealed the toxic spiritual energy clinging to the whole ThetaHealing program and "infecting" those coming into contact with it results from Vianna's motivation and spiritual condition. Instead of connecting people to God, he said she's actually connecting them to her negative "energy force." Some practitioners report (and Mina agrees) this is actually a dark, negative 'entity,' meaning a human person in spirit world (e.g., Trisha Howell; http://fraudthetahealing.com (accessed: 2018-05-07)) along with increases in physical ailments and spiritual dysfunctions (ibid). According to Mina, her 'negative—ill-intentioned—energy,' infused into ThetaHealing, results from her "grudge against humanity" for her physical ailments (harm). This is similar to the imagined though poorly understood psychology of computer virus creators (e.g., "Chapter 5—Malware: Can Virus Writers be Psychologically Profiled?" in Kirwin and Power 2012, 79–85; Chad Perrin, "10+ reasons why people write viruses," *Tech Republic*, May 4, 2009; https://www.techrepublic.com/b log/10-things/-10-plus-reasons-why-people-write-viruses/ (accessed: 2018-10-10)).

50. [64] I'd crankily missed 2016's REFUEL thanks to the hybrid battery failing in my fancy Prius. A conversation with my dad while driving to day two of 2017's REFUEL twitched my antenna, so I asked him on a lark if he'd had anything to do with the October 2016 battery fail and, *surprise!* he'd sabotaged it. That immensely shocked me on a moral *and* technical level. I mean, *Dad*! But, how? Some people in spirit world go to immense trouble to affect our life situations in positive or negative ways per their motivation. Throwing spiritual monkey wrenches isn't any different from the physical version most of us experience at some point in life, so that wasn't so hard to buy into. Physical death is just a transition from one mode of living to another, from one type of body and one set of physics to another. Why would our mind or attitude change when they're the same whichever body we're using? Even when now having the option of Mina's healing, some of the daily-dying (EN 42:180) refuse it. Our body, environment, and awareness of a bigger reality than we ever imagined might change, but our heart and mind not necessarily so much. We're still human, after all. But how my dad killed my hybrid battery: in simple terms, he'd made himself an 'energy vampire' much as such people drain our physical energy and drained susceptible cells in my HV battery until at least one triggered the onboard computer that disabled the car. Mina said it was quite a bit of effort for my dad to accomplish, so he had to be serious about not wanting me to go to REFUEL 2016.

51. [64] My daughters instinctively disbelieved the suicide tales and spent months delving deep into the murky world of Japanese heavy metal, eventually deciding both were murdered and their best guess by whom. They were discerning sleuths, and opened an energy testing conversation with Hidé and Taiji on Tuesday, October 10, 2017. Each provided details of their lives and the day's events leading up to their deaths, and their reactions to their dead bodies unexpectedly confronting them. They explained their murders, Taiji by a colleague and Hidé by a rival band member. Taiji had felt drawn to our house months earlier after hearing "there's this girl going to do something big," and his friend Hidé tagged along. That Tuesday wasn't their first visit. Weeks before, Ayako's bedroom light switch began to now and then physically move itself to the 'off' position (Hidé trying to get her attention). She'd stalk over and slap it back on. I was frankly a little skeptical. I never thought she was lying; perhaps mistaken? "No!" she spat. "When your light goes out and you find the switch in the off position—well, what then, Dad? Was I mistaken my light was even *on*?" Then she felt touches on her skin, saw someone very "dark" standing over her bed in the half-lit groggy hours of the morning (that was Taiji, still rip-roaring mad over his murder, hence of pretty 'dark' energy), heard noises, and generally felt haunted. She couldn't sleep and increasingly felt unsafe. She finally broached her angst on the ride home from church one Sunday whereupon, arriving home, I marched to her room and

militantly commanded whoever was hanging around to "get the F— outta here!" Ayako said she slept her best in months that night.

Only during their marathon sessions with Hidé and Taiji Tuesday and Wednesday did the girls figure out they were behind many of these events. It's a huge effort for spirit people to manipulate physical objects, and one Hidé only occasionally managed. He admitted I'd scared "hell out of him" when I'd ordered him out. He'd cleared off for weeks before tiptoeing back in, the sneak. Judging by Ayako's eventually renewed comments about spirits in her room, his timeframe sounded about right. She introduced him to me midweek just before the Big Event. Recalling the intensity of my spiritual energy when I'd kicked him out of Ayako's room, he refused to enter my bedroom where I was then in bed vainly attempting sleep (he was resentful and bitter over his murder; that depresses one's spiritual energy relative to another not having that negative emotion). He preferred speaking from the door—a little head-start distance twixt us—though I can't imagine why. What was I going to do? It's not as if I could kick his ghostly seat through his immaterial crown. He had the upper hand all around (I was forgetting my spirit self (body) can directly interract). Not your usual paranormal encounter, I suppose. Eventually, we got friendly. As angry as Taiji still was at being murdered in his fifties, Hidé's murder in his young thirties evoked such eviscerating emotions that, even three decades later, reminders overwhelmed him. Ayako partially healed both, though Taiji "backed off after I'd just healed three things because it was all so hard for him." The Big Healing then finished the job. Spending time with the girls seemed cathartic for them both. Our "death-convos" triggered their emotions less and less. Ultimately, they decided to "just stay away" when their respective murderers inevitably arrived in spirit world. "Taiji says what's done is done, Dad," Ayako sagely said. Yep, life goes on, here *and* there.

52. [65] Until then, the girls thought they were part African through their mom. Instead, they found that, despite her looking African, she was Carib Indian (Polynesian) paired with Caucasian plus Japanese, Korean, and Chinese through their great-great grandmother *Obāsan*. In their minds, the ancestry surprise outweighed my spiritual, religious, cosmological, and anthropological shocks that sometimes left me moping around the house. "At least you weren't deceived about where you came from, Dad," they'd artfully chuckle. But they left no doubt just how ecstatic they were to be Asian. Mina says modern Hawaiians are closest to how some American Indians used to look, and North American Indians had both curly and straight hair that tended to straighten through intermixing with Europeans. He said that when Europeans arrived there were "approximately 19 million" Indians in today's geographical United States (~6.79M today; USCB; https://worldpopulationreview.com/ countries/united-states-population (accessed: 2022-04-18)) with, as of 2021, ~98.5% dying from oppression, war, and related causes, up from ~60% had Europeans never arrived.

53. [65] I was aching to tell my dad's tale to my children—his own grandchildren after all—but he flat out refused permission for weeks. When he relented, they yawned. Still, it was a shocker for me. I recall him pontificating years ago on the moral turpitude of pilots returning to his WWII aircraft carrier with bubbly stories of strafing Japanese civilians on the beaches and elsewhere. I always thought that was the source of his strident claims to pacifism and his snarled "No!" when I'd wondered back in 1981 if he'd fight or kill to defend my mom and sisters from rape or murder. I was 22 years old then, and could only look upon his pacifism with incomprehension and, frankly, revulsion. The story he now recounted in the car—retested with Ayako several times including while writing this endnote to be certain I'd got it right—was that when he went to spirit world in 2012, someone spitefully told him (and he'd believed) that God was angry because he'd put providentially-important Sun-myung Moon's life in danger during his Pacific War service. To my dad, Sun-myung was the fruity, self-proclaimed Second Coming of Christ, but now . . . well, damn, maybe he was?

Here's the story. When young Sun-myung crossed by ferry from Japan to Korea across the Korea Strait, my father was at the same time prepping a carrier-based fighter for a mission. His intent while doing this work was that the plane and pilot kill "plenty of Japs." Soldiers or civilians, the distinction was without a difference. The revelation for me was that it was wholly out of character for the dad I knew based on the war's indiscriminate killing he'd tirelessly inveighed against. This aircraft spotted Sun-myung's ferry and reported it. I asked Mina if he'd ask the plane's pilot to corroborate. The pilot—whose name I didn't get permission to reveal—graciously did. He said he didn't know anything about my dad's situation, but that he did spot the ferry and reported it but didn't attack. Obviously, the ship safely arrived in Korea. Sun-myung said he never saw a plane overfly his ship, as he'd spent the voyage below decks. So, he was no help. Mina later said he was never upset with my dad because that's not his way. My dad's mal-intent was pretty small potatoes anyhow. Still practicing Emotion Code and ThetaHealing at this time—the Big Healing still being a few days away—I asked my dad if he wanted to be healed of this feeling of trauma and guilt. He did, and Mina healed him. Both Emotion Code and ThetaHealing are adamant that practitioners absolutely honor and respect the freedom of persons, and Mina confirms its importance. So, I learned to not only never attempt healing against a person's will or without their permission, but also to never share a person's information out of school. I argued (if you could call it that) with my dad several times for his consent to tell the girls and maybe others but he was resolute: *No.* Dang, I'd have to wait.

54. [67] This is an ancestral trace using spirit sources via energy testing. Born in 1921, *Obāsan's* Japanese name is Ai Akiō (what we'd thought was her ethnic *Amami* surname—as *Obāsan* had spelled it out for us—was actually a codeword for her living family). Her family had forcibly separated her from her daughter with a Chinese aristocrat in Beijing and sent her home in disgrace to Okinoerabu Island (沖永良部島), about forty miles north of Okinawa in the Ryukyu chain. American bombs killed her in July 1945 at the island's airport in today's town of Wadomari. She thought it was probably a June 30th raid I'd read about online, but wasn't entirely clear anymore (we've found that people can't always recall details of their physical lives over time, as happens anyway while alive). She felt crushed and bitterly angry with her family, even if not one bit with Americans for killing her, and couldn't forgive them or overcome her grief at having been separated from her baby daughter. At that point, we were healing people using Emotion Code techniques but not yet realizing we could simply skip right to asking Mina to do it. El was eager to relieve *Obāsan's* suffering, and I did the Emotion Code work in spite of her extended family—we counted well over thirty people—loudly arguing over how she was characterizing them. They refused en masse to be included in the healing and derided her for even wanting it. Well, funny thing. Her experience of having her trapped emotions released—particularly heartbreak and fear—and experiencing from Mina what it would feel like to live without them was so profound and transformative, and her 'energetic' response so electric, that El sensed the family now clamoring for it, too, as if shocked from a daze. All but three obstinate holdouts, that is. When Mina then healed *Obāsan's* extended family—here, the trapped emotions were primarily guilt, shame, and the like—these last three threw in the towel. We got quite a (not roundly appreciated) laugh out of that.

   All the anger, enmity, resentment, hurt, despair, sorrow—all of it—disappeared as this family transformed as Mina infused them with how it would feel to live with emotions and beliefs opposite to what they'd been living with. They forgave each other and themselves, felt love and acceptance for and by each, and released any hatred from World War II. *Obāsan's* older brother Kengo, for example, an inveterate joker, had died a coerced *kamikaze.* My daughters felt tears and emotions pouring from this family and especially their new BFF *Obāsan.* Their new energy and mood played across my daughters' faces and through their energy and body language. This vignette, along with my Uncle Joe's (EN 44:181), illustrates from our practical experience that people are people, here or in spirit world, and that not everyone wants, or is ready, to be healed of trauma. But when they are ready, Mina doesn't wait. He applies no conditions or judgment. He just heals, loves, and cares. If you think you're special because your 'sins' are so base that Mina—'God'—could never want to heal, or love, or talk to you, well, you're selling him and yourself short. You don't have to apologize, repent, change, promise the moon, or anything. You simply need let go your sorrows and woes; even subconsciously (or via your spirit self) is sufficient. Then ask Mina to heal you and he will.

55. [68] ". . . on July 2 [1945] the Japanese military announced a *levée en masse* of civilians. 'In less lofty terms,' [Edward J.] Drea writes, 'these woefully untrained children, old men, and women were beasts of burden who cleaned debris after air raids, portered supplies on their backs, and, armed with bamboo spears, were used as cannon fodder. Americans had witnessed them in all these roles on Okinawa.' On Okinawa, Japanese forces had sacrificed the Okinawan people, 200,000 of whom perished" (Ferrell 1994, 212, io). Also, "Many Okinawans died at the hands of the Japanese, who used them as human shields or forced mass suicides. Masahide Ota, a former governor of Okinawa, said he

uncovered World War II archives that Imperial Japan considered Okinawans not to be pure Japanese and therefore expendable. 'Imperial Japan used Okinawans as a sacrifice. We have not been treated as human beings but as goods to be used,' he said" (Matthew Carney, "Okinawa's horrific World War II history driving battles with US and Japan," Australian Broadcasting Corp., May 15, 2015; https://ww w.abc.net.au/news/2015-05-15/caught-in-the-middle-okinawa-still-battling-japan-and-us/6473054 (accessed: 2018-09-13)).

56. [69] El, on fire to be a singer and model, had months earlier reached out to and met online Japanese megastar Akiō (a pseudonym) with whom she developed a mentoring friendship. After I went to sleep, the girls learned they're his second cousins through his still-living grandmother, who is *Obāsan*'s younger sister (aged 5 at *Obāsan*'s 1945 death; she'd heard stories but never knew what happened to her older sister and brother Kengo (EN 54:184). El immediately messaged Akiō using *Obāsan*'s *Amami* surname that, in reality, is a family codeword. Unsurprisingly (except to my daughters), he went radio silent for a week. They fretted on pins and needles, thinking he must've cut them off as crazy Americans with a superstar fetish. Then he replied that he'd been shocked and dismissive of El's claim but the codeword had prompted him to visit his spiritualist grandmother still on Okinoerabu Island (沖永良部島) to hear what she had to say. He then tracked down other extended family. To his great surprise, they verified the familial connection. According to Akiō, his grandmother wept at her sister's "spitting image" in Ayako's photo (who was close to *Obāsan*'s age at death). Akiō was pretty shook. He and the girls then started getting to know each other as family.

57. [70] Since before the Middle Ages. Even so, Jesus continued to work with Christians and others receptive to him as he really is. According to Mina, this amounts to "exactly" 73 Christians and 681 non-Christians.

58. [71] Hidé spent the evening in Japan attempting to influence his "troublesome" adult son to mend his ways. When he 'portaled' into our house at a sleepy 2:30 AM, he was cross and ready for the Emotion Code healing session El had earlier promised him "tomorrow." "It *is* tomorrow," he declared. She laughed. I studied the wall clock. Exhausted, she nonetheless stood by her word after I'd gone to sleep. For the girls, Hidé and Taiji were already family and their issues were becoming ours. El knocked on the door as I lay in bed dropping off. Hidé wanted to formally meet (EN 51:183). "He's very nervous, Dad," said El, explaining his disinclination to step into the room. I consistently seemed to have that effect on these guys. Well, I sure wasn't climbing out of bed so we exchanged pleasantries long distance. I finally got to sleep around 3 AM wondering to what I'd awake.

59. [71] Her real name. Unlike *Obāsan*'s family's rejection, *Obāsan*'s lover *Yéyé* (爷爷; FN 45:71) was the scion of a wealthy political family that happily received their baby daughter. One of *Yéyé*'s sisters (now one of Ayako's spirit guides) reared her with love and acceptance while, joked Ayako, *Yéyé* "just made money." In 1953, his sister secretly paid their own 14-year old daughter's passage on a freighter out of China (at this point, he'd had no money himself) to give her a shot at surviving the Communist takeover. His family stayed behind "for honor"—not abandoning China for Taiwan—after which, according to him and Mina, the Communists burst into their home and shot them all because *Yéyé* was secretly helping the anti-Communists (who'd assassinated an official and his family; *Yéyé* and his family was payback). She ran out of money at St. Vincent and the Grenadines in the West Indies. *Obāsan* said it seemed to her that St. Vincent, tucked out in the middle of Cold War nowhere, was "a place of peace and safety" after their tumultuous lives in war, rebellion, and Communism's showdown with the West. Her daughter quickly birthed an illegitimate child with a Vincentian of African descent. She then married a Carib Indian man at age sixteen and produced my daughters' grandmother Martina in 1955, but died soon after of yellow fever. We used Emotion Code with her, too, healing her trapped emotion of sadness which Mina completed by 'downloading' his perspective on how it would feel to live with its opposite.

Chapter 6 – In the Hurricane's Eye

60. [73] Frederick Douglass' writings remorselessly pointed this out to me while writing "Cain and Abel" (Master's Thesis); see Douglass 1845, 5; DuBois 1969, 136; Myrdal 1964, 123, 607, 1197). Writing this endnote got me curious, though, so I checked my lineage. No African, Central or South

American, or Caribbean, but—*wow!*—Mina says I'm 10% Natchitoches from the larger Caddo tribe of Louisiana; he entered my maternal Cajun French grandfather's ancestry around 1850. The Indian Ayako frequently saw around our Virginia house is a 19th-century Natchitoches ancestor—and my paternal great-grandfather is Chiricahua (*Aiaha*) Apache, the famous Geronomo's older (and only) sibling, whom I call Shasha (*SOL* FN 236:202).

61. [74] Mina had a biological body before entering spirit world in Mother's universe, and before creating ours. He said his ethnicity is what we might call "archetypal Japanese." Don't think that didn't enthuse my two daughters.

62. [74] Technically, this isn't an unusual concept for Unificationists. My mandatory post-seminary 40-day retreat during summer 1998 saw me at the Unification Church's undeveloped *Cheongpyeong* Heaven and Earth Training Center's (천주청평수련원) compound on the mosquito coast of *Cheongpyeong* Lake (청평호반) near Seorak (설악), South Korea. My class arrived to incessant rain and some of Korea's worst-ever flooding. Our sodden hideaway's dearth of hygiene and proper plumbing cheered on a cauldron of infectious diseases that swamped our health and landed me in the *smoking* ward of a rural hospital with a severe but misdiagnosed lung infection, which I thought stood good odds of making me an ex-pat statistic. Leading up to this amusing respite, I found myself participating in a daily, hours-long traditional shamanistic ritual called *ansu* (안수) or *chan yang* (찬양, 'praise'). Participants sit in a line back-to-front cross-legged or on their knees and bitch-slap out the spirits residing in their body to a cadent song set to a steady, booming drumbeat, each body-part-specific slap alternated by hand claps to keep the rhythm. The person behind you takes care of whacking your back and you the one in front. These spirits are considered bad for the simple reason their presence selfishly disrupts your own spirit, body, and life. *Ansu* can be painful and outright debilitating as folks get carried away and pound hell out of themselves and their partner.

One day, mine compelled me to threaten to break his arms before he managed—some people think they have a religious duty to really let you have it—to ease up his blows. It was a bone-bruising, black-and-blue experience. Did it evict these spirit squatters? Well, taking a desperate break along the back wall in the midst of *ansu* one day, I saw 'angels.' They stood alongside each seated participant in the seven rows, thirty deep, rhythmically bending at the waist to yank forth a spirit trespasser, then doing actress Reese Witherspoon's *Legally Blonde* (2001) 'bend-and-snap' to fling them off like cotton bolls to the basket. *Ansu*'s purpose seems to be to make it too miserable for a spirit person to remain ensconced in your body, to shake them sufficiently loose that an 'angel' can haul their grasping selves out. Unificationists figure if it looks like you're being beaten to death, your bad spirits will abandon you like rats a sinking ship. *Ansu* made it almost too painful for *me* to remain in my body. And then we discovered we could simply ask Mina to accomplish the same outcome in a painless instant for all parties. I couldn't believe it.

63. [75] Brent Swancer, "The Mysterious Real Zombies of Haiti," *Mysterious Universe*, St. Leonards, NSW, Australia, August 5, 2014 (https://mysteriousuniverse.org/2014/08/the-mysterious-real-zombies-of-haiti/ (accessed: 2018-08-20)).

64. [77] Moon 1996, 12, 381–409. Also, ". . . Moon declared himself the Messiah . . . [and] 'humanity's Savior, Messiah, Returning Lord and True Parent'" (Charles Babington and Alan Cooperman, "The Rev. Moon Honored at Hill Reception," *The Washington Post*, June 23, 2004, A01).

65. [78] An important salvific component in *Divine Principle*'s Growth Stages (1996, 40–5). Like other ironies in Sun-myung's spiritual career, Mina says the Blessing actually produced spiritually elevated children. However, children conceived after the October 14, 2017 Big Healing are automatically 'blessed' in that sense and spiritually advanced (generally) over their parents. Unificationism's Blessing of Marriage is now redundant.

66. [78] Soon after the Big Healing, Mina said the various 'levels' of physical-born spirit world (*SOL* § 3.1.2.1.3:359; *SOL* § 1.2:521) had naturally recombined into the single 'level' he'd originally intended as healed spirit people 'energetically' transformed, raising their 'vibration.' At the time of Helen's death, that epochal event was still years in the uncertain future. For us, now, it was still some eighteen hours away.

67. [78] See *ansu* (EN 62:186).

68. [79] Mina said that before the Big Healing less than one million people worldwide (including Ayako) were free of spirit people 'infesting' them, their spiritual energy being too strong for it. That's less than 0.0132% of the estimated 2017 global population. Since the Big Healing, spirit people generally no longer 'infest' people on Earth nor 'feed off' their energy. However, the physics between 'low' and 'high energy' ('vibration') means a 'higher-energy' person in the physical world can be 'energy'-siphoned simply by the presence of 'lower-energy' spirit persons (interacting similar to high- and low-pressure air systems), but it's rarely intentional. One might liken it to the exhaustion one feels after an emotionally intense event.

69. [79] "There was never malice in this situation," Mina said, because these spirit persons were "trying to survive" their flyblown situations. They acted in fear, desperation, and emotions similar to *Real Love*'s "drowning man" analogy (Baer 2003, 15–17): "[a] drowning man doesn't mean to hurt other people; in his state of mindless panic, he simply can't seem to stop himself from grabbing anything or anyone that might help to keep his head above the water. His fear is so overwhelming that he doesn't think for a second about the harm he might cause others as he saves himself" (ibid, 29).

70. [82] Mina says guardian 'angels' are not capable of stopping spirit persons from 'infesting' our physical bodies or removing them if they do (SOL § 3.2:566). But if such a person in their subconscious believes they're in the wrong—the way criminals who avoid capture then plead guilty after capture—there's an implicit subconscious permission for correction. An 'angel' can then pull them out even if consciously they don't want to leave (as with *ansu*; EN 62:186). Mina, of course, doesn't operate that way. Instead, he works to heal them so they leave naturally.

71. [82] Besides Helen, my currently known spirit guides are the following. A French ancestor who preferred anonymity. "Well," I drawled, "I'm calling you Frenchie, then." She took it in stride. At least, I didn't get a *no* push. Eight months later, she decided to drop her veil, although I stalled three months before energy testing her deets. Her name is Daphne Giles (d. 1430). There's my other best Unificationist friend Godwin D'Silva (real name; d. 2007) who joined the squad in March 2018. Then my best friend from the US Coast Guard, Billy Roberts (real name; d. 2015 per he and Mina), came on board in June 2018. Helen continues her long earthly practice of pulling no punches when I seek her advice. Godwin is his same patient, considerate self. Billy, I hadn't seen nor heard since 1980. Since then, others not listed here have joined me as well as the girls.

Chapter 7 – Doom Ride

72. [90] It is perhaps shocking that Mina and his wife Ag'poprje (SOL § 2.2:341) didn't educate the first 'angels'—their direct offspring—about the finer points of how to live—though they fully answered any questions—because they "were new to parenting and universe creating" and hadn't appreciated what needs be conveyed or the consequences of not doing so. They'd made a command decision not to influence their children's minds in any way, although concluded that stinting on that aspect was counterproductive since, with the Big Healing, they've been addressing it. Until then, no 'angels' were aware of Mina's unique awareness–experience of all that happens amongst humanity and the universe and 'quantumly entangles' everything and everyone. However, he doesn't look into people's *minds* because it's sacred and inviolable. Unless he's already aware, whenever we ask him what a person—say, Michael—was thinking or being motivated by, we always need wait as he actually converses with the person before answering us. The 'energy' of their conversation will often pendulum us around before settling into stillness and then his response. From the Cardinal's (all universe builders, SOL FN 130:110; including Mina's) point of view, creating—building—a universe is analogous to building a large, multi-generational house for one's children to produce a multi-generational family that never moves out. If you view the universe through that metaphor, it is perhaps easier to comprehend.

73. [90] Ms. Medium's spirit self doesn't agree with or support what her physical self is doing in this respect, but takes a hands-off approach. Michael and Lucifer felt she should be trying a lot harder to rein in her physical self's behavior. As a result, she doesn't feel so welcome, hence "rarely visits" these 'angels.' I discovered this when conflicts in my energy testing revealed her physically asleep and her

spirit self disagreeing with Mina's description of her situation. In many ways, the physical pressure to survive and thrive along with erroneous beliefs—mindset—drives our physical choices. Absent that, our spirit self often has different attitudes, priorities, even personality from our physical self (e.g., Hitler *SOL* CH. 40:605).

74. [93] There's no such thing as 'negative energy.' For energy to be 'negative,' it must vest with intention. Hence, 'negative energy' is 'ill-intentioned energy.' Ms. Medium could see Michael with Ayako and wondered, Ayako said, "Why is he following this little girl around?" Ms. Medium infused her— "She really let me have it!" Ayako jested—with 'negative energy' because she saw that Ayako was important to Michael. She didn't like Michael, so she vented her dislike on Ayako, too. Secondarily, Ms. Medium knew Ayako would become better and stronger—more successful—than she, although Ayako didn't even know how to use her spiritual prowess at the time. Ms. Medium wanted to derail her development and keep it that way. She invested Ayako with ill-intention at every opportunity so she'd never be able to develop herself. Having been knocked flat for nearly two months from interacting with Ms. Medium at the ThetaHealing Basic DNA workshop, she'd paralyzed Ayako's spirituality for months more. Even if a person dislikes one, if they have no intention of harm then there is no harm. Unconsciously harming someone merely in consequence of one's dislike doesn't happen. If one feels 'negative energy' or spiritual harm, it's because a person consciously (or subconsciously) intends it. Absent Ms. Medium's ill will, the three of us could've interacted with her all day long without any ill effect beyond her 'negative' ThetaHealing 'energy.'

75. [93] The eight clair senses are seeing, knowing, hearing, emotional feeling, tasting, physical feeling, touching, and smelling. We three experience more or less of these to greater or lesser degrees as we've improved or developed from scratch since 2017. Ayako remains the most advanced amongst us.

76. [94] For example, why did these 'angels' (as we then-understood their reality) tell us that God can only love them through human beings? If human beings don't care about angels then, practically speaking, it means neither does God. Yet God is supposed to be the God of Love. This sort of astral subordination is really enslavement. It contradicts the premise of freedom. If a human wants angels to be free and directly loved by God, for instance, it would contradict the created order and be unattainable. No free will but only bounded will. This sort of illogic raised significant conundrums for us as to God's consistency, logic, reason, and his heart. Frankly, Ms. Medium did a great job creating a sense of majesty and we felt overawed in the presence of such angels. But it was falderal. Interacting with Mina, Michael, and Gabriel ourselves produced a completely different experience, one where God and angels were not majestic, superior–subordinate deities but human, personable, friendly, loving, equal, and free, and most important, entirely consistent as well as supremely logical, rational, simple, and understandable in their descriptions of a very comprehensible universe. When it came to whom to believe—Ms. Medium or ourselves—even if we excluded our own personal experience and just stuck to the data, there was no contest. Logic and reason alone demanded we defer to Mina's account over Ms. Medium's own.

77. [94] *The Urantia Book* 1955, 1, 42, 10. The book claims Uversa is the capital city of the *Orvonton* "superuniverse" of which our universe, *Nebadon*, forms a part (ibid, 1). Most of this work is ridiculous in its torturous complexity and supernumerary elitism whereas Mina's story of life is simple, straightforward, and egalitarian. But I was knocked flat when Mina said Uversa is an actual city in spirit world that spans both its physical-born and spirit-born iterations (*SOL* § 3.1.2.1.3:359; *SOL* § 1.2:521), and that a spirit person living there had legitimately delivered the textual quotation even though the content doesn't comport with reality. He added that some facts scattered through the book—not Orvonton—are correct. That said, the following passage from the book rings sensible enough as it relates to Mina's perspective on mediums. "Information and intelligence, gleaned from even high sources, is only relatively complete, locally accurate, and personally true. Physical facts are fairly uniform, but truth is a living and flexible factor in the philosophy of the universe. Evolving personalities are only partially wise and relatively true in their communications. They can be certain only as far as their personal experience extends. That which apparently may be wholly true in one place may be only relatively true in another segment of creation. Divine truth, final truth, is uniform and universal, but the story of things spiritual, as it is told by numerous individuals hailing from various spheres, may sometimes vary in details owing to this relativity in the completeness of knowledge and in

the repleteness of personal experience as well as in the length and extent of that experience . . . Truth is . . . both replete and symmetrical . . . The wise philosopher will always look for the creative design which is behind, and pre-existent to, all universe phenomena" (ibid, 42).

Franchezzo says much the same thing in Farnese's allegedly spirit-received *A Wanderer in the Spirit Lands* (1901). Admittedly, the *Urantia* authors—as spiritualists are wont to do from our perspective— could have built off this work, so a second opinion here is not necessarily a *second* opinion. "In the spirit world . . . there are a great number of different schools of thought, all containing the great fundamental eternal truths of nature, but each differing in many minor details, and also as to how these great truths should be applied for the advancement of the soul; they likewise differ as to how their respective theories will work out, and the conclusions to be drawn from the undoubted knowledge they possess, when it is applied to subjects upon which they have no certain knowledge and which are still with them as with those on earth, the subject of speculation, theory, and discussion . . . The waves of truth are continually flowing from the great thought centers of the Universe, and are transmitted to earth through chains of spirit intelligences, but each spirit can only transmit such portions of truth as his development has enabled him to understand, and each mortal can only receive as much knowledge as his intellectual faculties are able to assimilate and comprehend. Neither spirits nor mortals can know everything, and spirits can only give you what are the teachings which their own particular schools of thought and advanced teachers give as their explanations. Beyond this they cannot go, for beyond this they do not themselves know; there is no more absolute certainty in the spirit world than on earth, and those who assert that they have the true and only explanation of these great mysteries are giving you merely what they have been taught by more advanced spirits, who, with all due deference to them, are no more entitled to speak absolutely than the most advanced teachers of some other school" ([sic], Farnese, 90). Mina says this excerpt is largely albeit not fully true, although the book itself is not spiritually revealed but an aggregation of stories woven into a single storyline that gives a "partially correct view of spirit world." To know which is which requires energy testing the book line-by-line.

Still, we found the foregoing affirmed by our experience. When speaking with spirit human beings, we learned of their spirit world encounters and the truths about spirit world they'd gleaned from them. When speaking with 'angels,' we received a 'higher,' more universal understanding of spirit world, though even 'angelic' viewpoints reflect their own personal experience over the broader objective reality that Mina conveys who, by definition, has the singularly comprehensive understanding of our universe. When speaking with Mina, we learned in all respects the reality of how he, the universe, 'angels,' and human beings exist. But don't think for a moment that what we've learned from him and presented here and in *The Story of Life* represents all there is to know about such topics because the subject is vast beyond belief. For example, if we were to take Hidé's experience regaining consciousness after his drugged strangulation (EN 51:183) and extrapolate that to a truism for how all human beings recognize their transition to spirit world, we would be committing a fallacy. If, however, we include Mina's knowledge of how the transition from the physical to spirit works, on average, in all cases, then we'd have the larger context for which Hidé was describing only his part, and one colored by his personal circumstances.

78. [95] It's a simple logic. No compulsion means no judgment or punishment because even its threat— distant or vague—is coercion. Neither is there any moral law, as that not only eviscerates freedom but necessitates judgment and punishment of violators, the threat of which is also coercion. Mina provides no judgment or punishment himself, but individuals can and do provide it to the self (as self-coercion) and to others. This is a common social engineering technique evident in the 20th and 21st centuries and the foundation of political 'liberty through law.' But coercion is alien to Mina. If you deal with him, you'll find it's never part of the program. You might compel yourself because you generate a personal duty or fear, but that's on you. Mina creates no standard by which one might feel compelled to duty or fear an outcome. Humans alone craft the compulsions we know. Ultimately, this logic dictates there's no such thing as sin. We three certainly felt a personal duty to pass Mina's message to Ms. Medium, mostly due to the heartistic bond we'd built with him. But what if we'd chosen not to? We'd have simply carried on with Mina, the 'angels,' and spirit family and friends. If Mina thinks his message crucial, he finds another means to deliver it without holding our unwillingness or inability against us, all the while continuing our relationship so long as we want one.

We can say this because he did ask us to do other things at which we failed, forgot, let slide, or ignored without any diminution in our relationship—none we could perceive anyhow.

79. [95] For example, *Obāsan*'s eldest brother whom the girls call *Idaina-oji* (great-great uncle in Japanese, which he prefers to plain old generic *oji-san*, 'uncle', and whom I call "Gruncle One" on account of the multitude of great uncles) joined the Unification Church in the late 1950s after listening in on Divine Principle lectures while visiting Earth. When I showed up in St. Vincent and the Grenadines many years later as a Unificationist, he saw an opportunity to 'restore' his lineage by connecting his great-great niece with me and my lineage through the Blessing of Marriage. This is the Church's marital method of restoring people to God through separating them from Satan via spiritual conditions that rectifies Adam and Eve's sin and heals their lineages of 'fallen' nature, original sin, and historical resentments, and then producing Blessed Children free of original sin entanglements to forge disparate lineages into united, spiritually-restored families. But the Blessing is redundant as of the Big Healing October 14, 2017 (EN 65:186; SOL FN 545:639). Children conceived since then naturally surpass 'Blessed children.' *Idaina-oji*'s puppeteering—if I'm being indulgent . . . well, okay, he didn't exactly put a gun to my head to marry her—introduced me to drama and trauma I might have avoided despite it bringing me children I adore and would never unmake, regardless. This sort of back-office intervention in our physical lives is common with spirit persons who are motivated by all sorts of prosy reasons to guide, inspire, harass, help, hinder, harm, or otherwise manipulate our lives absent our knowledge and permission (SOL § 1.3:473). Mina and the 'angels' don't engage in this rank behavior because it short circuits our freedom and is thus an unloving therefore harmful act.

80. [95] Not in its modality (sway test, healing regimen, etc. which pre-dates ThetaHealing; Howell 2007, ibid, par. 9), but as regards the adverse 'energy' ThetaHealers call 'Creator' to which practitioners are taught to connect. Our personal experience—Ayako recognized (and Mina confirmed) it at the Basic DNA workshop straight off—is that this energy is not the 'Source' energy of God or the universe but a personal, 'negative ('ill-intentioned') energy' afflicting those who imbibe it. Former certified ThetaHealer Trisha Howell alleges ThetaHealing founder "Vianna—with the help of her husband Guy Stibal, a dark shaman—befriended an entity called Creator. Vianna has a special relationship with Creator, a being she claims is God but which has been experienced by hundreds of former ThetaHealers as a dark entity that subtly takes some of practitioners' energy in exchange for 'healings' . . . Vianna and Guy use Creator not only for their own personal gain but also to keep practitioners in line." (ibid, par. 8–9). According to Mina, Vianna's 'Creator' is just a malevolent human being in spirit world using and harming others for his own purposes, but had "moved on" from Vianna and ThetaHealing by the time we encountered her. The 'negative energy' developed through this spirit person's association remains—is even growing—because he says Vianna and ThetaHealers keep adding to it through their personal-gain intention and because, as an 'energetic poison,' the more it's used the more it grows. ThetaHealing started as a 'using' rather than a 'healing' modality. Certified ThetaHealer instructors who don't know this aren't lying, per se. The modality itself is tainted. No matter how beneficial when pure, any corrupted medicine taints the patient. One could wonder if Mina, 'angels,' and the spirit persons with whom we interact aren't who they claim, and it wouldn't be unreasonable to do so. We have. Besides analyzing their message, if one builds reasonable energy testing competency (SOL § 2:625), one can develop sufficient evidence to suit oneself either way. Mina hasn't sickened or disturbed us, however, and is doing all the healing without us, plus insists we don't charge money for our part in it.

81. [95] This is how we discovered Ms. Medium's underside, because we quite naturally asked Mina, "Hey, what's going on, here?" Mina had us go through our refrigerator and pantry item-by-item where he identified all the foodstuffs Ms. Medium's clinging 'toxic energy' had spoiled and were food-poisoning Ayako. The fresh vegetables from her garden, several recently-bought batches of more than sixty-four store eggs, jars of sealed, unopened peanut butter, and other typically 'unspoilable' foods—nothing frozen, interestingly—I peevishly carted to the landfill.

82. [95] Ayako was content with Mina's initial non-biological diagnosis. On the other hand, I revisited it over most of the weeks involved. No matter how I formed my queries, however, his answer was consistent and emphatic: it wasn't a biological infection but a 'negative energy' contamination. Similar

symptoms, different cause. For me, it was just hard to accept.

83. [95] Eventually, El admonished me that "Mina says stop asking him if you're 'connected.' We're always connected to him. Everyone is. When your chakras are off you just aren't hearing him." Right. But isn't not hearing the same as not connected? Sometimes we go round and round with definitions, Mina and I. He was really just advising patience. It took me awhile to get it, though.

84. [96] I emailed Moth Man. "You probably think this is nuts, but we drove home from church yesterday with me and the kids in the car, Hide Matsumoto ([El's] spirit guide/guardian angel), Taiji Sawada ([Ayako's] spirit guide/guardian angel), [Helen Smith] (my spirit guide), my Dad showed up when he came up in the conversation, Obaasan (the girl's great-great-grandmother from Japan) who's always around, and Lucifer, who, besides Gabriel, spends the most time with us of the angels (Michael's the quiet sort). The girls had the conversation going like a party. You could feel the energy and the family nature of it. The girls call them all 'the squad.' Funny. The girls can hear and feel touches . . . 'Lucifer, did you just pat my head?' 'Hide, did you POKE me?' . . . 'Who's yelling? My head's pounding from it!' And so on, the whole [roughly two-hour] ride down. This is my life now, [Moth Man]. Heh" ([sic] "Nov. 20," Email to Moth Man, Nov. 20, 2017).

In the car, we discovered spirit people can change their size, which makes sense since the spirit body is thought-based, manifested by mind. We could have ten or twenty people packed in—more, probably; we never checked on numbers beyond asking after people we knew or suspected might be aboard. At those Unification Church *ansu* sessions in Korea (EN 62:186) they'd told us spirit people hiding out inside physical bodies were as tiny as insect larva; well sure, how else could thousands of human beings crowd into your body, right? It all seemed a little farcical, then. But now we had Hidé, Taiji, our 'archangel' squad, Helen, Jesus, Sun-myung, family, and others telling us how big they were and where they were sitting (or standing) in my diminutive Prius. Additionally, they don't share the same space despite the different 'planes' of existence, because our physical body has a spirit body, which same space another spirit person can't occupy. When the girls figured it out, they asked things like, "*Obāsan*, is my leg in your space?", "Lucifer, you okay squeezed between us?", "Taiji, are you *really* sitting on the console?!"

At home where our house always seemed like spirit party central, my daughters developed sensitivity for where they sat or stood, or they'd ask for space on the sofa to squeeze in. Sometimes I'd plop onto the sofa without thinking and one of the girls would throw a fit. "Dad! You just made Gabriel move to the floor when you sat on him!" None of our spirit guests seemed put out by our faux pas. They're invisible to us, so what's the point? Taiji often stood behind the sofa for hours watching movies or YouTube music videos with us because there was no available seat—either empty or in a position where, were he physical, he could or would actually sit to see the television—or he didn't want to obstruct someone else. One doesn't lose such sensibilities just because one transitions to a pliable spirit body.

85. [96] Our household got the same way. Ayako dubbed these spontaneous convocations as "turn-up Tuesday," "wildin' Wednesday," and so on. No day was without spirit persons participating in meals, conversations, lectures, movies, book discussions, illuminating philosophical and theological ruminations, and whatnot. Sometimes Mina, the 'angels,' or others would stop me asking serious questions (or they'd ignore my zeal with playful answers) because they just wanted to "relax" and "hang out" in the new clubhouse they'd found. From dozens to thousands of spirit persons would 'portal' into our house, jamming whatever room in which we happened to be. Billions of spirit people coalesced outside our home day and night bodily and 'long-distance' via awareness out of curiosity, concern, or to experience the carnival atmosphere. The 'energies' got so strong at times that the closer we'd get to our house when returning home from a drive the stronger the cranial pressure or ear ringing or torso (especially stomach) sensations got, particularly with Ayako. It served as an early-warning system to expect a lot of spiritual activity at the house. Helen never would tell me exactly how many people showed up day-to-day because she didn't want me to "get a big head." Maybe she was justified but usually I was stupefied so many people crowded into my Q&A sessions with Mina, the 'angels,' Jesus, Sun-myung, and others. I just felt out of place. Still, El's declaration from Mina that I was now the most famous person in spirit world rang in my inflated ears a long while even if I had no independent way to 'know' it.

86. [98] 'Energy' drains aren't unusual. Psychic John Holland notes that "doing psychic work can make you extra sensitive, so you may occasionally feel tired or drained. Being sensitive comes with this work . . ." (Holland 2018, 124). I'm not sure he knows just how sensitive or draining it can really get. In these early days, we often relied on Ayako because she tested the fastest and most accurate. In the car with me driving and El still learning to hand test—not terribly motivated to learn, either, as she preferred sway testing—Ayako was our principal receiver.

87. [98] On this day, every physically living being—human, animal, plant, and smaller—capable of contributing 'energy' without being damaged did so, channeled by each of their guardian 'angels,' færies (SOL § 1.1.1.4:572), and other 'maintenance' spirits (spirit persons, all), from which Mina infused every physically- and spiritually-living thing across the physical and spiritual universe with healing 'energy.' The energy generated through physical processes is what powers spirit world (SOL § 7:211). An unprecedented event like the Big Healing required copious energy beyond the norm. Even so-called constants (which aren't actually constant) such as the speed of light and the Big-G temporarily fluctuated 'lower.'

88. [99] Some friends and acquaintances reported their marriage, relationship, or other aspects of their emotional lives inexplicably improved on the Big Healing day or shortly thereafter. My children happily discovered their mother, with whom they couldn't get along for most of their lives, dramatically improved within days until she easily got along with them. For the first time, they looked forward to visiting her.

Chapter 8 – Confrontation

89. [102] Lucifer has a deep-feeling heart, tender, embracing, and long-suffering. Naturally, he's sensitive to the hate, scorn, and accusation directed at him by millennia of 'angels' and humans mistakenly blaming him for the conditions of life. Driving home from church in Bowie, Maryland one day in November 2017, we spontaneously visited the Basilica of the National Shrine of the Immaculate Conception in Washington, DC, a beautiful Romanesque-Byzantine Roman Catholic church my daughters and I always loved to experience. Lucifer was riding with us, tagging along with our perennial companions Taiji, Hidé, and Helen not to mention our guardian 'angels' and others. To our surprise, the ingrained hatred for Satan and the 'energy' of desperation swirling around and throughout the building so overwhelmed Lucifer that after entering merely a few feet into a side vestibule, he was all palms out "Nope!" and went back to spirit world. Hidé started weeping almost right away. After awhile the 'heavy energy' did in Taiji, too. He sympathetically joined Hidé's tears and eventually tugged Ayako's collar to move us upstairs from the basement chapels and then outside.

It was a revelation to me that churches are so spiritually 'dark' and draining that the spiritually brighter can't take them. We traipsed around the lesser 'negative energy' grounds with a returned Lucifer and comforted our spirit friends in the natural, sunny beauty, shared our experiences inside, then decompressed before heading home. Most people can generally feel the vibes a person or place puts out. The stronger the vibe, the more likely they notice. Empaths or the spirit-aware are more sensitive to this, picking up vibes where no one else does, experiencing them in a personal, visceral way, particularly if they're unaware they're empaths. Emotive energy in places like churches where humanity pours out its grief, fear, frustration, sorrow, guilt, shame, hate, and desperation that's rarely countered by unconditional love, joy, or psychic release infuses and affects a sensitive psyche the way a vicious drug hits one's biology. Ayako (and less so, El) could always feel this 'energy' at the Basilica but realized they'd been blocking it out to enjoy the architecture and environment. Me—well, on reflection I could see how the basilica affected me when I'd visited before but, unaware then that I'm an empath, I chalked up my inexplicable feelings to other, conventional, causes.

90. [104] 'Angels' are used to this sort of treatment from physical persons, of course, and nobody more so than Lucifer. That doesn't blunt the hurt when a person sees yet snubs them. One might be surprised that people would knowingly snub an 'angel.' We sure were. But in spirit world, people snub God. In terms of emotive capacity, 'angels' aren't any different from you and me, though not as egocentric as physical humanity cut off from spirit reality.

91. [105] Mina said Ayako's current guardian 'angels' are a married second-generation couple, which

makes them Mina's immediate grandchildren, as are Lucifer and his siblings. Her original guardian 'angels'—who gave up their role to help quieten riots in spirit world following the Big Fracas—were Gabriel's fraternal twin sister and her third-generation husband. Mina said it's "a majority of 'angels' " holding these two sets of guardian 'angels' in such high esteem while the remainder see them as simply "regular."

92. [113] Mina was egging us on, not face palming over our emotions. He saw ThetaHealer's response as a "likely but not necessarily foregone" conclusion. Ayako's efforts reasoning with her was as pointless as Sisyphus thinking he'd reach the top. Our effort (all things being equal) ultimately won't bear fruit in the physical world with either ThetaHealer One or Two. They are as they are, though as Mina has told us before, "It's never sure till it's sure."

93. [119] ". . . She heard the death bells ringing /And as they rolled they seemed to say, / Hard-hearted Barb'ry Allen . . ." from *Barbara Allen*, Traditional Scots, ca. mid-17th century (Emmylou Harris, *Songcatcher*, compact disc, NY: Vanguard Records, 2001; and Dolly Parton/Altan, *Heartsongs (Live From Home)*, album, NY: Columbia Records, 1994). Ms. Medium's hard-heartedness toward Lucifer and Michael (who feels our comparison here resonates) is ironically the very epitome of religion's critique of Satan and the Sinner vis-à-vis God.

94. [121] Late in December 2017, Ms. Medium hooked Ayako into a lengthy conversation at Sunday church where she touched and hugged her and transferred so much 'toxic energy' to Ayako that it dampened her chakras and shut down her energy testing for close to four months. Similar close proximity along with Ms. Medium's lengthy embrace at church in April 2018 snapped my own chakras shut within the hour. Five weeks of virtually no spiritual communication later, they'd recovered enough that Mina could open them for me and I could resume sway testing. Only in late September did my finger testing ability—a subtle, 'energy'-sensitive methodology (more so than sway or hand testing; *SOL* § 2.2.1.3:629)—return. I had to exercise it like a withered arm. Mina pegged it 86% accurate within a couple weeks, however. People don't really notice 'negative energy,' instead chalking its effects up to random disease and misfortune, yet it can be quite toxic to the body and mind. Acknowledging Ms. Medium's toxicity isn't a slam on her character or personality—I liked her, all things being equal—but simply our awareness of her 'energy' intention and its effect on us. We didn't yet know how to build the spiritual equivalent of a hazardous environment suit, so keeping our distance was all we had for protection.

Chapter 9 – Revival Ride

95. [128] "In order to become a Sunnie, you have to free yourself completely from all shackles and become a real, true entity . . . What is the difference between Moonies and Sunnies? There is an important difference. The moon receives light and then reflects it, while the sun is the generator of the light and gives it out everywhere. Therefore, the difference between Moonies and Sunnies is also obvious. The Moonies are those who can only gain their strength from Father [Sun-myung], receiving his light and encouragement, then giving it out. But, for Sunnies it doesn't matter whether Father is present or not. Sunnies are dynamos themselves, giving out light to the world whether I am here or not . . . The wish of Heavenly Father, as well as my own desire, is for you to become such a Sunnie. Don't stay too long on the Moonie level; promote yourself to a Sunnie" (Moon 1987, par. 3).

96. [128] In my first Unification Church rebellion in 1984—rising from a culmination of confidence over self-doubt in the tradition of Martin Luther (Armstrong 2011, "A History of Darkness"; and Young 2017, "The Doubts of a Leader")—I wrote my own version of Luther's Ninety-five Theses (1517) slamming the church's corruption, violence, and abandonment of its own teachings. In the dead of night, I nailed—well, thumbtacked—my seven-page *A General Discourse on the Symbolic Relationship of Cain and Abel, Regarding its Theory and Misapplication in the Unification Church* to "the front doors of virtually every church center in the San Francisco Bay area" (McKeon 2024, 27). Local church leaders indeed tried to excommunicate its author but I'd thoughtfully signed my shot o'er their bow "as *Cassius*, a Roman jurist whom I thought embodied truth and fairness" (ibid, ia). Suspicions unquenched, they fell back on the all-purpose 'problem member' moniker to physically deny me entry to all Bay Area church centers, even for Sunday service. Unlike with medieval excommunication,

religious liberty obviates the threat of local government hounding me from the succor of my friends, which Martin Luther also avoided only because his friends were well armed. Many months later, I did get the satisfaction of an indirect apology from the local persecutorial ringleader although it came in a Sunday sermon they prevented my attending.

97. [135] After discovering my spirit guides Daphne (formerly Frenchie) and Godwin bicycling along with me on a Charlottesville, Virginia bike trail, our conversation provoked me to ask Mina, "When I quit procrastinating and get your actual name, can I also get your wife's?" *Yes, of course.* Then I asked, "Say, do you know Cosmo's name?" *Yes.* "Will you tell me his name?" *Yes.* "Great! Wait. You're, like, totally persnickety about getting permission from people before you do anything regarding them, so your *yes* means you already got Cosmo's permission to give me his name?" *Yes.* I said, "Aha . . . then . . . did you happen to also get his permission for me to mention him in the book?" Because, since we first discovered Cosmo's existence, he (like my obstinate dad) wouldn't give me permission to expose him. But how could I not discuss Mina's teacher (*SOL* § 3:343)? The logic was obvious. Readers would wonder. "Will he go for it?" I added. *Yes.* I'd only been making my case to Cosmo from the start. In my (possibly quetching) negotiations with Mina, his wife finally reached a "rocking-the-marital-boat" mind to "damn the permissions and full speed ahead!" ("Cosmo," e-mail to Moth Man, par. 3, June 19, 2018). As I ecstatically told Moth Man the next day, "Now I can move forward on that front with Mina's happy connivance" (ibid).

98. [136] There are people so abominable that no 'angels' will work with them, for example Hitler (*SOL* CH. 40:605), Stalin, and Pol Pot although not Mao Tse Tung, which took us by surprise. Here's what Mina said about that. Mao didn't care about the human cost of his policies. He knew suffering and death would result but was trying to accomplish good things for China and just didn't care how many suffered and died to do it. That separated him from the Stalin–Hitler-type crowd who target persons or groups for death (or slavery) unrelated either to accomplishing their national advancement or as an integral aspect of it. Brutality was gratuitous for Hitler, as it was unnecessary to his larger goals. Mao could accomplish his larger goals with little to no death and suffering but didn't care, thus it occurred. For Hitler types, death and suffering are integral to accomplishing their larger goals and brutality is encouraged and gratuitous. Aside from their own sense of duty, Mao's 'angels' overlooked his callousness and mass deaths as for them he didn't rise to the same egregious level as Stalin, Hitler, Pol Pot, and others once they'd crossed their individual Rubicons into Full Psycho Mode.

99. [136] It's hard to describe the sense of disconnection—wildly vibrating 'energy,' heat, prickles; floating, sinking, shifting sideways; spirit world light and seeing through closed eyelids; spirit arms and legs moving about till you're just out. The odd sensations and altered awareness were terribly disorienting and initially laced me with fear. When I couldn't quite get out of my body because I was distracted, had overeaten, or for whatever reason, my body sometimes felt cold, trembled, and electrified like an atomic reaction. It was impossible to sleep or relax even though tired and—as I'm doing now writing this endnote—I'd end up working all night on the book or otherwise distracting myself until 'normality' returned. If you've experienced any of this, or can empathize with the sensations described, then perhaps you imagine some of what El was going through.

100. [138] That's what spiritual 'gifts' are: learnable skills, not bestowed powers. Some folks (many more of which the public is unaware) are indeed inborn with what we'd call a talent or capability awaiting discovery and development. Many people experience the effects of their spiritual senses while it's still a latent skill without understanding the cause. They turn to prescribed or self-medication, or simply suffer anxiety, fatigue, headaches, 'hallucinations,' synesthesia, and so on. I've experienced some of these effects off and on throughout my own life but most especially since this amazing October 2017 week. For a list of the effects that spirit-awareness might induce, see https://psychickelli.com/signs -and-symptoms-of-the-spiritual-awakening-and-expanded-consciousness/ (accessed: 2022-01-30 (original URL accessed: 2018-06-13)).

Chapter 10 – Denouement

101. [150] On another day, we found Mina watching *Moana* (2016) with us. He remarked that, while he disliked the movie overall for its goddess Te Fiti's violent stolen-heart form as Te Kā—he eschews

violence in all forms and the film reinforced false good–evil, love–hate, peaceful–violent dualities—he loved its aesthetic, Moana persevering through loving freedom and consideration for (rather than from) others, and especially that Te Fiti looks like his wife, Ag'poprje (*SOL* § 2.2:341). That last bit really got my girls thinking.

Chapter 11 – A New Dawn

102. [157] For an overview and some literature on the topic, see Ingunn Karin Bendiksen, "Worldviews Shape Personality," *Science Nordic*, July 21, 2013 (http://sciencenordic.com/worldviews-shape-p ersonality (accessed: 2019-01-22)); Steven Chisham, "The Anatomy of a Worldview: The Eternal Self-Identity," *Creation Research Society Quarterly*, 49 (Spring 2012), 63–72; and Artur Nilsson, *The Psychology of Worldviews: Toward a Non-Reductive Science of Personality*, Lund University (2013).

103. [157] Micro-observation is the tendency to extrapolate larger reality from details including, counterin-tuitively, when studying complex systems holistically. Macro reasoning is a thinker's tendency "to mentally dilute reality expanding their vision of it to include finer details" [sic] instead of "mentally condens[ing] reality into clotted material, and giv[ing] their mindful attention to clots but not to the surrounding fluid" (Fell 2017, 100). Concepts like, *If there is a God he's benevolent and good*, or *Why is there something instead of nothing?* are perfect examples of fluid over clots. Science and philosophy end up denying intuitive awareness.

104. [157] An example of science talking out its arse is the way it uses biologism to casually convert the person into an organic object in a random world amenable to subjective value of the sort we apply to an inorganic machine. "The possibility of cloning from the nucleus of an ordinary cell undermines the idea that embryos are precious because they have the potential to become human beings . . . [as] every human cell contains the genetic information to create a new human being, the old arguments for preserving 'unique' human embryos fade away" (Singer 2005, 40). ". . . even if the life of a human organism begins at conception, the life of a person—that is, at a minimum, a being with some level of self-awareness—does not begin so early" (ibid, 41). Ostensibly arguing for the right to die, Singer is really preaching biologism to justify metaphysical assumptions about what constitutes a person in order to free the hand of science to do . . . whatever. However, even a cloned human body at inception automatically generates a new human consciousness attached to that newly cloned cell (*SOL* § 1.2.1.1.1:248). According to Mina, there's one planet in our universe that knows how to do this and they clone bodies for slaves, unconcerned that cloned human bodies house—integrate—an eternal ℘erson (the totality that is mind where mind is ℘erson, ℘erson defines Ɫife, Ɫife becomes ℘erson (*SOL* § 3:280; see also Ɫife force pg. 19)).

105. [158] Hilariously, Professor of International Health at Karolinska Institutet Hans Rosling (d. 2017) found that, regarding knowledge of world health, "the professors of the Karolinska Institute, that hands out the Nobel Prize in medicine . . . are on par with the chimpanzees . . . [mean $\pm$ confidence interval 2.4 ± 0.4 correct answers out of five total]" (Hans Rosling, "Debunking third-world myths with the best stats you've ever seen," TED, January 14, 2007, 2:16–2:27; https://www.youtube.com/watch?v=RUwSruAdUcI (accessed: 2019-01-17)).

106. [159] For example, "When I say 'noncomputational' I don't mean random. Nor do I mean incompre-hensible. There are very clear-cut things that are noncomputational and are known in mathematics. The most famous example is Hilbert's tenth problem, which has to do with solving algebraic equations in integers" (Penrose 1995, 244).

107. [159] Instructive here is the television series *Dark Matter* (Canada, Prodigy Pictures, *Syfy*, 2015–17), a metaphor for the human drive to know and survive—or to survive and know, take your pick—in which a group of six humans awake alone, without memory, on an automated spaceship who then devote themselves to just two principal activities: surviving and discovering their reality.

108. [159] See, e.g., University of Oxford philosopher Richard Swinburne as featured in "The Inductive Theist of North Oxford" (Holt 2012, 95–107).

109. [161] As of 2022, about 3.5% (4% in 2019) of spirit humanity still fear the certainty of an Accountableist God. About 5.8% (6% in 2019) still feel too overwhelmed by shame, embarrassment, and the like to

ask anyone in spirit world who can see or knows them for help and healing. As of 2024, the former are approximately 2.9% and the latter 5.7% of spirit humanity.

Chapter 12 – ET as a Mode of Inquiry

110. [165] "Remarks to the Commonwealth Club," par. 1–2, San Francisco, September 15, 2003.

111. [168] The most recent being 1917's alleged Miracle of the Sun involving 30–40,000 persons, which Mina calls a mass—collective—hallucination. On the other hand, the 'Phoenix Lights,' where a boomerang-shaped craft drifted over this city in Arizona in 1997, was spirit persons making spirit matter physically visible (which is the origin of UFO sightings). See, e.g., Le Bon 1896, 1–2, 6; Zusne et al. 2014, 117.

112. [171] Here's how it works. Ask a spirit person you trust to view the hands-free tire pressure gauge you're using to measure the air pressure in a particular tire. Without looking at the gauge yourself, query via ET—"Is it 30lbs? 33lbs? 35lbs?" or whatever—until you get a *yes* response. Check multiple times using different questions to be certain you correctly tested. Then, check the pressure yourself. If it's inaccurate, test the person's answers until you uncover the reason for the error. You might require a different gauge, perhaps you improperly tested, or the person you asked might be joking around, testing your abilities to maybe help you improve, or not as interested in helping as presumed. Remember, you're talking to people in a conversation. If correct testing exceeds statistical chance (50:50) then what do you have, subjective revelation or objective data?

113. [171] This last point is especially the case regarding 'special' revelation, meaning specific truths we can know via the supernatural, but especially from such revelators as, e.g., Zoroaster, Abraham, Moses, Jesus, or Muhammad as opposed to 'general' revelation, meaning generic truths we can know about God through nature (Rom. 1:10; Wis. 1:5 (Catholic)) unless there's some reference back to a 'special' revelation such as sacred scripture.

Works Cited

Explanatory Note: Works cited form no part (though some here and there do coincidentally agree in part with the text) of this book beyond short quotes or as a reference. They're representative of the background material that informed and guided our ET inquiries in areas where our awareness was deficient. Citation pages follow each entry as [cit. pg.#].

Armstrong, Chris R. 2011. "A History of Darkness." *Leadership Journal* 32 (4). Accessed June 12, 2018. https://www.christianitytoday.com/pastors/2011/fall/historydarkness.html. [cit. 193].

Ayala, Francisco J. 1995. "The Myth of Eve: Molecular Biology and Human Origins." *Science* 270, no. 5244 (December 22, 1995): 1930–1936. [cit. 176].

Baer, Greg. 2003. *Real Love: The Truth About Finding Unconditional Love and Fulfilling Relationships.* NY: Gotham Books. [cit. 187].

Burton, Richard A. 2008. *On Being Certain: Believing You Are Right Even When You're Not.* NY: St. Martin's Griffin. [cit. 180].

Dawkins, Richard. 1989. *The Selfish Gene.* (1976). Oxford University Press. [cit. 179].

de Chardin, Pierre Teilhard. 1959. *The Phenomenon of Man.* NY: HarperPerennial. [cit. 179].

Douglass, Frederick. 1845. *Narrative of the Life of Frederick Douglass an American Slave.* Boston: Anti-slavery Office. [cit. 185].

DuBois, W.E.B. 1969. *The Souls of Black Folk.* 17th ed. NY: NAL Penguin, Inc. [cit. 185].

Durkheim, Émile. (1893) 1984. *The Division of Labour in Society.* London: Macmillan Press. [cit. 179].

Edinger, Edward F. 1992. *Ego & Archetype: Individuation and the Religious Function of the Psyche.* Boston: Shambhala Publications. [cit. 179].

Farnese, A. 1901. *A Wanderer in the Spirit Lands by Franchezzo.* Chicago: The Progressive Thinker Publishing House. [cit. 189].

Fell, Elena. 2017. "Macro-Reasoning and cognitive gaps: understanding post-Soviet Russians' communication styles." *Journal for Communication Studies* 7 (1 [13]/2014): 91–110. [cit. 195].

Ferrell, Robert H. 1994. *Harry S. Truman: A Life.* Columbia: University of Missouri Press. [cit. 184].

Greenwood, Susan. 1990. "Émile Durkheim and C. G. Jung: Structuring a Transpersonal Sociology of Religion." *Journal for the Scientific Study of Religion* 29, no. 4 (December): 482–95. [cit. 179].

Heffernan, Margaret. 2011. *Willful Blindness: Why We Ignore the Obvious at Our Peril.* NY: Walker Publishing. [cit. 180].

Heidegger, Martin. 1962. *Being and Time.* Oxford: Blackwell. [cit. 47].

Holland, John. 2018. *Bridging Two Realms: Learn to Communicate With Your Loved Ones on the Other-Side.* Carlsbad, CA: Hay House. [cit. 192].

Holt, Jim. 2012. *Why Does the World Exist? An Existential Detective Story.* NY: Liveright Publishing Corporation. [cit. 195].

Howell, Trisha. 2007. *ThetaHealing is a Fraud and a Dangerous Cult!* Accessed May 7, 2017. http://fraudthetahealing.com/index.html. [cit. 190].

Le Bon, Gustave. 1896. *The Crowd: A Study of the Popular Mind.* NY: Macmillan. [cit. 196].

Learn, Joshua R. 2016. "No, a Mitochondrial 'Eve' Is Not the First Female in a Species." In *Smithsonian.com.* Smithsonian, June 28, 2016. Accessed July 19, 2018. https://www.smithsonianmag.com/science-nature/no-mitochon drial-eve-not-first-female-species-180959593/. [cit. 176].

Markus, Gabriel. *Why the World Does Not Exist: in conversation with Markus Gabriel.* Accessed December 22, 2018. http://christine-jakobson.squarespa ce.com/issue/world/markus-gabriel-interview. [cit. 94].

McKeon, Christopher. 1998. "Cain and Abel: A Spiritual Analysis of American Race Hate." Master's thesis, Unification Theological Seminary. [cit. 181, 185].

McKeon, Christopher. 2017–19. "October 13 (entered Nov. 10), 2017." In *The Diary of Christopher McKeon,* vol. VII. Unpublished; private collection. October 6, 2017–April 3, 2019. [cit. 179].

McKeon, Christopher. 2022. *The Story of Life: A Shocking Revelation About God and the Universe to End Fear and Liberate Humanity.* Rico, CO: Tõteppit Press. [cit. i, 2].

McKeon, Christopher. 2024. *Victim to Victor: Confessions of a Wrong-way Moonie.* Rico, CO: Tõteppit Press. [cit. iii, 177, 193].

Moon, Sun-myung. 1987. *When It Was Over, It Turned Out To Be Love.* True Parents Birthday at the World Mission Center Grand Ballroom, New York City. Speech, February 3, 1987. Accessed September 21, 2018. https://www.tparents.org/Moon-Talks/sunmyungmoon87/870203.htm. [cit. 193].

Moon, Sun-myung. 1996. *Exposition of the Divine Principle.* Color Coded. Revised 2006. NY: HSA–UWC. [cit. 4, 175, 181, 186].

Moon, Sun-myung. 1999. "Prayer and Declaration of the Liberation of the Cosmos (May 14, 1999)." Translated by Rev. Taek Yong Oh. *Today's World* (NY) 20, no. 6 (June): 11–12. [cit. 177].

Moon, Sun-myung. 2006. *Cheon Seong Gyeong: Selections from the Speeches of True Parents.* Family Federation for World Peace and Unification. eprint: 2009. [cit. 30].

Myrdal, Gunnar. 1964. *An American Dilemma: The Negro in a White Nation.* Vol. 1. San Francisco: Harper & Row. [cit. 185].

Nelson, Bradley. 2007. *The Emotion Code: How to Release Your Trapped Emotions for Abundant Health, Love and Happiness.* 1st ed. Mesquite, NV: Wellness Unmasked Publishing. [cit. 175].

Penrose, Roger. 1995. "Consciousness Involves Noncomputable Ingredients." In *The Third Culture: Beyond the Scientific Revolution,* by John Brockman, 239–261. NY: Simon & Schuster. [cit. 195].

Ruse, Michael. 2007. "Dossier Évolution et créationnisme: Intelligent Design Theory." *Natures Sciences Sociétés: Recherches et débats interdisciplinaires* 15, no. 3 (March): 285–286. [cit. 177].

Sheldrake, Rupert. 2012. *Science Set Free: 10 Paths to New Discovery.* NY: Deepak Chopra Books. [cit. 158].

Singer, Peter. 2005. "The Sanctity of Life." *Foreign Policy* (September–October): 40–1. [cit. 195].

Stibal, Vianna. 2011. *ThetaHealing: Introducing an Extraordinary Energy Healing Modality.* Carlsbad, CA: Hay House, Inc. [cit. 61, 64, 181].

Taylor, Steve. 2017. "Moving Beyond Materialism: Can Transpersonal Psychology Contribute to Cultural Transformation?" *International Journal of Transpersonal Studies* 36, no. 2 (September 1, 2017): 147–59. https://doi.org/10.2 4972/ijts.2017.36.2.147. [cit. 160].

The Urantia Book. 1955. Chicago: Urantia Foundation. [cit. 188].

Tiger, Lionel, and Robin Fox. 1974. *The Imperial Animal.* NY: Dell. [cit. 179].

Uebersax, John S. 2018. "The Monomyth of Fall and Salvation." In *Christian Platonism.* Catholic Gnosis (blog), December 10, 2018. Accessed January 1, 2018. https://catholicgnosis.wordpress.com/2014/12/10/the-monomyth-o f-fall-and-salvation/. [cit. 179].

Venema, Dennis R., and Scot McKnight. 2017. *Adam and the Genome: Reading Scripture after Genetic Science.* Grand Rapids, MI: Brazos Press. [cit. 44, 177].

Ward, Keith. 2002. *God: A Guide for the Perplexed.* Oxford: Oneworld Publications. [cit. 92].

Watts, Alan W. 1951. *The Wisdom of Insecurity.* NY: Vintage Books. [cit. 44].

Witzel, E.J. Michael. 2012. *The Origins of the World's Mythologies.* Oxford University Press. [cit. 178–179].

Young, Ben. 2017. "The Doubts of a Leader." In Ch. 5 "Famous Doubters." In *Room for Doubt: How Uncertainty Can Deepen Your Faith,* edited by Ben Young. Colorado Springs: David C. Cook. [cit. 193].

Zusne, Leonard, and Warren H. Jones. 2014. *Anomalistic Psychology: A Study of Magical Thinking.* NY: Taylor & Francis. [cit. 196].

Index

Example entries: **57**; 57f; e57. **Bold**: an entry's most pertinent page number; 'f': it's in the page's footnote; 'e': it's in the endnote number.